W9-CJN-814

Personalities and Policies

Personalities and Policies

STUDIES IN THE FORMULATION OF BRITISH FOREIGN POLICY IN THE TWENTIETH CENTURY

by

D. C. WATT

MA (OXON)

Senior Lecturer in International History,
London School of Economics and Political Science

LONGMANS

LONGMANS, GREEN AND CO LTD
48 Grosvenor Street, London W1
*Associated companies, branches and representatives
throughout the world*

© D. C. Watt 1965
except for
Essays 2, 3, 7 © *D. C. Watt 1963*
Essay 8 © *D. C. Watt 1958*
Essays 9, 12 © *D. C. Watt 1962*

First published 1965

*Printed in Great Britain by
Richard Clay (The Chaucer Press), Ltd.,
Bungay, Suffolk*

For Felicia

Contents

PREFACE   ix

ACKNOWLEDGEMENTS   xi

Introduction

Essay 1: The Nature of the Foreign-Policy-Making Élite in Britain   1

I. The Problem of Attitudes

Essay 2: America and the British Foreign-Policy-Making Élite, from Joseph Chamberlain to Anthony Eden, 1895–1956   19

Essay 3: American Aid to Britain and the Problem of Socialism, 1945–51   53

II. The Influencing of Opinion

Essay 4: Britain, the United States and Japan in 1934   83

Essay 5: Sir Warren Fisher and British Rearmament against Germany   100

Essay 6: Influence from Without: German Influence on British Opinion, 1933–38, and the Attempts to Counter it   117

III. The Impact of the Commonwealth

Essay 7: Imperial Defence Policy and Imperial Foreign Policy, 1911–39: The Substance and the Shadow   139

Essay 8: The Influence of the Commonwealth on British Foreign Policy: The Case of the Munich Crisis   159

IV. Contemporary Problems

Essay 9: Divided Control of British Foreign Policy – Danger or Necessity?   177

Essay 10: Entry and Training in the Administrative Class of the British Foreign Service   187

Essay 11: Security Procedures in the British Foreign Service   199

Contents

v. Bibliographical Section

Essay 12: United States Documentary Resources for the Study of British Foreign Policy, 1919–39   211

Essay 13: Some British and Foreign Materials for the Study of the British Foreign-Policy-Making Élite since 1918   223

APPENDIX

Some Members of the British Foreign-Policy-Making Élite, 1916–56   253

INDEX   263

Preface

THIS book is a by-product of an academic training compounded of equal parts of political and historical study followed by thirteen years' research and teaching in the field of twentieth-century international history. The author is by profession an historian and a student of international relations rather than a political scientist. His main concern, in publishing these essays, has been to bridge the gap between these two disciplines, by borrowing concepts from political science which might assist the elucidation of the historical problems which bedevil his field, in return for calling the attention of political scientists to a range of historical evidence which to some extent belies the assumptions on which so much of the theoretical discussion of political processes in Britain is based. The lot of a bridge-builder between disciplines is a hazardous and potentially unhappy one, and the author is well aware that much of what he has to say in these pages is controversial and contentious. In deciding to run the risks inherent in assuming this role the author's intention was less to settle old controversies than to provoke new ones. If he succeeds in provoking criticism and disagreement, or in stimulating his readers to re-examine the facts on which their assumptions are based, if only with a view to refuting the views here expressed, then his purpose is served. The old controversies have been too long with us, and the re-examination of old assumptions is, in the long run, the only alternative to intellectual stagnation.

The essays have been arranged in four main groups, preceded by an introductory essay discussing the nature, composition and social origins of the élite group involved in the formulation and execution of British foreign policy. The first two essays thereafter deal with aspects of the general attitudes to problems of foreign policy shared by that élite, using the case of the United States as an example. This is followed by three studies in the influencing of opinion within that élite. The third section deals with the impact of the Commonwealth on Britain's foreign and defence policies. The fourth discusses certain of the contemporary problems of British foreign policy and the policy-making élite. In the final section the author has attempted to indicate the nature of the materials available in this country and in the United States for the study of British foreign policy and the men who made it.

One final word. The vast bulk of the evidence on which these essays are based is historical and drawn from the years between the two world wars. This is inevitable in view of the comparative thinness of factual material since 1945 allowing of the kind of detailed discussion of personalities and policies here attempted. The reliance of the political scientist on such evidence in other fields is well illustrated in Robert Mackenzie's *British Political Parties* (1963) or in the works of Sir Ivor Jennings on the British political system, to take two examples of the best work on problems of contemporary British domestic politics.

Acknowledgements

THE author's thanks are due to the editors of the following journals for permission to use material which has previously appeared in their journals: the *Review of Politics* for Essay 2 (Jan. 1963); the *American Review* for Essay 3 (Apr. 1963); the *Journal of Commonwealth Political Studies* published by the Leicester University Press for Essay 7 (May 1963); the *Vierteljahresheft für Zeitgeschichte* for Essay 8 (1958); the *Political Quarterly* for Essay 9 (Dec. 1962); *International Affairs* published by the Royal Institute of International Affairs for Essay 12 (Jan. 1962). His thanks are also due to the European Association of American Studies and to the Rockefeller Foundation for financing research, parts of which have been included in this volume, and to the Director of the London School of Economics and Political Science for the year's leave of absence which enabled him to work through the American materials discussed in the bibliographical section to this book. To his professional and professorial colleagues, particularly to Professor W. N. Medlicott, the author is deeply indebted for advice, encouragement, and warnings. He would also like to acknowledge his indebtedness to Professors H. C. Allen, W. C. Robson and Kenneth Robinson of the University of London, Professor Max Beloff of the University of Oxford, Professor J. B. Duroselle of the Sorbonne, Professor Dietrich Gerhard of the Max-Planck Institut für Geschichte, Göttingen, Professor Ernst Fraenkel of the Free University of Berlin, Professor Max Silberschmidt of the University of Zurich, Professor Howard Ehrmann of the University of Michigan, Professor M. B. Fitzsimons of Notre Dame University, and Professor Arthur Link of the University of Princeton, who have at various times discussed parts of these essays with the author.

The author would also like to express his gratitude to his various sources of information within the British Foreign Service, who, for various reasons, prefer to retain their anonymity: and to his various typists who have battled so manfully with his highly personal calligraphy.

The author's thanks are due to the following persons for permission to quote from papers under their care or control: the Director, the Historical Office of the United States State Depart-

Acknowledgements

ment; the United States Navy Historical Division; the Royal Canadian Navy Historical Division; the Keeper of manuscripts, the Sterling Library, Yale; the Librarian, the University of Birmingham Library; the Trustees, the 11th Marquess of Lothian Trust; the Librarian, the Franklin D. Roosevelt Library; the Director-General, the Royal Institute of International Affairs.

The Nature of the Foreign-Policy-Making Élite in Britain

THE essays collected together in this book are to some extent linked by a common theme and a common thesis. The thesis is that Britain is essentially an oligocratic society,[1] one in which power is exercised by a minority of its citizens grouped together in a cluster of smaller groups, consistent enough in their membership over time for these groups to be treated not only as a political but as a social phenomenon, and for the characteristics of their social organization to be an essential element in the manner in which they perform their political functions. In any state, even in the most direct of democracies, the nature of political decision-making ensures that power is exercised only by a few. But in Britain those few form a continuous and recognizable grouping. They are also a good deal less responsible to and responsive to the main movements and currents of mass public opinion than their counterparts in other countries, and studies of such movements and currents do not necessarily have any bearing on the currents and movements of opinion among their ranks. They have, in brief, to be recognized and treated separately. Among these élite groups, this book concentrates on those persons and influences involved in the formulation of British foreign policy at various times and dates in the first half of this century.

The minority to which the previous paragraph refers is not, however, a united, self-conscious and self-interested social group. Nor is entry to its number closed to outsiders. There are different groups and different élites to be distinguished within the minority. In some cases the membership of such groups overlaps; in others it is almost completely disparate. The groups may be divided or united, at some moments at logger-heads with each other in fields where their interests conflict,[2]

1. *Oligocratic* rather than *oligarchic*, since it is the *exercise* rather than the *possession* of power which is at issue.

2. As, for example, the conflict of the 'Brass Hats' and the 'Frocks' during the First World War.

at others totally indifferent to one another's existence. Controversy, as, for example, that which rent Britain in November 1956 over the Suez crisis, takes place both within these groups and between them. Participants seek to influence mass opinion in their favour or to claim its support. But a thorough-going attempt to organize such support is the hall-mark of the group on the fringes, as the histories of the League of Nations Union or, at a later time, of the Campaign for Nuclear Disarmament amply demonstrate. The most serious debates, as, for example, that on British entry into the Common Market before the Labour party decision to oppose and the Commonwealth Conference of 1962 made it into a mass political issue, are apt to take place either in private or in the semi-private organs of communication employed by these groups. These last fall into three categories; the correspondence columns of the so-called 'quality press';[1] the clubs and institutes of London intellectual political society;[2] and the BBC's Third Programme. Their hall-mark is limitation of membership by approval – in the case of the press by the editorial staffs responsible for the selection of the letters chosen to appear in print; in the case of the BBC by the selection and approval of speakers and scripts; in the case of clubs and institutes by the normal procedures of restriction of membership.

The group interested in the formulation and execution of British foreign policy has been defined as an élite, that is, as a social group defined by and performing a political function. Its members can best be identified by reference to two sets of criteria: the positions and status occupied by them, which make their membership in and participation in the processes of the group *possible*, and the will to membership and the activities, which make their membership actual. The first approach provides us with a very significant division in the group, that between those who actually take decisions on the one hand and

1. The Correspondence Columns of *The Times* and *The Guardian* are most important in the daily press; of *The Observer* and *The Sunday Times* in the Sunday press; of *The Economist*, *The Listener*, the *Spectator* and the *New Statesman* among weeklies.

2. In addition to the clubs of Pall Mall and S.W.1 generally, such as the Athenaeum, the Carlton, White's, the National Liberal Club, one should mention the Royal Institute of International Affairs, the Institute of Strategic Studies, the Royal United Services Institute, the Royal Commonwealth Society, the Fabian Society, the 1922 Committee of Conservative MPs, etc. Perhaps the Common Room of All Souls College, Oxford, should be added, at least for the 1930s.

those who seek to influence them on the other. The second can only be decided by a consistent and detailed examination of the processes by which foreign policy has been made and influenced in whatever period of time is under examination. The late Lord Beaverbrook was certainly a member of this élite at one stage in his explosive career. But at the time of his death it was a long time since he had enjoyed any welcome from its members, his membership having ended essentially with the death of Bonar Law, his 'patron', if that word may be employed, and his subsequent conflict with Baldwin.

The first approach focuses essentially on the formal processes by which foreign policy is made on particular issues. The participants in these processes can be divided into four categories: political, diplomatic, bureaucratic and military. The *political* category comprises the elected politicians involved in the procedures by which decisions on matters of foreign policy are taken. The *diplomatic* includes the diplomatic representatives abroad and the senior staff of the Foreign Office. The *bureaucratic* includes those members of the domestic side of Government bureaucracy whose co-operation is necessary in the taking and implementing of decisions in the field of foreign policy. The *military* category covers the military, naval and air force advisers to the Government, their own policy planners, and their own representatives abroad, the Service attachés and the commanders of overseas stations in areas where sensitive issues of foreign policy may arise.

The first approach gives us, then, the following personalities *in the category of elected politicians*: *at the Cabinet level*, the Prime Minister, the Foreign Secretary, the Chancellor of the Exchequer, the Service and Defence Ministers, and such other Cabinet members who aspire to occupy or have already occupied such posts, younger expectants and elder statesmen, or who have been given special tasks in the field of foreign affairs, (as for example Mr Heath was made head of the British team negotiating on Britain's application to enter the European Economic Community); *at the junior minister level*, the Ministers of State, Parliamentary Under-Secretaries and Parliamentary Private Secretaries to the Secretary of State for Foreign Affairs; among the parliamentary opposition, the official party leaders, the parties' spokesmen of the moment on foreign affairs, finance and defence matters, and aspirants to those positions.

In the *diplomatic category* the formal approach should direct our attention to the processes within the Foreign Office by which incoming dispatches become outgoing instructions. The Foreign Office operates essentially on the collegiate system; that is to say that except for special categories of documents, incoming dispatches begin with the most junior deskmen and filter upwards to heads of departments, co-ordinating under-secretaries through the Permanent Under-Secretary, the senior career official in the Foreign Office, to the Minister. The junior will minute the document on the jacket in which it is filed by the registry on its arrival, attach past correspondence and perhaps suggest a draft reply, which will be commented on, accepted or amended by his superiors. For our purposes the important factor is that within the policy-making élite the flow of work unites together the junior and senior members of the administrative grade in the Foreign Office with their political heads. The process of posting from the Foreign Office to Embassies abroad, and back, the mechanism which makes of the Embassies and Legations abroad the channel of communication with foreign governments, as well as the providers of information on the country to which they are accredited, even with the twentieth-century vogue for ministerial diplomacy combine to make the personnel of the Foreign Service a crucial and permanent element in the formulation of British foreign policy; while their position in London very often makes for the closest personal contacts and friendships between them and their political masters.[1]

In the *bureaucratic category*, one must distinguish between three groups. Firstly, there are those whose interest in the general efficient functioning of government leads them to intervene in the field of foreign affairs. Secondly, there are those whom the expansion of foreign affairs and diplomacy in this century to include economic and financial matters, has permanently involved, willy-nilly, in the formulation of foreign policy. Thirdly, there are those whom some shift in a particular problem, or the emergence of some crucial issue over a limited period, may involve for a time in the formulation of policy.

Foremost among the first group, if group be not too magnificent a word for it, must come, in the interwar years, the occupants of the positions of Permanent Under-Secretary to the Treasury and of Secretary to the Cabinet and the Committee of Imperial Defence.

1. Two examples must suffice: the close friendship between Stanley Baldwin and Sir Robert Vansittart witnessed to in the latter's memoirs; and the regular personal correspondence with his ambassadors contained in the papers of Sir Austen Chamberlain in the University of Birmingham.

By a 'Treasury Minute' of 1919, the Permanent Under-Secretary of the Treasury, then Sir Warren Fisher, was recognized as 'Head of the Civil Service', under which at that time the Foreign Service was subsumed. Over his activities and use of this position, serious allegations have been made by at least two former members of the Diplomatic Service and the Foreign Office at that time, Sir Walford Selby[1] and Mr Ashton Gwatkin.[2] It is worth noticing, since these allegations have often been accepted uncritically, that Sir Walford Selby's views have been denied,[3] and that during the period of which he wrote he was himself abroad[4] and his allegations were based on hearsay, which was critically wrong in one crucial instance, in that it assumed Fisher, who was as pathologically hostile to Germany as Sir Robert Vansittart, was a supporter of appeasement. Ashton Gwatkin's main point of opposition to Sir Warren Fisher lay over the issue as to whether the Foreign Office should have its own economic section or continue to rely on the system by which economic matters were dealt with by the Department of Overseas Trade, over which the Foreign Office and the Board of Trade exercised an uneasy condominium. As an advocate of a unified Civil Service, Fisher opposed duplication of function within the departments of state. The Foreign Service was, however, formally separated from the Home Civil Service in the 1944 reforms, and therefore from control by the Permanent Under-Secretary for the Treasury.[5]

Much less controversy has attached to the figure of Lord Hankey, who held both the Secretaryship of the Cabinet and of the Committee of Imperial Defence until his retirement in 1938. Yet a detailed study of British disarmament policy in the 1920s, and of British policy towards international security,[6] would reveal that his role in these fields was the reverse of self-effacing, and that he carried, by virtue

1. Sir Walford Selby, *Diplomatic Twilight* (1953).
2. F. Ashton Gwatkin, *The British Foreign Service* (Syracuse, N.Y., 1950). Criticism was also voiced in the House of Lords by the Earl of Perth, formerly British Ambassador in Rome (125, *Hansard Parl. Deb., H. of L.*, cols 224–52). Lord Tyrrell denied that Fisher had ever interfered during Tyrrell's service as Permanent Under-Secretary (ibid., col.275).
3. 516, *Parl. Deb., H. of C.*, cols 151–2.
4. As was Lord Perth at the time of which he spoke.
5. Sir Warren Fisher's role is examined in more detail in Essay 5 below.
6. For some hints see Douglas Johnson, 'Austen Chamberlain and the Genesis of the Locarno Agreement', VIII, *University of Birmingham Historical Journal*, no.1 (1961).

of his tact, the trust he inspired, his position as organizer and drafter of CID reports to the Cabinet, and his long continuity in office, a degree of weight in the private counsels of the Cabinet greater than that of all but the most determined Cabinet ministers.

The second group must include the senior officials at the Treasury,[1] at the Bank of England and at the Board of Trade for all economic and financial affairs. Before 1914 such officials would tend to be consulted only in matters such as the international control of Greek, Egyptian, Chinese or Turkish finances, when such issues assumed temporary prominence in international politics. But after 1918 the issues of war debts and reparations, the Dawes and Young loans, the foundation of the Bank of International Settlements, the implications of Britain's return to the gold standard, the impact of the world depression and the financial strain of the British rearmament programme brought such officials as Montagu Norman, Sir Frederick Leith-Ross and Sir Horace Wilson[2] into the centre of the decision-making process. Once the Second World War had broken out, financial and economic affairs became a central and critical part of international negotiation, and the personalities and views of Lord Keynes and Lord Cherwell and, at a lower level, Lord Robbins and Professor James Meade, to mention only a small number of the British economic advisers and negotiators, become as important as those of Britain's professional diplomatic advisers and representatives. Since 1945, the need for Britain to be represented on the OEEC, the IMF, ECE, the World Bank, GATT, and in the negotiations on EFTA and the European Economic Community,[3] have still further enmeshed the principal economic and financial departments of state in the conduct of British foreign policy, so that one must assume this now to be a permanent phenomenon.

The third group comes from those departments of state whose

1. See, for example, the obituary of Sir David Waley in *The Times*, 5 January 1962, from which it appears that the major part of his career was spent in financial negotiations consequent on his position in the division of overseas finance in the Treasury.

2. Respectively Governor of the Bank of England, Chief Economic Adviser to the British Government, and Chief Industrial Adviser and subsequently Permanent Under-Secretary to the Treasury.

3. Of Britain's three 'flying knights', the three senior career civil servants on the British delegation which conducted the abortive negotiations in Brussels 1961–62 on British entry into the EEC, only one was a diplomat, Sir Pierson Dixon, the British Ambassador in Paris.

fields occasionally encroach on or are encroached on by international problems. The Colonial Office, the Commonwealth Office and before 1947 the India Office, which assumed at times a foreign policy virtually independent of the Foreign Office,[1] enter so regularly into this category that they should perhaps be classed with the second group. International commodity agreements or questions of agricultural tariffs may bring in the Department of Agriculture and Fisheries. International air transport, radio, cable and wireless communications similarly bring in the Ministry of Transport and the Post Office. But no department of state can be altogether immune from the need suddenly to produce an expert capable not merely of advising a British delegation to an international conference but on occasion sitting down and negotiating with other experts on the everyman-his-own-diplomat principle so universally accepted today.[2]

The *military category* is of obvious importance in wartime coalitions or in peacetime alliances. The attempts made by the League of Nations in its early days, and by the United Nations also, to equip themselves with military advisory committees on which the great powers predominated must be seen as operating on a similar principle, whether the committees operated, as under the League of Nations, to advise on problems of disarmament, or, as in the early days of the United Nations, to advise on the provision of a UN military force. The military category also includes those members of the armed services engaged on representative duties abroad, in the function of attachés to British diplomatic missions, or as members of military missions charged with advising foreign governments on the build-up of their armed forces and those at home engaged in regular contacts with foreign attachés. A third sub-group must include those whose job it is to advise the Government on strategic matters, that is the Chiefs of Staff, since 1924 formally embodied in the Chiefs of Staff Sub-Committee to the Committee of Imperial Defence, and any subordinates that may have been incorporated into the Committee of Imperial Defence secretariat or its network of subordinate committees. The directors of the Service planning divisions and their deputy-

1. Especially on issues connected with the Persian Gulf, the Red Sea, Arabia, Persia and Afghanistan.
2. Eight home departments have representatives appointed as members of the staffs of British missions to foreign countries, and no less than twenty are primarily responsible for relations with technical international organizations.

directors were so incorporated in the 1920s and 1930s. A fourth sub-group must include those military men whose function it is to advise the British Government on intelligence of a political or politico-military nature. A fifth sub-group must include commanders on foreign stations where sensitive issues of British foreign policy are likely to arise. The China station was throughout the 1920s and 1930s such a station, both as regards relations with the United States, and as regards relations firstly with the Chinese revolutionaries from 1926 onwards, then as regards relations with the Japanese.

The effect of the entry of these various groups into the foreign-policy-making process is to produce a group at the top of each of the three armed services almost as experienced in, familiar with and capable of advising the Government of the day on matters of British foreign policy as the diplomatic advisers of the Government. Two examples may suffice, both taken from the Royal Navy, the careers of Admiral Sir Howard Kelly and Admiral Sir Charles Little. Admiral Kelly was British naval attaché in Paris before 1914, and served with the 9th Cruiser Squadron during the First World War. In 1919–21 he served as head of the British naval mission to Greece, and did a great deal to maintain Anglo-Greek relations on an even keel despite the political upsets of that period in Greece. From 1927–29 he served as British naval adviser in Geneva to the British delegation to the pre-paratory commission for the disarmament conference. He played a major part in the disastrous and ill-conceived Anglo-French compro-mise of 1928 on naval disarmament which brought Anglo-American relations to one of the lowest levels reached in the twentieth century. From 1929–32 he served as Commander-in-Chief on the China station, playing a crucial part in the negotiation of a cease-fire after the Japanese naval landings in Shanghai in the spring of 1932, and preventing by his display of firmness and resolution any danger of the local Japanese naval commanders, who were more than a little out of hand, attacking either the ships under his command or the Inter-national Settlement itself. At the same time, the explosive nature of his comments on the state of the Singapore naval base played a con-siderable part in persuading the Government of the day to speed up the completion of that base's development. He must be regarded as one of the leading representatives of the Francophile group within the Royal Navy in the interwar years (they also included Sir Roger Keyes, Vice-Admiral Somerville, Admiral Sir Dudley North and Admiral Sir Andrew Cunningham), the influence of which was one of the factors which at times prevented bad Anglo-French relations from becoming worse.[1]

Admiral Sir Charles Little must by contrast be counted as one of the Americophils. He played a very considerable part in allaying the United States Navy's suspicions of British naval rearmament in 1934–35, when the needs of the European situation dictated the revival of British cruiser strength to a position which, when claimed in the disarmament negotiations of 1927–29, had aroused the deepest suspicion and antagonism in American naval circles. He succeeded, too, in creating excellent personal relations between himself and Admiral Standley, then Chief of Naval Operations to Roosevelt, so much so that Standley withdrew all objections to the British cruiser programme.[2] In 1937 Admiral Little was appointed Commander-in-Chief on the China station. Admiral Standley wrote to Little's opposite number, the Commander of the American Asiatic Fleet, Admiral Yarnell, recommending Little to him as co-operative and pro-American in November 1936, and the two Admirals, Yarnell and Little, were to co-operate very effectively in the period following the Japanese attack on China in July 1937.[3] Similar examples may be taken from the other services.

So far, attention has been confined to securing an ostensive definition of the membership of the foreign-policy-making élite in the strictest sense, that is those formally and constitutionally involved in taking the actual decisions the flow of which may be said to make up the substance of British foreign policy. But even a 'positional' definition of the élite cannot stop simply with those in official positions. There are three sources of pressure upon these men which are so regular and themselves so easily identifiable that they must be included in any enumeration of those whose position would lead any observer

1. This paragraph is based mainly on the unpublished memoirs of Admiral Sir Howard Kelly preserved in the National Maritime Museum, Greenwich. For the locations of the British and American collections of private papers and manuscripts used in these studies, the reader is referred to Essays 12 and 13 below.

2. This passage is based mainly on the records of Anglo-American naval discussions printed in *Foreign Relations of the United States, 1934*, vol.1, and *1935*, vol.1; on material in the *Norman H. Davis papers*; on material in the *US Navy General Board Papers*; on Admiral Chatfield's memoirs, *It Might Happen Again* (1947); and on private information from Lord Chatfield.

3. *Admiral Yarnell Papers*, Admiral Standley to Yarnell, 12 November 1936; Admiral Yarnell to Admiral Leahy, 12 September 1937.

automatically to include them among the élite in default of evidence to the contrary.

The sources of these pressures are threefold. Firstly, there are the party foreign-policy discussion groups and 'ginger groups' both inside and outside of Parliament. Secondly, there are the editors, leader-writers, columnists and foreign correspondents of the so-called 'quality press'. Thirdly, there is the Crown and its advisers. It should be emphasized that each of these sources of pressure has, on occasions, played a sufficiently important part in the processes by which British foreign policy is formulated, to qualify them for inclusion in any 'positional' definition of the foreign-policy-making élite. One can only decide on their actual claim for membership, however, if the influence they exact is direct, positive and persistent over a sufficiently long period of time for it to become recognized. To take one illustration: the rebel group of up to twenty Conservative MPs headed by Captain Waterhouse who were so opposed to an Anglo-Egyptian agreement in the first years of the post-1951 Conservative Government as to earn the nickname of the 'Suez Group' certainly can claim to have exercised an influence over the course of British policy. But the pressure was negative, indirect and 'outside' the élite group. In most respects the group's members were typical members of the Conservative party's right wing and of the very wealthy, powerful and influential social circles from which that group was drawn. But no one who has studied the formulation of British policy towards Egypt over this period can fail to recognize that the 'Suez Group' were not of the particular élite who formulated that policy. They were, in fact, outside it and regarded by its members as a set of unmitigated nuisances. Similarly, the Union of Democratic Control on the left of the Labour party during its first brief period of office in 1924 were revealed as being outside the circle of Labour party leadership though, in their own eyes, if not in anyone else's, they were ready to step inside the boundaries of the élite. Ramsay MacDonald could pass over Morel, the Union's leading figure, and most eloquent pen. The 'ginger group', in short, must command the confidence of the leaders of the party, as the Campaign for Democratic Socialism did in the last years of Hugh Gaitskell's life. It must operate within, not against or outside, the leadership.

A similar line could well be taken over the role of the press corps, though the justification for such a position would be much less strong. Among the 'serious' press are journals such as *The Times*, whose editors over much of this century have broadly conceived it to be their duty to support the Government of the day, at least in the field of foreign affairs, and to expound its views. With this purpose, their diplomatic correspondent is widely believed to receive additional briefing from the Foreign Office Press Department. But there are similarly journals such as *The Guardian* whose editors have conceived the duty of their paper to lie in an almost diametrically opposite direction. The ranks of these 'quality' daily papers have been sadly thinned since the turn of the century, and besides these two probably only the *Daily Telegraph* and, in its own field, *The Financial Times*, qualify among those published in London, with a handful of provincial and Scottish papers, the *Birmingham Post*, *The Yorkshire Post*, *The Scotsman* and the *Glasgow Herald*. The press corps is swelled by the three national serious Sunday papers, the political weeklies and the older and more serious monthlies and quarterlies about whose influence it is extremely difficult to speak much later than the mid-1920s, the heyday of such journals as the *Round Table*, the *Nineteenth Century and After*, the *Contemporary Review* or the *Fortnightly*.

The importance of the press corps lies in two rather different directions. Firstly, it provides a source of foreign news and information and its interpretation to which ministers and the political members of the élite have as frequent recourse as they do to the dispatches of Britain's representatives abroad, and the intelligence summaries and assessments of the various British intelligence agencies. Indeed, the first news of a new move by a foreign government may well be taken by ministers from the press reports, which they may be presumed to read at the breakfast table, rather than from the dispatches or confidential print which await them at their offices. The influence exerted by the foreign correspondents from whom such reports originate needs no emphasis.[1] But a second and more important influence exerted by the representatives of the serious press lies in the contribution they make towards the debate on foreign policy in Britain and their role as originators of proposals and ideas.

To take the former function first: it must not be assumed, as diplomatic historians are sometimes too ready to assume, that the intellectual processes by which decisions in the conduct of British foreign policy are formulated can be traced entirely from a study of

1. *The History of 'The Times'*, vols III and IV, seem to suggest that there has been a decline here since the great days before 1914; but the evidence is difficult to assess.

Foreign Office dispatches and the record of Cabinet debates. Nor can it be assumed, however, as political scientists are apt to assume, that the press represents 'public opinion' as opposed to the opinion of those in power. The serious press in Britain only really represents 'public' opinion in the sense that it represents opinions which have been made public by the act of their ventilation in the pages of the press. The debate which precedes or accompanies the formulation of any major move in British foreign policy takes place as much in private as in public, and that part of it which appears in the serious press represents only the visible part of the iceberg, or, to vary the metaphor, only one side of the polylogue,[1] out of which the ultimate decision or abstention from decision may emerge.

In this debate, individual members of the press corps may emerge as the mouthpieces, or the 'ideas men' of particular politicians or sides in the debate. The usual assumption is that the journalist acts as the politician's mouthpiece, that his leading articles are, as the phrase goes, demi-official or 'inspired'. But the assumption is a dangerous one. Perhaps the most famous example of this is *The Times'* leading article of 7 September 1938 calling for a retrocession of the Sudeten areas of Czechoslovakia to Germany, which was widely assumed at the time to have been a *'ballon d'essai'* floated by the pro-appeasement wing of the Cabinet, but has been conclusively shown to have originated with the Editor of *The Times*, Geoffrey Dawson, himself.[2] Generally speaking, the relationship between Dawson and Neville Chamberlain seems to have been much more that of a staff officer with his commanding officer, rather than that of a politician with his 'stooge'. The flow of ideas and attitudes came *from* Dawson rather than *to* him. The relationship between Beaverbrook and Bonar Law appears to have been rather similar. That between Lloyd George and Lord Riddell, on the other hand, approximated much more closely to the classic model, with Riddell acting as Lloyd George's mouthpiece, and occasionally, as at Versailles, or at Washington in 1921–22, as a kind of demi-official Public Relations Officer.

But it is not necessary for the relationship between press and politician to be as close as in these instances for the members of the press corps to continue to exercise a significant influence on the formulation of foreign policy. Except where a journal for some reason finds itself completely ostracized by officialdom and their political

1. If there can be monologues and duologues, there can also be polylogues.
2. *The History of 'The Times'*, vol.IV, part II, 929–31.

heads, the serious press acts in two ways to set the general climate of opinion in which the individual decisions for the foreign-policy-makers are taken. The peculiar difficulty in assessing the precise degree of influence the press exerts lies in this, that the press acts both as an originator of ideas (or as a commentator on ideas originated elsewhere), and as an echo-chamber for such ideas, so that it may both originate and perpetuate a particular climate of opinion. Nor is it averse to trying deliberately to set the tone or to define the concepts within which debate on a particular issue in foreign policy may be carried on, either by representing inference as certainty[1] or by organizing a correspondence which might otherwise not have taken place. At the very least, the press's leader columns can tend to be composed not for the bulk of its unofficial readership, but for a small number of persons in positions of power or influence.[2] A careful reading of the serious press can thus reveal a great deal about the general climate of official opinion which the press is attempting to influence.

The third source of pressure on the foreign-policy-making élite comes from the Crown and its closest advisers. In this field an outsider has to walk more warily than in any other. The extent of the Crown's influence is in general almost impossible to assess, even when it is clear that the monarch was not without views on the issues before his Government. The most plausible hypothesis is that which imputes most influence to the Crown on issues on which the Cabinet is uncertain, divided or willing to be pushed. It is known, for example, that King George V was thoroughly in favour of good Anglo-American relations in the summer of 1921 when one section of his Cabinet bitterly resented American claims to naval parity with Britain.[3] At the end of his reign, equally, he was opposed to any British action over the Italo-Abyssinian crisis likely to involve Britain in war.[4]

1. The interested press supporting British entry into EEC were not altogether faultless in this respect.

2. In the summer of 1960, a leading journalist, then campaigning for a British entry into EEC, told the author that the leading articles he was then writing were aimed at fifty men at most (whom he could name if necessary), in positions of influence in the City of London.

3. *Charles Evans Hughes Papers*, Frank Harvey (US Ambassador in London) to Hughes, 8 July, 11 July 1921; *US Navy General Board Papers*, Vice-Admiral Niblack, USN (commanding US Naval Forces in European waters), to Secretary of the Navy, 18 September 1921. In both cases direct conversations with King George V were being reported on.

4. Viscount Templewood, *Nine Troubled Years* (1955), 159–60. For other instances of royal activity see Sir Harold Nicolson, *King George V* (1953),

Edward VIII had given considerable evidence of supporting an Anglo-German *rapprochement* before his accession, and the Nazis, and not only the Nazis, believed that his influence was thrown in the scales during the Rhineland crisis of March 1936 to support those who opposed any British action likely to encourage France to take forcible action to secure a German withdrawal.[1] George V's interventions in the Irish negotiations in 1921 and in the formation of the National Government in 1931 are a little outside the scope of this essay, though neither are entirely unconnected with foreign affairs as such.

The influence of the Crown is exerted less in direct contact with his ministers or senior civil servants than in letters written in the name of, and by, his private secretary, whose own personality must obviously be of importance here.[2] In addition, the Crown can attract its own private group of advisers, though constitutional propriety and monarchical discretion will obviously limit both their number and their influence.[3] Their role is to be seen, not as that of sinister and unconstitutional *éminences grises*, wire-pullers to whom the King listens rather than to his constitutional advisers, but as providing a slightly different element in the forces going to make up the general climate of opinion within the foreign-policy-making élite as such. There are some indications that their influence manifests itself more through their relationships with senior officers in the armed forces than in any relationships with senior civil servants in the Foreign, Commonwealth or Home Civil Services.

438, 439, 521–2; Sir John Wheeler-Bennett, *King George VI, His Life and Reign* (1958), 419–20, 422–3, 424. In 1930, Henry L. Stimson, US Secretary of State, mentioned a conversation with King George V to Prime Minister Ramsay MacDonald, who 'manifested great excitement and said the King had no business to talk politics but he was constantly doing it and he worried all his Prime Ministers by so doing' (*Henry L. Stimson Diary, European Trip*, 1930, entry of 25 March 1930).

1. *German Foreign Ministry Archives*, Leopold von Hoesch (German Ambassador in London) to Berlin, 11 March 1936 (6710/E506679). See also *Documents on German Foreign Policy, 1918–45*, Series c, IV, document no.531.

2. See, for example, Sir Robert Vansittart's reply to a letter from Lord Wigram in November 1935 reproduced in Nicolson, op. cit., 529. For a general discussion of the role of the Sovereign's Private Secretary, see Wheeler-Bennett, op. cit., App.B.

3. Lord Esher seems to have exercised a certain influence of this nature in the early years of George V's reign.

This attempt to enumerate the members of the foreign-policy-making élite in Britain has hitherto proceeded entirely by enumerating various official and unofficial positions whose occupants might be *expected* to play a part in the internal debate on foreign policy, and the processes by which a general line is laid down or individual decisions formulated and executed in the field of British foreign affairs. Such a definition can only cover the potential membership of the élite over any given period of time. To define its actual membership there is no substitute for ostensive definition, a definition which can only develop from a detailed knowledge of and examination of the actual processes by which British foreign policy was, in fact, formulated over the period in question, an examination which must be preceded by an evaluation of what, in the totality of British contacts with other countries and with international agencies in the period, was of sufficient importance to enter into the definition of 'foreign policy' as such, what issues were of major significance and what only of minor or routine significance. The task is very much handicapped for students of British foreign policy by the exigencies of the fifty-year rule, deliberately designed in so far as its formal embodiment in the Public Records Act of 1958 is concerned, to protect the anonymity of the civil servant.[1] Nevertheless, the task is not impossible, if the historian will accept that his conclusions can only be tentative, and that that academic fantasy, the 'definitive study', is beyond his grasp.[2] All that is required in addition to this is patience, some use of interviewing techniques, knowledge of the British social structure and practices and a study of British foreign policy over a fairly lengthy period – fifty years for example. The second essay in this collection attempts such an examination, and the reader may judge for himself the advantages and the very considerable limitations of this approach, whose real defence can only be that it approximates more than any other to the reality of the processes by which foreign policy is formulated in the open oligocracy that is Britain.

1. See D. C. Watt, 'Foreign Policy, the Public Interest and the Right to Know', *Political Quarterly*, XXXIV, no.2 (April 1963), for the background to, and implications of, this Act.
2. See the Bibliographical Section, Essay 13, for indications as to some of the source materials available.

PART I

The Problem of Attitudes

America and the British Foreign-Policy-Making Élite, from Joseph Chamberlain to Anthony Eden, 1895–1956

THE great majority of work hitherto attempted on British attitudes to America falls into two main divisions: (*a*) studies, usually of American origin, of movements in the mass of British opinion;[1] (*b*) studies of the radical and politically 'nonconformist' elements in British political society.[2] Both of these suffer from certain major defects which reduce their value as contributions to the understanding of the various developments of Anglo-American relations, the former because as argued in the preceding essay the social structure of British political power does not weigh mass movements of opinion very highly, the latter because in the sixty-one years from 1895–1956 radical elements have controlled British foreign policy for a mere eight years and disputed control only for a further six.

Properly to account for these defects would require a separate essay in itself. Three points only can be made here. Historians of the recent past are few on the ground in Britain. Only a handful have touched on Anglo-American relations, and those usually impelled by idealist or quasi-ideological considerations.[3] In Britain, the dominant

1. Two excellent illustrations of this are R. H. Heindel, *The American Impact on Great Britain, 1898–1914* (1940), and Armin Rappaport, *The British Press and Wilsonian Neutrality, 1914–17* (Stanford, 1951).

2. Henry Pelling, *America and the British Left, from Bright to Bevan* (1956); Henry R. Winkler, 'The Emergence of a Labour Foreign Policy in Great Britain, 1919–29', *Journal of Modern History*, xxviii (1956); *The League of Nations Movement in Great Britain, 1914–19* (Rutgers, 1952); L. W. Martin, *Peace without Victory, Woodrow Wilson and the British Liberals* (New Haven, 1958); Elaine Windrich, *British Labour's Foreign Policy* (Stanford, 1952); M. A. Fitzsimons, *The Foreign Policy of The British Labour Government, 1945–51* (Notre Dame, 1953).

3. The works of Professor Denis Brogan and Professor H. C. Allen exemplify this. The former was for a considerable time connected with the

antipathy between historians and those who attempt theoretical studies of society based on historical example has resulted in the study of attitudes to America being left rigidly to the latter; in the past, at any rate, these have tended to maintain a radical dislike of and a consequent refusal to examine the functioning and ideals of the quasi-oligarchic structure of British political society; if there has been examination, it has not been with any aim to understand, only to condemn. In America students of Anglo-American relations have worked under two handicaps, one of a conceptual, the other of a methodological nature. Conceptually, many Americans find it difficult to visualize a society where the 'public' varies as much from moment to moment as it does in Britain, and where opinion is weighted by the social processes of its expression as much as votes used to be in pre-1918 Prussia.[1] Methodologically, the lure of that well-known academic myth, the 'definitive study', offers its own inducements to study those who express their views on policy in public rather than those whose comments are confined to archives and private papers closed by the Official Secrets Act.

The title of Henry Pelling's study referred to above suggests that the subject of this essay should be 'The British Right and America'. This would be mistaken for two reasons: (*a*) the British Right in internal politics is often no nearer the process of foreign policy formation than the British Left; (*b*) the British Left, as a radical movement dedicated to change, was interested in America first as a model to

---

British Liberal party. As a radical Glaswegian Scot, his outlook and background are far from conforming to the orthodox pattern of the British political élite. Professor H. C. Allen is an avowed and doctrinaire supporter of Anglo-American union. Nevertheless, his *Great Britain and the United States: a History of Anglo-American Relations, 1785–1952* (New York, 1954) is the indispensable introduction to any serious study of Anglo-American relations.

1. Two recent examples of the limitations experienced by some American scholars in attempting to penetrate or understand the mentality of the British political Right are the otherwise excellent works, Leon D. Epstein, *Britain – Uneasy Ally* (Chicago, 1954), and Marjorie Bremner, 'An Analysis of British Parliamentary Thought Concerning the United States in the Post-War Period' (Ph.D. thesis, London, unpublished, 1950), both of which give the impression of swallowing and repeating the myths about British Conservative 'experience' in foreign affairs and unity of opinion and social origin, neither of which will stand up to a moment's examination even in the periods they are dealing with.

copy, then as one to avoid; but while the British Right, like the French, is often equally radical, it is also nationalist and patriotic and to concentrate on the advocates of copying foreign models would mean dealing not with the orthodox Right but its lunatic fringe; the British Right while being imperialist has also been nativist. Thus, a study of right-wing attitudes to America would be open to the same objections as have been launched at studies of the Left. It would not necessarily touch on those who make the British Left so much as those whom A. J. P. Taylor called 'the proponents of an alternative foreign policy'.[1] The theme of this paper must be the attitudes of those who are the proponents of the orthodox foreign policy.

Pelling was interested in the attitudes of those he studied to America as the embodiment of a revolutionary idea of society. The nature of the élite here examined renders that approach pointless. As they are defined by their political function, their 'attitudes' to America must be defined as attitudes to America as a factor to be considered in the formation of British foreign policy. The words 'foreign policy' and 'Anglo-American relations', however, are ambiguous, as a brief comparison of Anglo-American relations in 1896 and 1956 must show. In 1896 Anglo-American relations were bilateral, separate from the main stream of British foreign policy. In 1956 they impinged upon every field of British policy. A study of the development of the attitudes of this foreign-policy-forming élite to America, therefore, must cover not merely attitudes to America as such but the place allotted to America in the general formulation of British foreign policy.

The year 1896 has been selected as the opening date,[2] for the impact of President Cleveland's message to Congress on the Anglo-Venezuelan frontier dispute marks the opening of British awareness of American expansion and emergence on the scene as a world power. The date is not without significance in Britain. Only a year earlier the electorate had definitely and finally abandoned the values and inactions

1. A. J. P. Taylor, *The Trouble Makers. Dissent Over Foreign Policy, 1792–1939* (1957).
2. By contrast with American historians who have preferred 1898, the year of the Spanish-American War. It is noticeable that the main work on Anglo-American relations in this period has been done by Americans or Canadians: R. H. Heindel, op. cit.; L. M. Gelber, *The Rise of Anglo-American Friendship, 1898–1906* (1938); Charles S. Campbell, *Anglo-American Understanding, 1898–1903* (Baltimore, 1957). The year is selected because it marks the opening of active American imperialism in the Spanish-American War.

of Gladstonian foreign policy, and returned the Salisbury–Joseph Chamberlain union of Tories and Liberal Unionists to power; the culminating period of British expansionist imperialism was at hand, a period which was to see the capture by the ideals of imperialism of that section of the Liberal party which was to be from 1906 onwards the driving force in British foreign policy, the period of Fashoda, the Boer War and the Anglo-Japanese alliance.

It is also the only period of Anglo-American relations to have been studied in detail in the light of the British and American diplomatic archives.[1] It could be argued that such concentration has been misleading, since it has enabled historians to take a period in which, on the whole, Anglo-American relations prospered as indicating both that the process would continue and that this continuance was in some way inherent in the special nature of the relationship. A casual glance at the period 1906–12, or, indeed the 1916–22 period would shed a very different light on such arguments. In 1907 the British Ambassador Sir Mortimer Durand was recalled under American pressure.[2] The mission of his successor, Lord Bryce, was in the short run a failure marked by disputes over the Newfoundland fisheries, over sealing and other issues, and clouded at its end by the Senate's defeat of Grey's Anglo-American arbitration treaty and by Congress' unilateral denunciation of the Hay–Pauncefote Agreement on the Panama Canal.[3] Woodrow Wilson to his credit reversed this immediately after his inauguration, but there was a good deal of friction over his Mexican policy.[4] Theodore Roosevelt came to be detested by many British and his friend Senator Lodge, who with him killed

1. The recent opening of the British Foreign Office, Admiralty and War Office Archives has still to result in any published work on Anglo-American relations.

2. Sir Percy Sykes, *The Right Honourable Sir Mortimer Durand* (1926). Durand would not fit into Theodore Roosevelt's 'court'. Roosevelt was desperately anxious that Durand be replaced by his personal friend, Cecil Spring-Rice.

3. On Bryce see H. A. L. Fisher, *James Bryce* (New York, 1927); Lord Percy of Newcastle, *Some Memories* (1958); and Beckles Willson, *Friendly Relations; a Narrative of Britain's Ministers and Ambassadors to America, 1791–1930* (Boston, 1934). 'He had the quality of liking to make long and rather dull speeches on commonplace subjects which I know to be a trait that would make him popular with the American masses', wrote Sir Charles Hardinge who originally proposed him (Lord Hardinge of Penshurst, *The Old Diplomacy* (1947), 132).

4. A subject of first-class importance as yet unstudied.

the arbitration treaty in the Senate, was even more disliked.[1] The Anglo-American relationship was not stable, and it was consummated largely by a succession of British surrenders.

It is refreshing to find that the most recent British study in this field makes this its main theme.[2] Campbell argues that once America turned from isolationism to thoughts of her 'manifest destiny', that is, to imperialist expansion, conflict with Britain was inevitable; moreover, that the American challenge to Britain was so unmarred by doubt or self-criticism, so inspired with a confidence in American righteousness that the subsequent British 'surrender' needs special explanation, when contrasted with the sense of outrage expressed by British opinion against the much less far-reaching self-assertion of Wilhelmine Germany. He finds its explanation in five factors: firstly, British surprise at America's action and a consequent refusal to believe that after thirty years of peace there could be any new cause of disagreement; secondly, a general assumption of mutual goodwill, based on slowness to adapt to American intervention, and British preoccupation with Europe. German, French and Russian imperialisms were seen as a renewed extension of the 'struggle for mastery in Europe' and the consequence was that, practically and psychologically, concessions to America were easier to make, since they were irrelevant to that struggle. Thirdly, as American action took place largely within the framework of the Monroe doctrine, acting in isolation from Europe, there was no question of America linking with Britain's European rivals; fourthly, American brusquerie could be easily rationalized in terms of the Darwinist social theories of the day as the product of adolescent ignorance of the rules of the game, where similar German, French or Russian action would only be interpreted as studied insults; and finally, all this could be masked as squabbles within the 'Trans-Atlantic Anglo-Saxon family'. Campbell emphasizes that this feeling of 'kinship' (*'Anglo-Saxonia contra mundum'* as the journalist W. T. Stead put it at the time of the Spanish-American war) was far stronger in Britain, where it dominated thinking on the Anglo-American relationship, than in America, where, although

1. Admiral Sir John Fisher saw Roosevelt and Lodge as 'bitter foes' of an English-speaking federation, 'England's two greatest enemies' (A. J. Marder, *Fear God and Dread Nought*, ii (1961), 456). Even in 1901, Valentine Chirol of *The Times* could describe America as 'the most serious opponent of England' in conversation with the German diplomatist, Holstein.
2. A. E. Campbell. *Great Britain and the United States, 1895–1903* (1961).

racialism played a part, in general race was less important than the belief that England and America shared in the spread of progressive civilization based on the democratic virtues of political freedom and social equality. It is interesting to find exactly the same point being made about British Conservative parliamentary thought in the 1945–50 period.[1]

This analysis is in refreshing contrast to most previous work in the field because of its concentration on British opinion and because of the contrast it draws between the British and American interpretations of the 'special relationship' both countries professed to see in Anglo-American relations. It is the aim of this paper to argue that this analysis could be carried much farther, into the social and intellectual bases on which the 'special relationship' then postulated actually rested. Three hypotheses will be advanced; firstly that, in the social field, the attraction or repulsion of Britain for America or *vice versa* seems to be very closely connected with changes in the social basis of political power and influence in each country, especially among those sections of the political élites most concerned with foreign relations; secondly, in the field of intellectual developments, that British policy towards America (and indeed British foreign policy generally) shows just as marked an interaction between realism and idealism as that with which studies of the content and ideas of American foreign policy have familiarized us;[2] and thirdly, that the fluctuations in each field are concurrent and may be connected causally.

The remainder of this study proposes to concentrate on the British side of the relationship; its purpose is to explain the change from a state of affairs when Anglo-American amity was in political terms broadly a relationship between British imperialists and American Republicans as in 1900, to that of the 1950s when most shades of British opinion would have elected the Democratic presidential candidate in both the 1952 and 1956 elections and welcomed the result of the 1960 election. It is based essentially on British political and diplomatic memoirs,[3] British and American diplomatic documents and such biographical details as are given in the *Foreign Office*

---

1. Epstein, op. cit.; Bremner, op. cit.

2. For example, Robert E. Osgood, *Ideals and Self-interest in America's Foreign Relations* (Chicago, 1953).

3. All British diplomatic memoirs and biographies, and all relevant political ones have been consulted. Military and naval memoirs have not been so thoroughly covered.

Lists and in *Who's Who*. It does not profess to be based on any statistical sampling or to be exhaustive. Rather its aim is to advance a hypothesis which would have to be verified by sociological methods of investigation.[1]

To take the social hypothesis first: the Anglo-American *rapprochement* in the 1898–1906 period rested very much on the accident that political control in each country rested, however precariously, in the hands of men belonging to social groups of very similar outlooks, men who thought in terms of a 'deferential society'. These groups had become increasingly linked by intermarriage and the prevailing freedom of international travel. Increasingly, the 'season' in London was a 'must' for socially ambitious Americans, while a small, though increasing, number of the British élite were beginning to include America in a special Grand Tour, which took in Ottawa and Niagara Falls, Washington, New York and the Chicago meat canneries.[2] It is hoped that some returned with more than the Liberal Whig, Lord Crewe, of whom his biographer recorded: 'he brought back with him a short travel diary, an attitude of amused tolerance for the Americans, a list of the hotels in which they had stayed, a self-compiled glossary of Americanisms, and two recipes for making John Collins' and a whisky-rum-and-angostura-bitters cocktail.'[3] It was, however, the same Lord Crewe who remarked in July 1915 to the Russian Ambassador that he believed it would be very difficult for the United States to assume an attitude entirely hostile to England, for the *better element in American public opinion* would not accept such a departure from tradition.[4] Lord Curzon, Foreign Secretary from 1919–22, and again from 1922–23, brought back an American wife; but his attitude to America remained hostile. There were a large number of other intermarriages (some 140 by 1914),[5] and at least one

1. One extremely important theme which has only been touched on here is the channels of information and experience of America available to and used by the political élites in Britain.

2. Some went on, retracing Mr Phileas Fogg's steps, to the Grand Canyon, the Yosemite Valley, San Francisco and on to Asia on a round-the-world trip.

3. James Pope-Hennessy, *Lord Crewe, 1858–1945; Portrait of a Liberal* (1955).

4. Benckendorff to Sazonov, 1 July 1915 (*Mezhdunarodnye Otnosheniya*, Series III, VIII, no.223). As Lord President of the Council, Crewe was temporarily in charge of the Foreign Office in Sir Edward Grey's absence.

5. The figure is from H. C. Allen, op. cit. See also Elizabeth Eliot, *They All Married Well* (1960). The marriages did not always serve to strengthen

significant American immigration, that of the Astor family, who came first to acquire *The Observer* and its brilliant editor, Joseph Garvin, the intellectual inspiration of the Conservative party between 1908 and 1913,[1] and then in 1922, *The Times* itself.[2] Astor père left America in an excess of dislike for its press, which had harried him unmercifully, for a land where the mass press could be ignored. His son and daughter-in-law both entered Parliament, and their home, Cliveden, is part of the legend of British foreign policy in the 1930s.[3]

The change in British politics with the great Liberal victory in 1906 did not have the shattering effect on Anglo-American relations that the advent of Wilson was to have in America in 1913. The Liberal party was an alliance between three elements: reformist Whigs of the same social tradition and background as those whom they had supplanted; social *arrivistes* of Jewish or 'self-made' vintage, whom their enemies called the 'radical plutocracy'; and regional and lower-class discontent, *petit bourgeois*, agrarian and industrial working class. Of these elements, the first had largely been captured by imperialism in the decade immediately after 1900 when they looked in vain to Lord Rosebery for leadership. The second and third were largely uninterested in foreign relations. There was a fourth group, that of the intellectual *arrivistes* such as Asquith, Haldane and Reginald McKenna. There was also a group of radical intellectuals less interested in power than in proselytization, who propounded an 'alternative' foreign policy of the type described by A. J. P. Taylor.

Anglo-American relations. American readers did not well receive remarks in the vein of Oscar Wilde in *The Canterville Ghost*: 'For Virginia received the Coronet, which is the reward of all good little American girls, and married her boy-love. . . .' On one future American President, Hoover, the knowledge of such marriages had a contrary effect: 'The cynical remarks upon American ladies who bought titles would be hard for those ladies to bear. It added wormwood to American listeners to learn the justification of such titled gentlemen which was that sacrifice must be made to repair their family fortunes' (*The Memoirs of Herbert Hoover* (New York, 1952), I, 126–237, and also ch. 10 *passim*). See also the very astute comments of Lord Percy of Newcastle (op. cit.), a member of the British Embassy in Washington under Bryce, later Minister in various of the Conservative Cabinets, and a close friend of Baldwin.

1. A. M. Gollin, *The Observer and J. L. Garvin* (New York, 1960), 301–3.

2. *The History of 'The Times'*, vol.IV, part II.

3. See on Cliveden: T. H. Jones, *A Diary with Letters* (1954); Sir James Butler, *Lord Lothian (Philip Kerr) 1882–1940* (New York, 1960); Maurice Collis, *Nancy Astor* (1960); Michael Astor, *Tribal Feeling* (1963).

But before 1916 this group had little or no influence on the formulation of foreign policy. The William Jennings Bryans of British
Liberalism were excluded from power. The intellectual *arrivistes*,
however, were only the Liberal wing of a general phenomenon in
British politics at this time; their opposite numbers in the Conservative party are in many ways more significant. But before examining
them it is as well to look briefly at the second hypothesis propounded,
that of the interaction of realism and idealism.

The realist tradition in British foreign policy enters into the formation of British policy in two ways. In the Foreign Office and
among the political élite, it stems from the aristocratic tradition of the
eighteenth and nineteenth centuries, with Lord Salisbury as perhaps
its greatest exponent. Its basis is a concern for British national and
individual interests and a refusal to become so involved in the affairs
of one part of the world as to be unable to see in what priority these
interests should be judged. Being aristocratic, it was neither chauvinist nor nationalist; its concern for individual British interests was
benevolently paternalist, that of the landowner for his tenants rather
than of the racialist for his fellows. Empiricist in tradition, it dis-
claimed ideology of any kind and remained contemptuous both of
amateurism and of intellectualism.

Its main strength obviously lay in the Foreign Office, though it has
been a weakening force there since the 1920s.[1] But it continues inevitably to find a way into discussions of foreign policy, via the
Service ministries and the Chiefs of Staff committees, whose job is
the relation of foreign policy to British strength, a point of view
particularly well entrenched in the Admiralty. It was the Admiralty
that in 1901 advised the Cabinet that with the accepted relative study
of naval strength, in order to place Great Britain in a position to
acquire the command of the seas on the coast of America it would be
essential that the neutrality of the European powers should be
assured.[2] This judgment was made at a time when it was obvious that
no such assurances could be given; the obvious deduction was that, if

1. Lawrence Durrell's fictional portrait of the British Ambassador in
Egypt in the 1930s, whom he calls Mountolive, in the third book of his
Alexandria tetralogy, is very perceptive: 'Mountolive had indeed been rather
shocked by opinions [those of the novelist, Pursewarden] as clear-cut as they
were trenchant, for he at the time shared the prevailing egalitarian sympathies of the day – albeit in the anodyne liberalised form then current in the
[Foreign] Office' (*Mountolive* (Pocket Books Edition, 1961), 49).
2. Cited in Charles S. Campbell, *Anglo-American Understanding*.

27

such an assurance was not possible, conflict with America must be avoided. In 1903 the Admiralty advised the War Office that if there were European complications they could not guarantee the command of the seas at the opening of hostilities with the United States; the real significance of this, it added, was 'the necessity of preserving amicable relations with the United States'.[1] These arguments were essentially of a strategic nature, and said nothing of 'alliances', natural or otherwise. The Anglo-American *entente* in this view was what the Anglo-French *entente* was originally meant to be, a settlement of differences, nothing more.

Idealism entered first on the political plane. It came in two brands. First was the Anglo-Saxonism of the publicists, going back to Seeley, Dilke, E. A. Freeman and even to Dicey, and finding its most popular expression in the Poet Laureate Alfred Austin's effusion on the Spanish-American War, in W. T. Stead's *Anglo-Saxonia contra mundum*, and in Kipling's bitter attack on the Conservative Government's participation in the German debt-collecting naval demonstration off Venezuela in 1903. It ensnared more extraordinary political figures, in Admiral of the Fleet Lord Fisher and Salisbury's nephew, Arthur Balfour, the Conservative leader. Theodore Roosevelt's great circle of friends included many of this point of view, enshrined literally in the title and theme of Churchill's *History of the English-Speaking Peoples*.

Second and more important, however, is the administrative imperialism of Indian and Egyptian origin, the latter of particular importance. Lord Cromer was its first exponent, Lord Milner its first great prophet with his study of Cromer's administration in Egypt. As Cairo lay within the terms of duty of the Foreign Service,[2] its outlook influenced the diplomats also. To India went the later Foreign Secretary, Curzon, and Hardinge of Penshurst, a future Permanent Under-Secretary of State. From India came the unfortunate Sir Mortimer Durand. The ethos of administrative imperialism supported good Anglo-American relations, as a means of strengthening Britain. Although idealist in its devotion to the Empire and in

1. I am grateful to my colleague, Dr Bourne, for providing me with this quotation from War Office files recently deposited in the Public Records Office.

2. An extraordinarily large proportion of the most successful figures in the British Foreign Service in this period served terms of duty in Cairo, where the nature of the British occupation made their jobs quite unlike those of the normal diplomatic post.

much of its personal attitude to America in the more narrow field of foreign affairs, this position is essentially realist in approach. In essence it was hostile to democratic procedures as tending to produce weakness, divisions of counsel and compromise, rather than the model administrative solution. It disliked the American system and American press as embodying the rule of an ill-educated plebs. It looked with near contempt on the Americans' inability to handle their colonial problems in Cuba and the Philippines. It despised them for their inability to produce an élite civil service on the British model, and Roman history was read so as to equate political corruption with decadence. As a school of thought it could have no time for America except as a possible ally.

Administrative imperialism is principally important to this study for its offspring, neo-imperialism. Milner took with him for his period of reconstruction in South Africa after the Boer War a group of young men known as the 'Kindergarten'. In South Africa they imbibed briefly the pan-Anglo-Saxonism of Cecil Rhodes. But a far greater influence on them was Joseph Chamberlain's imperial tariff movement and the movement for an imperial federation. This group was to be of immense importance in Tory politics because apart from Garvin they were to be for nearly forty years Toryism's only effective doctrinal body. All were publicists of the first order. Leo Amery, the only one to achieve really high office, was already on *The Times*. Lord Lothian founded and edited *The Round Table*. Lionel Curtis became the prophet of Chatham House. Dawson edited *The Times* from 1922 to 1941, exerting unparalleled influence on both Baldwin and Neville Chamberlain.[1] John Buchan ended as Governor-General of Canada. F. S. Oliver, Grigg, Brand and others acted as their influential seconds.[2]

The group as a whole set itself one aim—the creation of an imperial super-state, in which all the races of the Empire were to be penetrated by British traditions and British purposes, wedded with whatever individual contributions their original cultures could bring

1. See Sir Evelyn Wrench, *Geoffrey Dawson and Our Times* (1955); *The History of 'The Times'*, vol.IV, part II. See also 'The Influence of the Commonwealth on British Foreign Policy: the Case of the Munich Crisis', Essay 8, below.

2. On some grounds, George Lloyd, High Commissioner in Egypt 1922–30, and first head of the British Council, may be counted in this group, although he kept aloof from most of its activities. See Colin Forbes-Adams, *Life of Lord Lloyd* (1948).

to enlarge this. This imperial super-state was to adopt what had been best in the Roman Empire, including its universal citizenship, and the imposition of the Pax Romana.

The aim of the group gave it a triple interest in the United States. Firstly, it was in their view incontestable that to a large degree the United States had succeeded in the absorption and unification of a great mass of different peoples and traditions. It was a great federation. Secondly, the group subscribed largely to the theories that the two countries shared a common culture and a common purpose.[1] Thirdly, the group realized that their aim could only be achieved by maintaining British predominance over Europe, especially against the European tyrannies in Germany and Russia, which, they believed, were challenging Britain's position. This they felt America would help them to do. Again and again one finds in their writings the idea of an Anglo-American world hegemony. Britain and America together could dominate the world, widening and strengthening the Pax Britannica, the world order on which they set so much store.

As a group, they were, almost to a man, intellectual *arrivistes*, with little besides their intellectual powers to recommend them to the social oligarchs who advanced them. Up to 1912 this group, though occasionally resentful of individual American actions, was pro-American. On the other side of the political fence its members were supported by the Whig families, already noted, who responded to American idealism, by the 'radical plutocracy', the social *arrivistes* who saw in American society methods and models they would have liked to impose on their own,[2] and by their own equivalents in the Liberal party.

The advent of Wilson in 1913 and his appointment of Bryan as Secretary of State changed all this. British opinion began with high hopes of Wilson, but his and Bryan's behaviour in the vital 1914–16 period was a terrible disillusionment. There had been preliminary difficulties in Mexico and Colombia, but the vital point was American unwillingness to endorse the British blockade of Germany and Wilson's refusal wholeheartedly to espouse Britain's cause against Germany. Spring-Rice, the pan-Anglo-Saxon, whose attitude alone

1. The influence of Bryce is of considerable importance here. F. S. Oliver wrote a biography of Alexander Hamilton that was not without its influence.
2. Although both supported the Conservative party before 1914, Northcliffe and Rothermere, the press lords, are in other respects characteristic of this type.

in the Foreign Service was akin to that of the 'Kindergarten', had arrived in the Washington Embassy too late to find his friend Theodore Roosevelt in power. His position was unenviable in the extreme. A dedicated anti-German, an ideological patriot, he had to swallow Wilson's and Bryan's suspicion of Britain's motives in entering and fighting the war. At the same time, he was well aware of the way in which Wilson's own freedom of action was limited by the victory of the Southern and Mid-Western radicals, whom Wilson's victory had brought into power in Congress. He thus found himself in the unenviable position of seeming to Wilson a mere British chauvinist, while in Britain he was regarded by the more traditionally-minded realists of the Foreign Office as too pro-American.[1]

The turning point in Anglo-American relations came in 1916. Three factors were at work.[2] Firstly, the difficulties made by America, and that able and intelligent group in the Foreign Office blockade section who put American goodwill above perfection of the blockade, progressively alienated the Admiralty which was rarely pro-American anyway.[3] Secondly, the failure of Wilson to react in a bellicose and chauvinistic manner to German submarine measures led the younger neo-imperialists, who were of the opinion that Britain was fighting America's battles as well as her own and defending their common traditions against alien authoritarianism, to be progressively embittered and contemptuous in private, even though they preached

1. See his letters to Grey of 30 May and 14 July 1916, and to Maurice de Bunsen of March 1916. 'I thought the Bird [Sir Eyre Crowe, then head of Blockade Division in F.O., subsequently Permanent Under-Secretary] would raise an angry beak at my pro-American tendencies.' *The Letters and Friendships of Sir Cecil Spring-Rice*, II (1929).

2. Ernest R. May, *The World War and American Isolation, 1914–17* (Cambridge, Mass., 1959) is an indispensable introduction to this period and the first book on this subject to come out of America in which intelligent comment is not deafened by the noise of grinding axes.

3. Admiral Beatty was at least sympathetic towards individual Americans. Neither Jellicoe nor Wemyss, his successor as First Sea Lord, had any time for America, Wemyss finding Americans 'tiresome and sententious' despite his school friendship with Sir Esmé Howard, Baron Howard of Penrith, one of the few Foreign Office men who understood America at this period (Ambassador 1924–30; Councillor in Washington 1907–8). See Howard's *Theatre of Life, 1863–1936* (1935–36), and Victoria, Baroness Wester Wemyss, *The Life and Letters of Lord Wester Wemyss* (1935). On Beatty see Lord Vansittart, *The Mist Procession* (1958), 319. Lord Robert Cecil was the Minister of Blockade. See Viscount Cecil of Chelwood, *All the Way* (1949), 129–40. Hoover pays tribute to him in his memoirs.

amity in public.[1] Thirdly, the Liberal Government's position was steadily weakening in the face of Conservative pressure that allied with the 'radical plutocrats' and the irresponsible patriots on both sides of the party line. Both Asquith and Sir Edward Grey set great store on the maintenance of Anglo-American amity. But the increasing war psychosis induced in Britain by the appalling casualties (a factor consistently underestimated by every American writer), which fell with peculiar heaviness on the upper middle and upper classes who provided the volunteer officers for the armies of 1915 and 1916 before the introduction of conscription, made it progressively easy for Asquith's and Grey's enemies to use Service opinion against them. In December 1916 Lloyd George forced Asquith out of office, and the Coalition which he formed was to govern until 1922, when he in turn was forced out of office by a revolt in the Conservative party. Neither the Coalition nor its successors were to be pro-American in anything except public oratory.[2]

The Coalition consisted of three main groups, so far as its driving power was concerned. Firstly, there were the neo-imperialists acting directly on the new Prime Minister, Lloyd George, through Amery, Lothian and Grigg, his private secretaries, and also through their

1. Arthur Willert, *Times* correspondent in Washington 1910–19, to Dawson, 22 January 1915: 'I feel it incumbent to be more pro-American in print than in private. I do resent rather the sordidness of the American attitude.' The same to the same, 5 March 1915: 'We must never forget that in the United States we have perhaps the weakest government she has ever suffered under, fighting unscrupulously, stupidly and incessantly to save itself in the next Presidential election.' Dawson, early 1917: 'Personally, I believe that nothing would be so popular here as a real anti-American outburst and the sacking let us say, of poor old Page's house.' See *The History of 'The Times'*, vol.IV, part I. British informants in America, a legacy from the 1900s, tended to be Republicans, who assured them that Wilson could not last in power.

2. 'Of course Anglo-American relations were "paramount" and all that, but Macdonald was exceptional in meaning it' (Vansittart, op. cit., 318). Vansittart was head of the American department in the F.O. 1924–27, Deputy Under-Secretary and Principal Private Secretary to Baldwin and MacDonald 1927–30, Permanent Under-Secretary 1930–38, and married an American as his first wife. Grey was adamant on doing nothing to disturb Anglo-American relations. 'We wish in all our conduct in the war to do nothing which will be a cause of complaint or dispute as regards the United States Government; such a dispute would indeed be a crowning calamity . . . and probably fatal to our chances of success' (Grey to Spring-Rice, 3 September 1914, cited in G. M. Trevelyan, *Grey of Fallodon* (1937), 356).

idol, Milner. Secondly, there were the 'radical plutocrats': North-cliffe, Rothermere, Riddell from the press, the Geddes brothers, Lord Cowdray, Lord Rhondda and many others from industry, to name only a few. Third was a group that can best be called the 'irresponsibles'. These were men without party loyalty, or political party (as opposed to personal) principle. After his period as a radical legislator had ended, Lloyd George was certainly one. F. E. Smith (Lord Birkenhead), Sir Edward Carson, Sir Robert Horne and in methods, at least, Churchill, for all his later advocacy of Anglo-American amity, must be counted among these. One should perhaps add to them the 'passive irresponsibles', such as Montagu and Reading, who in 1917 replaced Spring-Rice as Ambassador to Washington. The distinguishing mark of this group was a chauvinistic patriotism, a contempt for idealism and a delight in the exercise of power for its own sake, particularly the last.

Wilson's attempts at mediation in the course of 1916 impressed this combination of opinions in the worst possible light. For a time, it is true, Grey and his group were able to negotiate, but the course of these negotiations[1] made it clear that, despite some wavering at home (owing to the appalling casualties in the first battle of the Somme), the main thing to keep them going on the British side was the hope of American intervention. Wilson's move from private to public mediation, the speech of May 1916, and the Peace Note of December 1916, were received with anger by all groups of British opinion, by none more strongly than the traditional realists who had by then settled into a rooted hostility to Germany on a par with their earlier hostility to Russia.[2] The need not to alienate Wilson completely dictated a friendly reply[3] from the new Foreign Secretary, Arthur

1. Ably described in May, op. cit.

2. 'A great piece of impertinence' (*The Diary of Lord Bertie of Thame, 1914–18* (1924), entry of 21 December 1916). Bertie was Ambassador in Paris, 1905–18. 'Frankly a piece of impertinence' (Hardinge of Penshurst, op. cit., 207). Hardinge was Permanent Under-Secretary in the Foreign Office. An 'outrage', unless the American Ambassador in Berlin had told Wilson that Germany could fight another five years (*Journals and Letters of Reginald, Viscount Esher* (1938), IV, entry of 24 December 1916). A professional '*éminence grise*', Esher was close to the Court, a friend of General Haig and in regular correspondence with Captain Hankey, Secretary to the Cabinet.

3. 'We shall be obliged to reply with civility and suppressed anger' (Bertie, op. cit., entry of 20 December 1916). Pressure was, in fact, on the British press to restrain hostile comment (Blanche Dugdale, *Arthur James Balfour* (1936), III, 188–9).

Balfour, a consistent pro-American of neo-imperialist sympathies, one of the few in the new Coalition. But although complete alienation was avoided, the rejection of his offer and the fall of Grey convinced Wilson that British intentions about the future were to be regarded with as much suspicion as those of Germany. He was already beginning to equate British navalism with German militarism,[1] and from this period dates his determination to use the Allies' dependence on America as a weapon to force their acceptance of the kind of peace he desired.

It is against this background that the period of Wilson's ascendancy must be judged. The political direction of Britain's foreign relations was divided between the 'irresponsibles', the 'neo-imperialists' and the 'traditional realists' who, while remaining the weakest party in that direction, at least until Lord Curzon took over the Foreign Secretaryship in 1919, were strongly entrenched in the War Office, the Admiralty and the Foreign and Diplomatic Services. On Wilson, neo-imperialists and traditionalists were of one mind.[2] Pro-American neo-imperialists had seen Britain and America as allies, approaching a quasi-federal relationship. Wilson's attacks on British blockade practices, enshrined in his doctrines of 'Freedom of the Seas', represented to them as to the traditional realists, a direct assault on British power, the act of an enemy rather than an ally. Thus, whatever their personal feelings and friendships, Wilsonianism made nonsense of the 'special relationship'.

Good relations with America were only maintained by the sheer necessity of avoiding an open break in the circumstances of 1917–18. Lord Reading can claim some of the credit,[3] but much more must go

1. See the remarks of the American Ambassador in Turkey, Morgenthau, to Esher, op. cit., entry of 11 August 1917, and more significantly Colonel House's attempt, on Wilson's instructions, to force Britain publicly to accept the principle of the freedom of the seas, by threatening a separate peace with Germany, in October–November 1918 in the negotiations for the drafting of armistices with Germany and Austria.

2. It is significant that the main formal embodiment of Anglo-American amity in the 1900–12 period was the oligarchic Pilgrim Trust. In 1917–18 it was the middle-class English-Speaking Union founded by the Irish journalist and protégé of Northcliffe, Sir Evelyn Wrench. See his *Struggle, 1914–19* (1935).

3. *Rufus Isaacs, First Marquess of Reading, by his son* (1945). Of a Jewish fruit-importing family, Isaacs rose by his brilliance at the bar to be Liberal Lord Chief Justice; Ambassador in Washington 1917–19; Viceroy of India; and Foreign Secretary 1931.

to Sir William Wiseman, a British Intelligence Officer attached to the Washington Embassy,[1] who between 1917–19 acted as the only channel by which any genuine Anglo-American conversation could be carried on. For his main contacts in England, Wilson turned to the intellectual radicals of the Liberal party, and the few idealists from the older political élite, whose innate respect for law was leading them to envisage some kind of supranational organization. The latter were impelled towards him anyway, as Grey had been, by sympathy for his ideals. The former were obvious allies since they fitted in so clearly with Wilson's favourite technique of mobilizing the people against the 'special interests'.[2] In so acting Wilson was setting the stage for what was to be the basic pattern of Anglo-American relations in the 1930s and 1940s, the transatlantic alliance of American 'liberals' with British Liberal–Labour radicals, that is, between the northern Democrats and the British centre. The group that he contacted was to prove of extreme importance in the 1920s and the 1930s. Rejecting Lloyd George and the Coalition, its members were to move into the Labour party, and in the atmosphere of the 'Secret Treaties' and the Stockholm Socialist Congress they had already formed links with Labour's pacifist wing. And as the Labour movement entered political life unprovided with any doctrinal attitude to foreign affairs, it was to be a ready victim of the sophistication and experience of these ex-Liberal radicals and their Union for Democratic Control, whose social and intellectual antipathy to those who made traditional foreign policy fitted easily with Labour's suspicion of the upper classes. Moreover, both groups, idealist oligarchs and intellectual radicals, were to unite in the League of Nations Union, the single most important and influential pressure group in British foreign politics between the wars.

In the meantime, however, Anglo-American relations on the political plane were to plummet to as low a position as they had ever occupied. Wilson was variously regarded as a new Rousseau,[3] 'Buddha in a frock coat',[4] concerned only to increase American trade with

1919

1. Sir Arthur Willert, *The Road to Safety* (New York, 1953), *passim*; Lord Murray of Elibank, *At Close Quarters* (1946).
2. On the League of Nations movement see Winkler, *Journal of Modern History*, XXVIII. On Wilson's connections with the British intellectual radicals see Martin, *Peace without Victory*.
3. Esher, op. cit., entry of 27 January 1917.
4. Esher, op. cit., to O.S.B., 16 November 1918.

Germany,[1] a bungling amateur, 'tiresome and sententious',[2] and the Peace Conference itself a fiasco.[3] The crowning disaster was Wilson's inability to achieve the necessary majority in the Senate for the ratification of Versailles. The reactions of all circles of British élite opinion were summed up in a memorandum prepared by Sir Cecil Hurst, legal adviser to the Foreign Office, and circulated to the Cabinet by Lord Curzon.

The principle for which the Allied Powers in Paris purported to be struggling and the basis on which they posed as contracting was that of substituting the principle of sharing in common the obligations of the civilized states for the condition of affairs which had prevailed up to the time of the war of mere individual regulation of international relations. Once the principle is admitted that one or more of the Great Powers is to stand outside the settlement the inevitable result must be to reintroduce the old state of affairs with all the uneasy conditions which have prevailed in Europe for the last two decades. . . . To the British Empire the exclusion of the United States from the obligations under Article x means that burdens may have to be supported single-handed which no government would lightly undertake without an assurance that the other great states would do their part, more particularly its great commercial rival across the Atlantic. . . .[4]

1. *The Private Papers of Douglas Haig, 1914–19* (1952), entries of 20–1 February 1919.
2. Wemyss, op. cit.
3. 'The Paris Conference has at any rate succeeded in this, that a future war upon a bigger scale becomes inevitable. It is something to have dispelled all doubt upon that point. It is not precisely what Wilson set out to do' (Esher, op. cit., to L.B., 16 June 1919). It is interesting to find Esher in agreement with the radical liberal aristocrat, Commander Kenworthy, RN, MP, who on 6 June 1919, said that the Versailles Treaty had turned the peace into 'a just and durable war' (cited in R. B. McCallum, *Public Opinion and the Last Peace* (1944), 51). Kenworthy, later Lord Strabolgi, was a serving naval officer until 1919, when he entered Parliament as an Asquithian Liberal. In 1927 he joined the Labour party. See his *Sailors, Statesmen and Others* (1933).
4. *Documents on British Foreign Policy*, Series I, v, document no.399. Viscount Grey was sent over on a despairing mission to try to secure a détente in Anglo-American relations, but despite the strong recommendation of Colonel House, Wilson refused to see Grey, ostensibly on grounds of ill-health. It was at this period that the second Mrs Wilson established her ascendancy over the ailing President, and succeeded in turning him against House himself. Grey insisted on employing a member of Lord Reading's staff whom gossip alleged to have spoken slightingly of Mrs Wilson and of the President. See Sir Maurice Peterson, *Both Sides of the Curtain* (1950);

The triumph of the Republican and isolationist elements in Congress and in the country in defeating the Treaty ushered in a prolonged period of strained relations. During their campaign against the Treaty, Republicans had not hesitated to point to Wilson as the victim of British guile and to appeal to the anti-British sentiments of the Irish and German voters; while the Democrat administration was far from being Anglophile in its views, and regarded Britain's efforts to regain some of the economic position she had enjoyed during the war as presaging an Anglo-American trade war.[1]

The victory of the Republican party in 1920 would not have improved matters had not the new Secretary of State, Charles E. Hughes, a Republican of the prewar type, fought a bitter rearguard battle against Congressional pressure, the big Navy pressure of Denby, the Republican Secretary of the Navy and an obscurantist and Nationalist Congress. His task was not aided by the attitude of the British Coalition Government. During the first four years after the war, the control of British foreign policy lay at issue between the 'irresponsibles' and the traditionalists, between Churchill, Birkenhead and Lloyd George on one side, and Lord Curzon and the Foreign Office on the other. Neo-imperialism was temporarily in eclipse, for Lord Milner had resigned and Lloyd George had evaded the control of the junior ministers and members of his secretariat who still held to its ideas. Their position had been still further weakened by the disaster suffered by the Treaty of Versailles at the hands of the Senate. The Senate action deprived them of any renewal of earlier hopes, in the war years and during the Peace Conference, of a joint Anglo-American condominium as law-givers to the non-Anglo-Saxon world.

In the conflict between 'irresponsibles' and traditionalists, America figured only as one of many factors in the power-relationships which bore on Britain. The paralysis of American government under Wilson's political dotage was matched by an almost criminal neglect

---

William Phillips, *Ventures in Diplomacy* (Boston, 1952), 91–2; *State Department Papers, Decimal File, 1919–29*, US National Archives, File 704.41111/303,304,305,314 1/2.

1. Indeed, Republican leaders had warned Lord Reading that the charge that Wilson was a victim of British guile would be a consequence of very obvious British co-operation with Wilson at Versailles (*Frank L. Polk Diary*, entry of 26 April 1919). Wilson, on his part, attempted to prevent the appointment of Sir Auckland Geddes as British Ambassador in 1920, because he believed promotion of a trade war to be the reason for Sir Auckland's appointment (*Polk Papers*, Wilson to Frank L. Polk, 3 March 1920).

D

of Anglo-American relations in Britain. The 'irresponsibles' were mainly concerned with foreign affairs as a field in which to win victories that would enhance their declining position on the domestic front. The traditionalists were mainly concerned with Britain's position in the Middle East, with restraining French intoxication in victory, and with attempting to curtail British commitments to match Britain's resources. In this a number of issues dear to national chauvinism, supremacy at sea, the control of oil resources[1] or wireless and cable communications and the like, all displayed more in terms of public bragging than in positive action, were allowed to embitter Anglo-American relations and reinforce American suspicions of Britain.

The question of the renewal of the Anglo-Japanese alliance, the deep embitterment of Japanese-American relations by naval competition, and the alarm of the Dominions, especially Canada, expressed at the Imperial Conference of 1921,[2] led to the summoning of the Washington Conference, and the conclusion of the Washington Treaties, as much a peace settlement between Britain and America as between America and Japan. A major part was played in its successful convention and conclusion by a temporary reconjunction of the elements in both countries which had brought about the prewar détente. The American delegation was led and dominated by Secretary of State Hughes and Assistant Secretary of the Navy, Colonel Theodore Roosevelt Jr, with the assistance of Elihu Root, and of Senator Lodge returned to the Anglophilia of his youth. Aided by the intelligence of the Maine-born Admiral Pratt, Hughes ignored the chauvinism of the American Navy and steered things so carefully as to deprive the chauvinist and isolationist Congress of any real weapons to use against the treaties finally concluded. On the English side, he was aided and abetted by the conjunction of a pro-American First Lord of the Admiralty,[3] a fundamentally realist First Sea Lord, Lord

1. For some illustration see J. de Novo, 'The Movement for an Aggressive American Oil Policy Abroad', *American Historical Review*, LXI (1956); Benjamin Shwadran, *The Middle East, Oil and the Great Powers* (New York, 1959).

2. See J. Bartlet Brebner, 'Canada, the Anglo-Japanese Alliance and the Washington Conference', *Political Science Quarterly* (1935); J. S. Galbraith, 'The Imperial Conference of 1921 and the Washington Conference', *Canadian Historical Review*, XXIX (1948); W. Farmer Whyte, *W. M. Hughes: His Life and Times* (Canberra, 1957).

3. Arthur Lee, Lord Lee of Fareham. As military attaché in Washington under the Embassy of Sir Julian Pauncefote he had become very friendly

Beatty, and the leadership of Arthur Balfour who headed the British delegation and could deal with Hughes, Root and Lodge on a basis of intellectual equality. In the disputes over Mesopotamian oil and the 'Open Door' in Iraq, the British company principally involved met its major American competitors in a deal carried out behind the backs of the State Department, which was forced to recognize a *fait accompli*. As a result pressure behind the public criticism of Britain in America was largely removed.[1]

From that date onwards, the foreign-policy-making élite in Britain accepted American isolationism. It became axiomatic that any British proposal made in Europe would not be based on the hope of American support, and that if American proposals were made it was best to let their proposers make the running. On both sides of the Atlantic, considerable ill-will or, at least, mistrust prevailed beneath the surface bonhomie of Pilgrim Trust dinners, at any rate, in those circles where political power resided.[2] In 1927–28, the years of the

---

with Theodore Roosevelt Sr, and was an honorary member of the latter's 'Rough Riders'. His wife was American. He had attempted various unofficial approaches to members of the new administration early in 1921. See Lee of Fareham to Colonel Theodore Roosevelt Jr, 11 March 1921 (*Colonel Theodore Roosevelt Jr, Letters*); Commander E. S. Land to the same, 27 May 1921 (*Admiral Emory Scott Land Papers*); Eugene J. Young, *Powerful America* (New York, 1936), 49–56.

1. Shwadran, op. cit. On the principal British negotiator, see John Rowland and Basil, Second Baron Cadman, *Ambassador for Oil, the Life of John, First Baron Cadman* (1960).

2. 'Gratuitous ill-will is an absorbing subject' (Vansittart, *The Mist Procession*, 318–19). 'As to America taking part in promoting security in Europe, I think the public is still quite unready for anything of the sort. Overriding all this is the attitude of purely political and Congress circles, and as to this, my view is that no progress is to be registered, perhaps even retrogression, on the question both of debts and security, especially of the latter' (Sir Ronald Lindsay to the Marquess of Reading, 23 October 1931, *D.B.F.P.*, Series II, II, no.277). Vansittart served as Head of the American section of the Foreign Office up to 1927. His wife was American. Sir Ronald Lindsay served in Washington as Second Secretary to Bryce, 1906–07, and as Ambassador in Washington 1931–39. Lady Lindsay was American. Attempts were made behind the scenes to influence both the Coolidge and Baldwin administrations, and to find a formula to reconcile their differences by groups headed by the Council for Foreign Relations in the USA and by Lord Lothian working through the Royal Institute of International Affairs in London (see *Lothian Papers*). The changes of régime in both countries made these efforts unnecessary.

ill-starred three-power Geneva Naval Conference and of the Anglo-French compromise of 1928, relations plunged to a new low. Only the advent of Stimson as Hoover's Secretary of State in 1929, and of Ramsay MacDonald's second administration in June 1929, made possible the general settlement of outstanding issues achieved by MacDonald's visit to Rapidan in October 1929 and the London Naval Conference of 1930. The settlement was made because both sets of political leaders were prepared to override their naval advisers.[1] Stimson was an uncharacteristic figure among contemporary Republicans. A former Secretary of War under Taft, he was a disciple and protégé of Elihu Root, and, possibly, the last representative of the pre-1914 Republican political élite. MacDonald's main virtue was that he failed in any respect whatever to conform to the American stereotype of the British ruling classes. But his political views and those of many of his Cabinet had been formed in the days of the Union for Democratic Control and the contacts between Wilson and the British radicals. Though tempered by the realism which comes with any tenure of office, he thrilled to Wilsonian ideals and sentiment. In turn, Hoover was one of the more prominent Wilsonian Republicans, at least, until fairly late in Wilson's career, and shared Wilson's predilection for assuming the moral leadership of the world, if such a position seemed open for applicants.[2]

But underlying this temporary and fortuitous conjunction of individuals powerful enough to override their service advisers and the nationalist and chauvinist press there were new social alignments on both sides of the Atlantic. Some time would have to elapse before these new groupings could adjust themselves to and adopt as their own the arguments for Anglo-American amity.

It would be an oversimplification to call the Republican era of the 1920s an era of businessmen. It is rather that the inter-regional balance of power inside America had shifted away from New York society and the east coast generally. The Republican party had lost the genteel oligarchic elements which controlled its foreign policy in

1. See Miss P. M. Shepherd, 'Anglo-American Relations during the Administration of Herbert Hoover, with Special Relation to Europe' (unpublished MA thesis, London, 1955); George M. Fagan, 'Anglo-American Naval Relations, 1927–37' (unpublished Ph.D. thesis, University of Pennsylvania, 1954); Raymond G. O'Connor, *Perilous Equilibrium: the United States and the London Naval Conference of 1930* (Lawrence, Kansas, 1961).

2. He later published a highly partisan defence of Wilson in 1918–19, *The Ordeal of Woodrow Wilson* (New York, 1958).

the 1900s. In Britain, Bonar Law's advent to the Conservative leadership in 1912, the elimination of the Asquithian Liberals as a serious political force in the 1918 'coupon' election and the gradual amalgamation of Lloyd Georgites and Conservatives during and after the Second Coalition, had similarly altered the balance of power inside the Conservative party. The overthrow of the Coalition in 1922 removed the 'irresponsibles' from power. This result was mainly the work of the young neo-imperialists and the new generation in the Conservative party. Stanley Baldwin, Austen and Neville Chamberlain, Bridgeman, Hoare, Eden, Sir Bolton Eyres-Monsell, Cunliffe-Lister, Duff Cooper were not members of the landed aristocracy, which had held the predominating power over the Premiership, the Treasury, the Foreign Office and the Service ministries before 1906.[1] The available evidence suggests that a similar change was beginning to take place in the Foreign and Diplomatic Services,[2] as a result of the reforms initiated in 1906 and 1918, when the two services were amalgamated; although it would take until the late 1920s before the new entrants began to attain sufficient seniority to affect the formulation and conduct of foreign policy.

This change in the social composition both of the diplomatic and political membership of the foreign-policy-making élite[3] expressed itself in a curious paradox. The political élite, while paying lip service to such ideals as pan-Anglo-Saxonism and the League of Nations,

1. The only attempt to classify this kind of group of which the writer is aware is made in Dr Bernard Semmel, *Imperialism and Social Reform* (Cambridge, 1960). In writing of essentially the same group in the pre-1914 era, Semmel distinguishes between financial imperialists and industrial imperialists, according to the main source of the individual's wealth. The classification, a little neo-Marxist in inspiration, is suggestive rather than entirely satisfactory.

2. Lord Strang, *The Foreign Office* (1959), 73. This allegation is, I know, flatly contradictory to the normally accepted view. But if one concentrates on parental occupation rather than educational background one can pick out Sir Robert Craigie, Ambassador in Tokyo 1937–41, whose father was a naval officer, and who entered the Foreign Affairs Office in 1907; Sir Maurice Peterson, whose father was Principal of MacGill University, Canada, entered the Foreign Office in 1912; Duff Cooper entered in 1912 and his father was a successful surgeon; Sir David Kelly, son of a Professor of Classics at Adelaide University, entered in 1913; Lord Strang himself, the son of a market gardener, entered in 1919; Sir Reader Bullard, entered in 1909 via Levantine consular service, his father a dock labourer.

3. No attempt has been made to extend the investigation to the Service ministries or the other sections of the foreign-policy-making élite.

retreated with a few exceptions into the narrowest kind of political reaction. America was written off as incurably isolationist.[1] When she moved into the field of world activity she became 'Uncle Shylock',[2] the reluctant Achilles, the obstinate amateur,[3] the 'uncertain ally'.[4] The Foreign Office, by contrast, began to show a quasi-idealist interest in both the League and the American friendship,[5] provoking the more traditionalist of the Tory party to animadvert to the loss of nerve of senior diplomats with American wives, unable to face strained relations with their in-laws!

But the political élite, though they might write off America as

1. 'It is always best and safest to count on nothing from the Americans but words' (Neville Chamberlain quoted in Keith Feiling, *The Life of Neville Chamberlain* (1946), 325). 'Rightly or wrongly, we were deeply suspicious, not indeed of American good intentions, but of American readiness to follow up inspiring words with any practical action' (Lord Templewood (Sir Samuel Hoare, Air Minister 1922–24, Foreign Secretary 1935, First Lord of the Admiralty 1936–38), *Nine Troubled Years* (1954), 263). 'The apparent contradiction . . . that those who had sought the easier and more secure position . . . of putting themselves out of the range of European turmoil and disturbance . . . should nonetheless claim to exercise full right of criticism and judgment in regard to matters for which they were unwilling to accept any measure of direct responsibility' (Lord Halifax (Lord Privy Seal 1935–38, Foreign Secretary 1938–40, Ambassador to the United States 1941–46), *Fulness of Days* (1957), 242). Despite his American connections, Vansittart came to share this scepticism towards American willingness to move from the utterance of pious sentiments to valiant action. Hoare, to do him justice, tried very hard to obtain American support, by invoking the Kellogg Pact at the time of the Italo-Abyssinian crisis, but with no success. See *Foreign Relations of the United States, 1935*, I, *passim*; and ibid., *1936*, I and III; also Herbert Feis, *Seen from E.A.* (New York, 1947), part III, *passim*; Hugh Wilson Jr, *For Want of a Nail* (New York, 1959).

2. A phrase which Hoover quite unjustly suspected British diplomats of propagating (*Memoirs*, II, 179).

3. The theme of Sir Arthur Bryant's study of Field-Marshal Alanbrooke's papers, *The Turn of the Tide* (1957).

4. John Biggs-Davidson, MP, *The Uncertain Ally* (1957).

5. Indications may be found in the diary of the young Foreign Office clerk (son of the very realist-minded Lord Carnock, Ambassador in Russia 1906–10, Permanent Under-Secretary in the Foreign Office 1910–16), Harold Nicolson, *Peace-Making 1919* (1933); in Vansittart's discussion of Anglo-American relations (op. cit). For the contrast between the Foreign Office's overestimate and Chamberlain's dismissal of President Roosevelt's letter to Chamberlain in January 1938, see Winston S. Churchill, *The Gathering Storm* (1948); and very noticeably in Lord Strang, *At Home and Abroad* (1956).

incurably isolationalist and prone only to consider domestic electoral considerations when formulating foreign policy,[1] could not leave America totally out of their considerations once the Far East and Italy began to confront them with the possibility that their obligations to institute sanctions against an aggressor under the Covenant of the League of Nations might have to be implemented. This brought them at once against the dilemma originally propounded by Sir Cecil Hurst in 1919. In 1934 Baldwin repeated the point:

Never so long as I have any responsibility in governing the country, will I sanction the British Navy being used for an armed blockade of any country in the world until I know what the United States of America is going to do.[2]

The dilemma led to one of the bitterest of the back-stage debates in the formulation of British foreign policy during the years of appeasement, over the degree to which British policy should conform to the needs of American goodwill. The problem became particularly acute twice, in 1934 over the possibility of negotiating an agreement with Japan,[3] and in January 1938 over the incident of the Roosevelt message.

It is an interesting reflection that it was among the pro-American group that many members of the hard core of those who wished to see a negotiation of Anglo-German differences, who supported at its strongest the policy of 'appeasing' Germany, were to be found. Their Atlanticism was essentially a form of isolationism on the American model, a withdrawal from European entanglements,[4] especially from any involvement in the maintenance of the 'rotten structure' of the Treaty of Versailles. This is the more worth emphasizing as the

1. 'I can form some opinion as to what France or Germany or Italy are likely to do in this or that contingency. Except in a narrow field, the course which will be taken by the United States is a riddle to which no-one – not even themselves – can give an answer in advance. But perhaps this is only saying that the United States has no foreign policy. The ship drifts at the mercy of every gust of public opinion' (Sir Austen Chamberlain (Foreign Secretary 1924–29), cited in Sir Charles Petrie, *The Life and Letters of Sir Austen Chamberlain* (1939), II, 321–4).

2. Speech at Glasgow, 25 November 1934, cited in A. W. Baldwin, *My Father: the True Story* (1955), 207.

3. This episode is dealt with in more detail in Part II, Essay 4 below.

4. This view is argued further in Essays 7 and 8 below, and in the bibliographical Essay 12 at the end of this book.

question of relations with the United States in this period is usually discussed in terms not of making British policy conform to American isolationism but of the alleged missed opportunity of enlisting American aid to oppose the dictators.

The alleged missed opportunity centres around President Roosevelt's proposal of January 1938 to summon an international conference at which the United States Government together with a number of prominent neutral states should draw up a kind of code by which international relationships should be regulated. Under the circumstances in which the proposal was made it seems so fantastically unreal that the real question must be what lay behind it. Chamberlain, seeing, one suspects, in this nothing but a new illustration of the naïve and verbose idealism which so many of the élite took to be typical of American attitudes to international affairs, rejected it out of hand without even recalling Eden, his Foreign Minister, who was then on holiday. He gave as his reason that the proposal would enable the dictators to evade the steady pressure he was putting on them for bilateral negotiations at which the existing sources of world tension could be ironed out. Eden, returning from his holiday at the urgent request of the Foreign Office, forced the Cabinet to withdraw Chamberlain's rejection and to encourage Roosevelt to follow up his proposal. This the President did not do immediately, and the subsequent German annexation of Austria and the outbreak of the Czech crisis which ended in the Munich Conference put the scheme out of court.[1]

The debate over the precise nature of Roosevelt's intentions in advancing these proposals is a bitter one, and one likely to continue so for some time to come.[2] This is not the place to pronounce upon it. What is of interest for this essay is the motives which led Eden to insist on a reconsideration of Chamberlain's original and rather cavalier rejection of the proposal, and which led him and Churchill to animadvert so bitterly on this as an act of supreme folly. These are revealed in the comments made in his memoirs, and in the extracts from the contemporary documents there quoted.

1. The course of the negotiations may be followed in: *F.R.U.S., 1938*, 1; Earl of Avon, *Facing the Dictators* (1962), 547–68.

2. See, for example: Sumner Welles, *A Time for Decision* (1945), 55–8; idem, *Seven Major Decisions* (1951), 19–44; Winston S. Churchill, *The Gathering Storm* (1948), 196–8; W. L. Langer and S. Everett Gleason, *The Struggle for Isolation* (1952), 19–27; J. McVickers Haight, 'Roosevelt and the Aftermath of the Quarantine Speech', *Review of Politics*, XXIV, no.2 (April 1962).

I had no doubt that the purpose of this move . . . was to put obstacles in the way of Hitler and Mussolini by the only method known to Roosevelt. . . . At the worst Roosevelt's offer would gain us time and bring the United States a little nearer to a divided Europe. . . . I told the Prime Minister that . . . this was probably as far as he [Roosevelt] felt able to go at the present time. Even if the initiative did fail, we should have gained immeasurably from this first American intervention in Europe and another might follow . . . . a risk of some confusion in the method which the President wished to employ and from the fact that his Government lacked an intimate knowledge of European affairs. . . . The Prime Minister, and most of his Cabinet, did not look beyond the Roosevelt plan itself, which admittedly might have failed, to the beneficent consequences which might have flowed from it. . . .

One may perhaps distinguish three elements in this. Firstly, there is the somewhat patronizing attitude taken towards the President's proposals themselves and towards American opinion. The proposals themselves would fail, displaying as they did both ignorance and unrealism. By this failure American opinion would receive 'instruction' in the real villainies of the world. As a result the immense powers of the American Presidency would be freed from the restraints imposed on them by the dominance of American public opinion by isolationist sympathies, and could be used for common Anglo-American purposes. One could not find a stronger illustration of the basic doctrines and assumptions of English pan-Anglo-Saxonism – the unquestioning identification of British and American leadership, the naïve assumption that British leadership would be welcome and acceptable, the identification of Anglo-American hegemony with the achievement of universal peace, and the optimist idealism about the influence of a united Anglo-American opinion as a deterrent against the use of force to upset the world *status quo*. The value of Roosevelt's initiative lay in the anticipated after-effects on American opinion of its expected inevitable failure. Against this it is not surprising in the circumstances that the dominant scepticism of the majority of the Cabinet (and their advisers outside the Foreign Office), as to the unlikelihood of anything more than verbal support being secured from the United States, prevailed.[1]

1. 'Reliance upon the anti-Axis sentiments of America would be just as much a delusion. . . . Reiteration of American moral principles was unlikely to make rulers tremble in Berlin or Rome' (Iain Macleod, *Chamberlain* (1961), 207). 'The plan appeared to me fantastic' (Chamberlain diary entry of 19–27 February 1938, cited ibid., 212).

The general attitude of the bulk of the British élite towards America led American observers, especially in the State Department, to conclude that British statesmen found America useful as their excuse for never taking the League seriously.[1] The interwar generation of American diplomats falls into two main groups, the professional diplomats like Gibson, Atherton, Armour, Marriner, Hugh Wilson and others who spent the bulk of their time in diplomatic posts abroad, and those who centred around the Council on Foreign Relations in New York, stayed mainly in the State Department or were active as political columnists or academic commentators. In sympathy and sentiment[2] the former group was at least mildly isolationist. The latter could be described as 'collectivists *manqués*', capable of reacting into strong isolationism, muddled unrealism and deep suspicion of Britain as displayed by Cordell Hull and Franklin Roosevelt in the early years of the latter's administration, a reversion to the worst aspects of the year 1920.[3] Both groups had passed through a common experience. They belonged largely to the American disillusionment with Versailles.[4] They shared in that extraordinarily influential school of American historiography, whose version of Versailles as the European betrayal of Wilsonianism still finds the widest acceptance in America. One and all can be said, as Lord Eustace Percy acutely noted,[5] to have shared in the suspicion that England's ruling élites were losing their moral fibre, 'going soft', becoming decadent. Few, if any, had any time for, or realization of, the changes that were overtaking relations inside the Commonwealth,[6] of the dilemmas which

1. Feis, *Seen from E.A.*, part III.

2. Most of them became isolationist Republicans in the 1940 election; while the latter group joined the 'All Aid to Britain Short of War' movement.

3. Especially in their belief in the revival of the Anglo-Japanese alliance. Only the perspicacity and intelligence of Norman H. Davis, a Democratic holdover from Hoover's disarmament delegation, saved matters.

4. Bullitt, Berle, Christian Herter, Joseph Grew, the Dulles brothers, Norman H. Davis, Walter Lippmann, among the most prominent. The point is acutely, if dramatically made, in Arthur M. Schlesinger Jr, *The Age of Roosevelt*, (Boston, 1957), I, 11–14. See also Percy of Newcastle, *Some Memories*, 70, 72.

5. Percy of Newcastle, op. cit., 31, 174. A curious instance of how history repeats itself is Joseph Alsop's remark in 1955 that the atmosphere in London 'stank of defeat'.

6. See the excellent, if critical, study by Neville Kingsley Mooney, 'American attitudes towards the British Empire, 1919, 1922' (unpublished Ph.D. thesis, Duke University, 1959).

accompanied these changes, particularly in the realm of foreign policy, economic policy and capital investment, or the way in which imperial preoccupations hampered the evolution of a strong attitude towards Nazi expansionism. Accustomed to thinking of Britain as a European power, they believed her to be shirking her European responsibilities. Not until 1940 had they any evidence to the contrary; 1940–41 were the halcyon days of Anglo-American amity.

President Roosevelt's administration tended to add to this group a third group in many respects actively hostile to Britain's role in international politics although in other respects very friendlily disposed towards Britain itself. These were 'liberals' in the American sense, disciples of Wilson and Bryan, desperately suspicious of the principal elements in British foreign policy, her imperial trade and financial policy and her possession of an Empire. It was a younger member of their number, J. Pierrepont Moffatt, who called the British Defence White Paper of 1935, the 'most defeatist document I have ever seen'.[1] Other members included General Patrick Hurley, who in a notable passage of arms with Winston Churchill in late 1944, tried to prohibit the use of Lend-Lease weapons to retake Hong Kong from the Japanese on the grounds that weapons provided by the United States should not be used to restore the British Empire;[2] Adolf Berle who tried to prevent the functioning of Sir William Stephenson's British Security Organization in the United States during the Second World War.[3] The issues which led them to the greatest suspicions of their opposite numbers in Britain were India, China, imperial preferences and, in the years immediately after 1945, the Sterling Area.[4]

In examining the role of these groups one is tempted also to return to Lord Eustace Percy's comments on Bryce's achievements during his tenure of the Washington Embassy; Bryce, he said, converted 'the bank balance of Anglo-American intimacy which had accumulated in the private diplomatic books at Washington into an investment in American public opinion', especially in academic and educated circles.[5] From his contacts developed the whole range of contacts

1. *Moffatt Papers.*
2. Sir Llewellyn Woodward, *British Foreign Policy in the Second World War* (1962).
3. H. Montgomery Hyde, *The Quiet Canadian* (1963).
4. See Essay 3 below.
5. Percy of Newcastle, op. cit., 27.

between the professional classes of both countries from whom in increasing measure the new diplomatists of the Second World War and the postwar years were to come.

The advent of members of the professional, university, 'egghead' class to positions of influence in America with the beginning of the New Deal and the role in the 1930s of the young men of the American delegation at Versailles have generally been recognized for some time. But the weakness of contemporary intellectual history in Britain has caused the corresponding developments in Britain largely to be overlooked. The British delegation at Versailles included the historians Toynbee, Namier, Webster, Sumner, Powicke, Prothero, E. H. Carr and Headlam-Morley as well as the able group of economists around Keynes.[1] After the war they came together with Lionel Curtis of the 'Kindergarten' to form the Institute of International Affairs. Although the Foreign Office was somewhat diffidently associated with its foundation,[2] its role was to provide a forum in which an educated opinion on foreign relations could develop. Futhermore it also built up a cadre of academic writers on foreign affairs who were to play a part in the great expansion of British official activity in the field of foreign relations. This expansion, in the changed circumstances of the 1940s, changed the nature of the British foreign-policy-making élite still more, by adding to it a permanent accretion of political economists. The Foreign Office, after years of struggle,[3] acquired an economic section, and the Treasury and Bank of England, previously only involved in diplomacy as a temporary measure in moments of world crisis and slump, found themselves committed to it *in perpetuo*.[4] With it this new inrush brought the political ideas of the British centre; and the way lay open for the second and third periods of Anglo-American co-operation, the period of drafting a European settlement, 1943–45, and the period of the Marshall Plan, roughly 1947–51.

1. R. F. Harrod, *Life of John Maynard Keynes* (1951). Another distinguished British historian, R. B. Mowat, served on Field-Marshal Smuts' staff.

2. Sir John Tilley, Chief Clerk in Foreign Office 1913–19; co-ordinating Under-Secretary over American Department 1919–21; Ambassador in Brazil 1921–26, in Tokyo 1926–31 *London to Tokyo* (1942), 94–5.

3. The theme of Sir Victor Wellesley (Deputy Under-Secretary in Foreign Office 1925–40), *Diplomacy in Fetters* (London, 1945).

4. See R. N. Gardner, *Sterling–Dollar Diplomacy* (Oxford, 1956); Sir Henry Clay, *Lord Norman* (London, 1957).

This new group was on the whole very favourable to Anglo-American co-operation. They echoed most of the view of the American critics of Versailles; and they believed strongly that the errors of Versailles could have been remedied had America not withdrawn into political isolationism. Those already active in international affairs, as through the I.L.O., the Public Commission for Refugees or the like, had maintained contact with Americans on matters of common interest. Those who entered the new fields of foreign affairs from academic or professional life found the relationship stimulating if trying. Most adhered instinctively to the doctrine of the 'special relationship', though they based this not on any naïve pan-Anglo-Saxonism but on assumptions of common intellectual inheritance, common points of view and common purpose.[1] While they were patriotic, they were not chauvinistic; they proceeded on the assumption that the aim of their diplomacy was to rebuild a common order, not so to 'cook' it as to extract the maximum advantage for their own country. They were the more embittered, as were their American opposite numbers, when they discovered the wide areas of difference that still existed on many matters, since such discoveries touched on the crudeness of their assumption that 'what is good for Britain (or America) is good for the world'. And being, despite their general intellectual sophistication, inexperienced in the new field of foreign relations, it was easier for them to believe their opposite numbers guilty of applying a double standard than to realize the inconsistencies in their own position. This explains much of the bitterness

1. Two more senior illustrations of this. 'Keynes . . . was not predisposed to admire the American way of life. Later influences, strongly and typically British, coming from his circle of Bloomsbury friends made him still less predisposed to take a kindly view of American civilization . . . and yet . . . amid the grim and terrible circumstances of the Second World War . . . he found something he had long missed in Britain . . . men who had retained their intellectual poise, men of strong conviction . . . men who believed that by rational discussion one could plan and achieve reform and carry forward the progress of mankind' (Harrod, op. cit., 4–5). 'It took me some time and several visits to America to get this notion [that the United States had a different social philosophy and a different political system] . . . firmly into my head. It took me rather longer to perceive that in spite of all the sharp contrasts between the American and the British ways of thought and action they were rooted in the same subsoil of ideas and ideals' (Sir Harold Butler, *Confident Morning* (1950), 162). This, of course, cannot be said of the older political leaders like Churchill, Eden and the Conservative Right who still thought in terms of the 'English-speaking peoples'.

that reigned in Anglo-American relations between 1945 and 1948.[1]

The second drawback to this great expansion of British official activity in the field of foreign relations and the expansion of Anglo-American contacts which went with it was a corresponding fragmentation of foreign policies into subjects and regions. This fragmentation made the friendly achievement of a common policy possible in one field, while in others the absence of co-operation was so pointed as to be capable of leading at any time to open hostility,[2] which could not, of course, be confined to the field in which it had arisen. Moreover, the new influx, being inexperienced in the practice of diplomacy and the nuances of close relations with nationals of other countries, brought with them an armoury of prejudices and quasi-ideological concepts. On both sides these were to prove a considerable impediment to close relations, except where positive and formal action was taken to create a supra-national organization in which contact was between individuals doing a job in a unified structure of jobs rather than between individuals as representatives of their nations.[3] First tried out in North Africa, this later technique became the pattern of all subsequent military co-operation, and was adopted in 1949 as the model for the organization of NATO; its achievement in creating in the British Army and Air Force a climate of Americophilia over the atmosphere revealed in Field-Marshal Lord Alanbrooke's papers[4] emerged very strongly in the Services' reaction to Suez. It is the more marked when contrasted with the poor state of Anglo-American co-operation in planning and executing the Pacific campaigns.[5]

It was this fragmentation which was to lead, after the six years' Labour party interlude, to the last stage in the see-saw of Anglo-American relations covered by this paper, the failure of Sir Anthony Eden's last years.[6] The story is told in the entries under the heading

1. The special case of Anglo-American relations between 1945 and 1950 is considered in more detail in the essay immediately following.

2. This fragmentation was raised to the level of a dogma by John Foster Dulles in his famous speech on 'colonialism' at the height of the Suez crisis.

3. Whether he originated it or not, this was General Eisenhower's major contribution to Anglo-American amity.

4. See Bryant, *The Turn of the Tide*, *passim*.

5. See Admiral of the Fleet Viscount Cunningham of Hyndhope, *A Sailor's Odyssey* (1951), 598, 612.

6. Earl of Avon, *Full Circle* (1960).

'Anglo-American Relations' in the index to Eden's memoirs. They read as follows: 'causes of friction . . . differences over Indo-China . . . threatened by search of ship for arms . . . importance of maintaining accord . . . differences over Iranian question . . . Mussadeq plays off . . . differences over Egypt and Sudan . . . differences over Arabia . . . differences over Middle East . . . differences over Suez question . . . "colonization" as a cause for disagreement . . . broken over Suez action . . . in unity over action in Lebanon and Jordan'.

This is not the place to recapitulate the troubled history of Anglo-American relations in the Near and Middle East. What is of interest in the relationship is that it seems to have masked a turn away from Anglo-American amity based on the British side on a quasi-ideological view of the relationship in which, to quote *The Times*,[1] 'Britain has much to give by way of counsel and initiative to the shaping, still tentative and uncertain, of a world policy, political and economic, at the summit in America'. The outburst of anti-Americanism which followed the failure of the Suez operation is still strong enough in our memories to make further discussion unnecessary. There have been signs in the recent British debates on the development of the European Common Market that realism has for the moment replaced the doctrine of the 'special relationship'.

In the period under study, Britain's relations with America have been conducted by an élite whose membership has evolved, but has, except for the interruptions of 1916–22, 1924, 1929–31 and 1945–51,[2] not admitted any element so alien as to be incapable of adaptation to its basic conception of Britain's position in the world. This élite's attitudes to America as a factor in world politics have evolved with America's own power and willingness to intervene. Such evolution has been governed on the intellectual plane by an interplay between traditional realism and the quasi-ideology enshrined in the doctrine of the 'special relationship'. It has been suggested that this interplay has, in part at least, varied directly with changes in the socio-political composition of the élite, especially as related to similar changes in the corresponding group in America. Thus the original approach to

1. 13 May 1948, cited in Epstein, *Britain – Uneasy Ally*. Note again the slight paternalism commented on above, p. 45.

2. In each case a slightly, though decreasingly, alien element was first added to and then withdrawn from the political membership of the group mainly by the electoral process: the 'irresponsibles' and some Labour leaders in the years 1916–18 and 1918–22, and Labour itself on the three other occasions.

Anglo-American amity was accompanied by the temporary control of foreign affairs in America by an east coast oligarchy. Under the Presidency of Wilson, this broke down and led gradually to the pheno-menon of the 1930s and 1940s, the *rapprochement* less of oligarchs and aristocrats than of meritocracy and meritocracy, though each, it is true, was by a curious paradox still led by oligarchs of the old type in Franklin D. Roosevelt and Winston S. Churchill.

ESSAY 3

American Aid to Britain
and the Problem of Socialism,
1945–51

In the previous essays a number of comments were made on the nature of the foreign-policy-making élite, in general, comments which could lead perhaps to the view that this approach tended to play down or neglect the role of public opinion in the formulation of British foreign policy. In this essay, therefore, attention is turned to the role British public opinion played in limiting and restraining the action of the British Government in relation to the United States in those six years, noted in the previous essay as constituting one of the lengthiest periods in which radical elements were in control of, or, better said, in a position to influence the formulation of, British foreign policy, the period from 1945–51, of the two postwar Labour Governments. As there already exist a number of excellent American studies of the attitude towards the United States of the Labour party and its supporting elements[1] this essay proposes rather to concentrate on the effect, if any, its alleged ideological differences with the United States had on the course of Anglo-American relations at a time when British dependence on the United States was almost absolute.

This essay must necessarily, therefore, concern itself with both American and British opinion, since its theme is the product of what has been called 'total diplomacy',[2] that is, that state of relations between states which occurs when popular participation in the processes of international relations is continuous, and those processes themselves impinge on most sectors of domestic political activity. The traditional view of international relations saw them essentially as relations between political administrations and their professional representatives. The first decades of this century brought a realization that governmental dependence on popular support and goodwill, even in the

1. See the sources cited in the previous essay in footnotes to pp. 19 and 20.

2. William T. R. Fox and Annette Baker Fox, *Britain and America in the Era of Total Diplomacy* (Princeton, 25 March 1952).

E

autocracies, was coming to act as a limiting factor on the freedom of action hitherto enjoyed, at least in theory, by governments in their relations with another. The foreign policy of a government came to be seen as the product of two sets of pressures: those of other governments and those of its domestic public opinion. The concept of 'total diplomacy' (even though the word 'diplomacy' is ill-chosen and confusing) implies interaction not only between government and government, and government and domestic public opinion, but also between public opinion and public opinion. It is this kind of interaction which the fact that Britain's Government was nominally at least 'socialist' introduced into the general field of Anglo-American relations after 1945, and particularly into the field of American aid towards Britain's economic recovery.

One could perhaps set out this hypothesis diagrammatically. The traditional theory saw international relations simply as:

government A ⇄ government B

To this was added in the first decades of this century the extra factors

public opinion A ⟶ government A ⇄ government B ⟵ public opinion B

The concept of total diplomacy makes these pressures circular rather than linear:

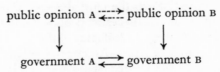

The nature of the problem this paper concerns itself with is generally held to have affected only the interactions indicated by dotted lines on the diagram.[1] The course of this paper will show that while there are definite exceptions which do not support this view it is at least

1. The author has been assured by British participants in the 1945 negotiations for the Anglo-American loan that the problem of 'socialism' played no part whatever in these negotiations. This is certainly strictly true. On the other hand, Lord Keynes' letter to Dalton of 28 October 1945 (cited in Dalton, *Memoirs, 1945–60, High Tide and After* (1962), 76–7, and preserved in the Dalton papers in the British Library of Economics and Political Science), shows that his American counterparts were coming to realize that the Labour party's domestic programme depended on substantial American aid; as do Dalton's contemporary comments written in the week he thought the Anglo-American loan negotiations were about to break down (*Dalton Diaries*, entry of 7 December 1945).

broadly true that, despite misgivings on both sides, 'socialism' did not arise as an issue in intergovernmental relations.

The problem itself can be resolved into two separate sets of problems: the nature of the two 'public opinions', and the nature of the issues comprehended in the word 'socialism'. One should begin by refining the concept of 'public opinion' a little and defining it in relation to the phenomena with which this paper is intended to deal.

Firstly, 'public opinion', whatever it may mean in the abstract, can clearly be broken down in practice into two separate sets of phenomena; firstly, the general state of opinion which limits actions and imposes criteria by which they are judged, what is often called the 'dominant climate of opinion', and secondly, particular pressures, representations and views on particular sets of issues. In the United States the concept, as employed in this paper, covers opinion within the Administration, within Congress, within the organized pressure groups to whose representations both Administration and Congress feel obliged at least to give an attentive hearing, and opinion in the press generally and among the corps of syndicated commentators especially, as well as grass-roots opinion. In Britain it covers opinion within Parliament, Whitehall, the press (the 'quality' press[1] being given more weight than the 'quantity' press), in constituency parties, trades unions, professional associations and grass-roots opinion whenever that seems to be crystallizing. In both cases, opinion among those elements on whose support the Administration relied is obviously more important than opinion among their political opponents.

In this period, 1945–50, opinion in this sense in the United States was more changeable and at times more disunited even than normally so. As the war ended, the Administration, shorn of its leader, a man whose leadership had in part at least thriven on the lack of common ground between those he led, apart from that provided by his leadership, was moving steadily away from the days and personalities of the New Deal. One by one, Henry Wallace, Harold Ickes, Henry Morgenthau, they dropped away from the Truman Cabinet. In their place came men much more representative of the reformist wing of

1. That is, to reiterate a point made in earlier essays, of national dailies at this date, *The Times*, the *Manchester Guardian*, *The Financial Times* and *The Daily Telegraph*: of national Sunday papers, *The Observer* and *Sunday Times*; of national weeklies, the *New Statesman and Nation*, *Spectator*, *The Economist*, *Tribune*; of others *Socialist Commentary*, *Forward*, *Political Quarterly* (then much more of an organ of Labour opinion than today).

American business, or even more simply of the Conservative Democrats of the South. One, somewhat hostile observer, has put it as follows:

Roosevelt's death left the 'economic Royalists' he had once so roundly scorned in virtually complete control as an incident to the staffing felt necessary in Washington while fighting an all-out-war.[1]

Another,[2] writing of Fred Vinson who succeeded Morgenthau as Secretary of the Treasury, has called him a 'homespun alumnus' of the House of Representatives, whose main idea was not to lead but to interpret the will of the people, which in his view was definitely unconcerned with international problems, being preoccupied with those of domestic reconversion, especially with the size of the national debt.

What remained of the Rooseveltian New Deal philosophy manifested itself in two fields only – the continued distrust of Britain's imperial policies, expressed often in the grossest overestimation of British strength in the postwar world,[3] and the continued economic liberalism preached by F.D.R.'s first Secretary of State, Cordell Hull. This was expressed in a determination to use American economic power in the postwar world to secure a liberalization of world trading and financial practices which, for its ruthless and olympian incomprehension of the real issues, can only be compared with the attitude adopted by President Wilson in the rather similar circumstances of 1918. The principal representative of this determination was the Under-Secretary of State, Will Clayton, who, as a result of the President's general inexperience and Byrnes' preoccupation with the political issues of peace-making, became the principal policy-maker on issues of international economics and finance in Washington. He differed from Wilson and Vinson only in being basically Anglophil. Otherwise his background and training as the self-made head of the largest firm of cotton-brokers in America gave him a 'passionate abhorrence of government interference in economic life'.[4] Like Hull

1. Robert A. Brady, *Crisis in Britain* (New York, 1950), 16.
2. Richard W. Gardner, *Sterling–Dollar Diplomacy* (Oxford, 1956), 193. Vinson came from Kentucky.
3. This is very noticeable in some of the position papers prepared in the State Department for the American delegation to the Potsdam Conference.
4. Gardner, op. cit., 197–8. See also Ellen Clayton Garwood, *Will Clayton. A Short Biography* (Austin, 1958), 11. Dalton's diaries are replete with instances of Clayton riding his hobby-horse, earning him the sobriquet of 'Doctrinair Willie' (see entries of 30 September, 5 October 1946 and 27 June 1947).

he was convinced that war sprang from economic imperialism, and that multilateral trade was the cure for war. In this view he was supported by a considerable body of opinion in America.

This complex of opinions was to change under the impact of the opening stages of the cold war in Europe,[1] especially with the emergence of the practice of 'bipartisanship' on major foreign policy issues, under the benevolent aegis of Senator Vandenberg. But the elements with whom the Truman administration co-operated did not lose their 'conservative' nature; rather the reverse. The Congressional elections of 1946 produced a Congress which Truman in his later 'radical' days was to call the worst in American history. The unexpected defeat of the Republican expectations of victory in 1948 produced a serious malaise in American conservative morale which, coupled with the disasters in China and the increasing bitterness of the cold war, even before Korea, was to lead to that period of national shame and hysteria we know as the McCarthy era. None of this was likely to ease the problem of obtaining Congressional support for American financial aid to 'socialist' Britain. For the matter of continuous financial aid from one country to another, if that aid be provided from public funds, perhaps more than any other issue involves the two countries in 'total' diplomatic relations.

The structure of power in the British Labour movement has so often been analysed that it needs little recapitulation here. It can best be described at this time as constituting a plebiscitary oligarchy. The 'leadership' is confirmed in power and policies by its support in the Parliamentary Labour Party (and in this it is no different from its Conservative rival) and in the annual party conference. In 1945 the leadership rested in the hands of five men, Attlee, the Prime Minister, Bevin, the Foreign Secretary, Dalton, the Chancellor of the Exchequer, Cripps, the President of the Board of Trade, and Morrison, the Home Secretary.[2] Of these, three, Attlee, Dalton and Cripps, came from the

1. See Gardner, op. cit., 250–1, for the part this played in securing Congressional approval of the Anglo-American Financial Agreement of 1946.

2. Alexander, the Minister of Defence, was by virtue of his ministerial post of express importance. But his position as leader of the Co-operative party, the political wing of the Co-operative trading and retail movement affiliated to, rather than part of the Labour party, seems to have excluded him from the inner ring. Bevan and Shinwell were also important though Shinwell was to come to grief over his mishandling of the fuel crisis, and Bevan was only to emerge as a major challenger to the leadership after the deaths of Bevin and Cripps and Dalton's resignation.

British professional classes, at a time when those classes had reached the apogee of their power and influence in Britain. The other two were, in different ways, political 'bosses' of a peculiarly British kind. Morrison had risen through his capture of the London Council for Labour, and Bevin through his dominance of the biggest and most heterogeneous of the trade unions, the Transport and General Workers.

The party they led to victory in 1945 was equally heterogeneous. In essence it was, and is, an alliance between organized trades unionism and the various long-standing radical strains in British politics, ranging from the aristocratic Catholic radicalism of Lord Pakenham through middle-class egalitarian radicalism, Fabian rationalist and 'planificatory' radicalism,[1] Nonconformist radicalism, the regional radicalism of south Wales, north-eastern England and central Scotland, to the intellectual neo-Marxism of the radical publicists and the emotional populism of the self-educated worker. These radical strains have tended to divide, the egalitarian radicals moving with the party leadership, the neo-Marxists and emotional populists entrenched in the constituency organizations and firmly in control of the radical press moving into conflict with it, and the 'planficatory' radicals caught uneasily in a situation upon which their own set of ideals left them peculiarly ill-equipped to decide. It is known that through the mechanism of the annual party congresses, the so-called Left could find a platform to voice its criticism of the party leadership and rebuke them for back-sliding in the practices of the true faith. It is equally a matter of common knowledge that the mechanism of the 'block-vote' enabled the party leadership, leaning upon the support of three of the five largest trade unions, always to defeat that criticism. It has, however, been too readily assumed that this trade union support would have been forthcoming, whatever the issues on which the leadership was criticized; that it sprang from feelings of loyalty and solidarity. No doubt in part it did. But the trades union leadership which provided the support had to face their own annual conferences. They were only able to stand off attack by the more militant idealists among their members by being able to show that the political leadership's policy accorded in part at least with party ideals and wholly with their members' interests. The need to ensure trades union support set limitations on the freedom of action of the Labour leadership

1. That branch of the radical intellectual movement which tends to believe in 'planning' as the solution of all ills.

58

analogous to those encumbering the Administration in the United States by the needs of 'bipartisanship' in Congress. In this the Labour Party Conference may be seen as playing a role analogous in some respects to that of Congress. Majority support for administrative policies was essential, criticism was both 'irresponsible' and 'grass-roots' in origin, and majority support had to be won, not 'whipped in', and won for policies as well as persons.

The main burden of the attacks to which the party leadership were subjected was, as has been remarked above, that the policies they were following were insufficiently in accordance with the 'tenets of socialism'. To define these tenets would be to embark on a profitless examination of low-level political metaphysics. For our purposes it is sufficiently revealing to consider the principal policies of the Labour Government. Central to these were the complex of issues connected with the maintenance of 'full employment', redistribution of income, nationalization and the improvement of welfare by state action in housing, public health and education. The different strands of thought represented in the Labour party reached agreement on these policies by different ways, some starting from the ideal of central planning (to which the experience of its successful employment during the war gave great popular appeal), some starting from a mildly conspiratorial theory of society which argued the need to bring the central concentrations of economic power under central control, and some from the position of emotive populism arguing that the resources of a country should 'belong to the people'.[1] These various strands of opinion were to move into violent opposition in the 1950s after the experience of six years of power; but in 1945 they were united on the three principles of the maintenance of full employment, the transfer to public ownership at least of the 'commanding heights of the economy' and the enactment by public action of the egalitarian welfare state. From this they went on in unison to agree on the need for central economic planning, and the maintenance of a cheap-money policy. Initial disagreement came on the international implication, not so much of these policies, as of the metaphysical 'socialism' which inspired them. Three sets of issues may be distinguished: firstly, the use of state trading practices, bulk-buying and long-term commodity agreements designed to eliminate economic fluctuations in international trade; secondly, the development of what may be loosely called a socialist

1. An excellent illustration of this is the Bevanite slogan of the 1950s on the issue of public ownership of land: 'God gave the land to the people'.

doctrine of 'imperialism', that is of British responsibilities within the Commonwealth; and thirdly, the idea of a 'socialist' foreign policy in political matters.

The first of these is the most difficult and obscure of all the issues dealt with by this paper. One would have thought that it would have been, of all issues, that most likely to lead to direct conflict between the Labour Government and the United States Administration, since it conflicted directly with the economic liberalism of Clayton and others. But the facts are that the practice of concluding long-term commodity agreements was continued by the Labour Government long after the conclusion of the Anglo-American Financial Agreement of 1946; that it never seems to have been a major issue in Congressional or Administration criticism of British policies; and that it was the least of the issues on which the Labour Government had to face leftist criticism.[1] The probable explanation is that the issues raised were swiftly shown to be totally unrealistic in the world of the late 1940s, as the fate of the International Trade Organization, supposed to embody these commitments, was speedily to demonstrate.[2]

The problems presented by the Labour party's beliefs in the Commonwealth were more persistent.[3] In the political sphere the

1. Criticism of the Anglo-American Financial Agreement on this issue was voiced in the debates on the ratification of the agreement by three Labour MPs, Norman Smith (a supporter of Social Credit doctrines), Jennie Lee, wife of Aneurin Bevan (somewhat ungrammatically); and R. R. Stokes (417, *Hansard's Parl. Deb., H. of C.*, cols 478, 673, 709). Criticism continued into the summer of 1946 in the *Political Quarterly*, and from the pen of G. D. H. Cole in *Reynolds News* (21 July 1946). See Aylmer Vallance, 'the Future of Anglo-American Relations', *Political Quarterly*, XVII, no.1 (January 1946), Alaric Jacobs, 'The Big Two and Ourselves', ibid., no.2 (April 1946); Gardner, op. cit., 229.

2. Dalton's diaries show that the British authorities firmly resisted all term bulk purchase agreement on Canadian wheat concluded in the summer of 1946, arguing that their policy was based on the purely commercial consideration that Canada offered lower prices than those quoted for American wheat. See *Dalton Diaries*, entry of 1 August 1946.

3. The existence of a British socialist version of the neo-imperialism usually associated with the Conservative radicals of the Balfour, Milner, Leo Amery school and the group which launched the periodical the *Round Table* before 1914 is entirely ignored by most non-British writers on British Socialism and unknown to Continental Socialists. Witness the conflict at the meeting of European Socialists in the Common Market in 1962 at Brussels between Mr Gaitskell and M. Spaak, and the genuine surprise with which the views of the former and the ignorance of the latter struck both.

action of the Labour party in speeding the transfer of power in India eased Anglo-American relations of one of its worst burdens. But in the field with which this paper is concerned it was to be a continuing problem. Labour attitudes to the Commonwealth in this period were compounded of two distinct lines of thought, both of them likely to affront American opinion. The first was the idea of a socialist 'Third Force' linking European democratic socialism with the socialist governments of Australia, New Zealand and the emergent members of the Commonwealth, which will be discussed later. The second was the development of the Sterling Area and the problem of the 'sterling balances', the wartime debts contracted abroad, especially to India and Egypt, which the Americans wished to see drastically written down, and in which desire they met with an outright refusal. The existence of the Sterling Area was calculated to arouse in the United States the widest possible range of Anglophobe prejudice,[1] and the dismantling of the Sterling Area's 'dollar-pool' was presented by spokesmen of the American Administration as the principal gain from the Anglo-American Financial Agreements in their attempt to secure Congressional approval.[2] Again they were to be defeated by events, in the swift reversal of the convertibility of sterling introduced in July 1947 and abandoned six weeks later.

The third set of issues were those connected with the desire for a recognizably 'socialist' foreign policy. In the beginning this was a compound of old millennialist beliefs in the capitalist and imperialist origins of war, and the conviction that the internationalization of socialism would lead to perpetual peace. Thus it was felt that the British Labour leaders would be the more likely to achieve agreement with the Soviet Union, that 'Left could speak to Left'. This view was not shared by the Party leadership,[3] but it was incorporated, nevertheless, into their election manifesto, and took strong hold of the imaginations of the intellectual neo-Marxist radicals like Crossman, Laski, G. D. H. Cole and the *New Statesman–Socialist Commentary–*

1. The loan 'would promote too much damned Socialism at home and too much damned Imperialism abroad', remarked Representative Celler (7 December 1945; Gardner, op. cit., 237).

2. See US Senate, Committee on Banking and Currency, *Hearings on Senate Resolution 138, Anglo-American Financial Agreement*, 79th Congress, 2nd Session.

3. With the exception of Dalton; see M. A. Fitzsimons, 'British Labour in search of a Socialist Foreign Policy', *Review of Politics*, XII, no.2 (April 1950).

Tribune–Political Quarterly school of writers. The obvious intransigence of the Soviet Union caused the Left to divide, a minority of fellow-travellers and crypto-Communists being forced into the open, while the bulk of the Left plumped for the idea of a democratic socialist 'Third Force', freed both from American and Soviet influence, and comprising western Europe and the British Commonwealth,[1] which should be able to hold the balance of power, if not to mediate between the two power-blocs of capitalism and totalitarian socialism. This school of thought (which has its echoes even today) was distinguished by its willingness to give the Soviet Union at its most Stalinist the benefit of any doubt as to its motives, while ascribing motives of doctrinaire capitalist imperialism to the United States. It could thus be relied on for consistent opposition to any measures of co-operation with the United States. In fact, it outdid the native British Communist party in calling the Anglo-American loan 'a vote for war with Russia', at a time when the only Communist MP, Willie Gallacher, was to speak in its support.[2]

To recapitulate: to be able to give aid to 'socialist' Britain the United States Administration needed to win the support of a Congress inclined at first towards a financial conservatism to which the Administration was itself highly susceptible, while being very hostile to all but 'liberal' doctrines of international trade and finance: to be able to ask for and receive American aid, the British Labour Government had to be able to guarantee full employment and the improvement of welfare to secure the support of sufficient trade union and general party support to be able to stand off the attacks of its doctrinaire Left. The principal issues raised in practice by British 'socialism' were on the continuance of British external financial controls, the 'Sterling Area' in fact, and the practice of state trading and commodity agreements. In America these were complicated by suspicions of British imperialism and a doctrinaire antipathy to Britain's 'socialist' domestic policy. In Britain these were complicated by doctrinaire suspicions of American 'economic imperialism' and the desire for a 'socialist' foreign policy. What needs to be traced now is the interaction between the one and the other. This can best be

1. This argument, put at its clearest in R. H. Crossman, 'Britain and Western Europe', *Political Quarterly*, XVII, no.1 (January 1946), was also adopted outside socialist circles. See evidence cited in Leon D. Epstein, *Britain – Uneasy Ally* (Chicago, 1954), 120–3.

2. See 417, *Hansard's Parl. Deb., H of C.*, cols 553–7 and 696.

done by considering three illustrations: the negotiations for the Anglo-American Financial Agreement of 1946; the Marshall Plan; and the 'devaluation' crisis of 1949. All of these fell within the period of Marshall aid to Britain which ended in December 1950. This did not end the period of American financial contributions to British financial recovery. But it is generally accepted that its continuance after 1950 was necessitated by the very changed conditions consequent on the Korean War and the upward rise of prices caused by the American crash rearmament programme and its accompanying stock-piling.[1]

The need for continuing American assistance to Britain after the end of the war in Europe and the Far East had been agreed upon between Churchill and Roosevelt at the Quebec conference in September 1944,[2] but no concrete steps had been taken to implement this agreement. The matter was rendered very urgent by the curtailment of Lend-Lease in May 1945 to what was necessary to Britain's participation in the continuing war in the Far East. Churchill had raised the question again with Truman at Potsdam on 18 July, and believed that he had obtained a sympathetic hearing. On 24 July 1945 Churchill wrote to Truman proposing immediate conversations, as the reduction in Lend-Lease payments, 'with Washington officials interpreting this in the narrowest sense . . . has reduced munitions and supplies to the vanishing point and has put us in a very difficult position'. Five days later Truman replied that he had instructed Clayton to take the matter up in informal conversations in London.[3] The day before this letter was dispatched, the Labour Cabinet had entered into office, Hugh Dalton becoming Chancellor of the

1. 'The speculative buying of raw materials which followed turned the terms of trade catastrophically against our western European allies and especially the United Kingdom and wiped out years of effort in expanding exports to pay for imports. It must have seemed to the United States' European friends as if Americans, with their apparently limitless stock of cash, had decided to buy a solution to the problem posed by their own lack of preparedness and their unwillingness to submit to economic controls strong enough to control inflation. They seemed heedless of the effects upon less affluent allies even when those effects were ruinous' (Fox and Fox, op. cit., 1).
2. Winston S. Churchill, *The Second World War*, xi, *Triumph and Tragedy* (1955), 138; Sir Llewellyn Woodward, *British Foreign Policy in the Second World War* (1962), 472–3; *Foreign Relations of the United States, The Potsdam Conference*, docs 537, 538.
3. Churchill, op. cit., 546, 547; Harry S. Truman, *1945, Year of Decision* (1955), 409–10, see also 145–7. See also Herbert Feis, *Between War and Peace, The Potsdam Conference* (Princeton, 1960), 26–30, 330–2.

Exchequer. Dalton, trained as he was as an economist, was well aware that the principal problem which would face Britain would be her balance of external payments;[1] he had, in addition, inherited the expert and experienced, though hardly socialist, Lord Keynes, the central figure in the wartime Churchill coalition's discussions with the United States on the pattern of postwar international economic and financial arrangements. On 14 August Dalton circulated to the new Cabinet a memorandum by Lord Keynes which painted the position of Britain's overseas financial prospects in grim terms, following it three days later by a proposal that talks should be opened at once with the United States on the need for continued financial assistance from the United States.[2]

The need was even more urgent than he had anticipated. Four days later, on 21 August, as a result of Japan's surrender and the end of the war in the Far East, Truman signed an order ending all Lend-Lease deliveries to Britain. The news struck the Labour Cabinet, filled as they were with the *élan* of victory, as a peculiarly bitter blow. The Prime Minister, Attlee, so far forsook his normal caution as to say publicly that the decision put Britain in 'a very serious financial position'. On the Left it revived all the fear of Wall Street, and played directly into the hands of those who regarded the fall of the last Labour Government in 1931 as the product of 'a bankers' ramp'.[3]

In this position the Labour Government turned inevitably to Lord Keynes. In his memorandum of 14 August he had prophesied a dollar deficit of perhaps $5,000 million to be incurred in the interval before a balance could be incurred between Britain's external liabilities and the moneys earned by a revived export trade. Without substantial aid from the United States on acceptable terms, the Labour Government would have to resign itself to a régime of much greater austerity than that imposed by the war, and to the indefinite postponement of its social and economic programmes. He thought, however, that by pointing out that without aid Britain could not enter into the system of international economic co-operation based on the principle of non-discrimination so much desired by the United

1. *Dalton Diaries*, entry of 17 August 1945. This also shows that he expected Lend-Lease to stop 'any time now, and the resultant gap will be terrific'.
2. Dalton, *Memoirs, 1945–60*, 69–70.
3. *Tribune* called it 'a calculated blow against the new Government directed from Wall Street' (31 August 1945). For similar evidence see Epstein, op. cit., 38–9. The accusation was revived by the Bevanites in 1952.

States, the US Government might be persuaded to grant Britain a grant-in-aid, or at least an interest-free loan of the sum needed.[1] With such arguments, even though some thought his estimates too pessimistic, he won reluctant Cabinet approval for negotiations with the United States. They opened in Washington on 13 September 1945.[2]

With the detailed course of the negotiations,[3] this paper need not concern itself. It will be seen from the proposals of Lord Keynes quoted above that on one count the line he proposed had already rendered the Government vulnerable to accusations that it was abandoning socialist practice in international trade. Hugh Dalton has left in his memoirs a graphic description of the crisis which arose in the Cabinet when Professor Robbins returned from Washington at the beginning of November 1945 with news of the baselessness of Keynes' hopes of a grant-in-aid or an interest-free loan. New instructions were given to Keynes after a prolonged debate in Cabinet, in which Dalton, Bevin and Cripps united to force their view of the impossibility of breakdown on the reluctant acquiescence of Alexander, Shinwell and Bevan.[4] The new instructions made even clearer the surrender to American demands for the progressive removal of discriminatory barriers to international trade. There was a renewed crisis at the beginning of December, produced by American demands which modified the Bretton Woods agreements to Britain's unique disadvantage. This was coupled with a demand, which Keynes and Robbins supported, for joint pressure on the holders of sterling balances for their cancellation. The matter came so near a break that Dalton began drafting a speech announcing this for Parliament. But his alliance with Cripps and Bevin was able to force acceptance of the American demands modified in a number of particulars, and without the proposal to cancel the sterling balances, which 'ran contrary to all British Labour idealism towards India', through the Cabinet. A large part was played in this resistance by fears that American hostility to the Sterling Area cloaked a 'desire to take it over themselves', according to Dalton.[5] The Anglo-American Financial Agreement was

1. Dalton, op. cit., 70–2.
2. Dalton, op. cit., 73.
3. Admirably summarized in Gardner, op. cit., ch.10.
4. Dalton, op. cit., 78–80. See also *Dalton Diaries*, entry of 6 November 1945.
5. Dalton, op. cit., 82–6. The crucial days were 3–4 December 1945. *Dalton Diaries*, entry of 7 December 1945.

signed on 6 December 1945, and submitted at once to Parliament for ratification. The subsequent debate saw the Government subjected to violent criticism from its own left, criticism which was to continue throughout the eighteen months to come, criticism which grew increasingly anti-American, and increasingly prone to depict the Government as being dragged at America's heels away from the paths of a proper socialist policy, as a result of its financial dependence on Washington. They were accused of 'subservience to American economic imperialism',[1] and of being 'dragged at the heels of American big business'.[2] In September 1946, a minority of two and a half million votes was recorded against policies 'tying the economy of Britain with that of capitalist America'. In November one hundred Labour MPs led by R. H. S. Crossman put down an amendment to the King's Address criticizing the Labour Government for subservience to the United States. Public opinion pollsters reported an up-swing of sentiment favourable to Russia and an 'alarming increase in anti-Americanism', two out of five interviewed being predominantly unfavourable, the remainder apathetic.[3] Early in 1947 Crossman and his supporters published the famous pamphlet *Keep Left*, criticizing the Government again for allying itself with a right-wing United States Government and a free enterprise system.

The course of the debates and hearings in the US Congress played a considerable part in exacerbating this sentiment. Even before the Financial Agreement had been concluded, a House Committee on Post-War Economic Policy and Planning had expressed concern over the nationalization plans of the British Government and proposed that American reconstruction aid should be only given to countries willing to abandon state trading practices.[4] Representative Celler's angry comment has already been quoted. Barney Baruch, the financier and friend of Churchill, wrote an open letter to Congress during the loan negotiations, warning against aiding Britain 'to nationalize its industries against us' and arguing that aid to Britain would be

1. Jacobs, *Political Quarterly*, XVII, no.2.
2. See Epstein, op. cit., 102–3.
3. Tom Harrison, 'British Opinion moves towards a New Synthesis', *Public Opinion Quarterly*, Fall 1947; H. D. Willcock, 'Surveys. Public Opinion Attitudes towards America and Russia', *Political Quarterly*, XIX, no.1. (January 1948).
4. US Congress, House Special Committee on Post-War Economic Policy and Planning, *Economic Reconstruction in Europe*, House Report 1205, 79th Congress, 1st Session, 12 November 1945.

wasted or employed on 'further policies incompatible with American principles of private enterprise'.[1]

In the Senate hearings on the Agreement, the spokesmen of the Administration, Vinson, Clayton, Acheson and the representatives of those American business interests favourable to the Agreement repeatedly emphasized that the loan was not intended to influence Britain's nationalization policy or to assist it, indeed that no such influence should or indeed could be exercised by the American Government. Nevertheless the Senatorial inquiries were able to extract statements that the loan would enable Britain to return to private trading practices (Clayton); that it would support 'our view of private enterprise' (Senator Fulbright confirmed by witness Flanders); that it would 'preserve free enterprise' (Senator Taylor confirmed by Acheson); that it would 'arrest the trend of nationalization'; that it is 'failure to make the loan that would be a victory of the Left' (witness Read, Chairman of General Electric Company).[2] Clayton had, in addition, to deal with a considerable body of private inquiries from business figures.[3] Criticism on the floor of Congress was even more outspoken.

Hugh Dalton has witnessed to the general effects on the Labour Government in 1947:

Of Congressional debate on our affairs we had had enough in 1946 when the Loan Agreement was under discussion. Though the Administration had then loyally backed us, we had had a bad experience with Congress. Many Congressmen had deployed lengthy, ill-informed, unfriendly and even spiteful criticisms of Britain. . . . Much of the criticism was not merely of Britain but of the actual British Labour Government and its policies. There had been talk of 'putting England through the wringer', by which was meant bringing heavy pressure on us to abandon our policy of nationalizing selected industries, and the 'creeping socialism' as some Americans called it, of our National Health Services and of our other Social Services. These suggested American interferences with our internal

1. He also called Keynes an 'irresponsible exponent of Socialist experimentation', which says little for his understanding either of Keynes or socialism (Gardner, op. cit., 193–4). Apparently he told Churchill in February 1946 that he was anxious to help, and did not want to jeopardize the loan (*Dalton Diaries*, entry of 25 February 1946).

2. US Senate, Committee on Banking and Currency, *Hearings*, 122, 392–3, 340, 368.

3. Gardner, op. cit., 238, quoting Clayton papers. Baruch was prominent in this correspondence.

policies angered me and my colleagues and made us still less inclined to risk further debate with Congress . . . we did not want a repetition of this which would have been damaging to our credit and to Anglo-American co-operation in general.[1]

British economic and financial policy in the years 1946–47 was marked by five characteristics, all of which can in some degree be traced back to the traumatic experiences of the Congressional debates on the Financial Agreement, and the rising tide of anti-Americanism in Britain which the agreement unleashed. Firstly, the Government became if anything more determined to insist on the primacy of the maintenance of full employment. At the London Conference of October 1946 on the charter of the new International Trade Organization, this insistence largely defeated American hopes of bringing the negotiations to a successful finish. The determination to demonstrate British independence manifested itself in other fields too, most notably in the resistance to American pressure to end long-term commodity agreements referred to above. It led also to a continuous pressure within the Cabinet by Dalton and Cripps for a reduction in overseas financial and man-power commitments, and an equal and bitter resistance to this from Alexander, which drove Dalton at one stage to threaten resignation,[2] on the grounds that the matter was being treated by Attlee with frivolity. It led to a rate of withdrawal of the moneys provided by the American loan at a much greater rate than had been anticipated. It led also in late 1946 and early 1947 to a much-publicized proclamation of success in recovery and in the export drive which was itself ill-received by those American circles which persisted in thinking in terms of economic warfare between Britain and the United States. This baseless and irresponsible optimism, shared in those Treasury and Bank of England circles which should have known better,[3] was to lead to the 'convertibility crisis' of the summer of 1947, just as the pressure to reduce commitments was to lead to the Truman doctrine and to Marshall's speech

1. Dalton, op. cit., 254–5. According to his diaries one prominent British banker with a long history of involvement in Anglo-American relations even proposed that Britain should ask the Irish Premier, de Valera, to make a public statement in favour of Britain getting the loan, as a means of countering Irish-American pressure.

2. His letter to Attlee of January 1947 is printed in Dalton, op. cit., 194–8.

3. The *Banker* boasted that Britain had 'handsomely lived up to its obligations . . . apparently to the surprise of American financial opinion' (cited in Gardner, op. cit., 312).

at the Harvard graduation ceremonies from which sprang the European Recovery Programme. Although it is chronologically inaccurate to do so, it is more logical to take the latter first since it marks the concluding phase of the bilateral Anglo-American financial relationship, ending in near-disaster what had begun amidst such ill-feeling and misunderstanding.

Convertibility of sterling was finally introduced on 15 July 1947. The Anglo-American Financial Agreement had stipulated its introduction within fifteen months of the agreement coming into operation, and this had been reluctantly accepted by the Labour Government after very considerable initial opposition and in the conviction that it would be impossible to fulfil. The gradual dismantling of the currency controls which had preceded the introduction of total convertibility had, however, produced no undue pressure on the pound, and the mood of irrational optimism which can only be considered as a psychological product of the accumulated strain of six years of war and two years of the aftermath fed on this. There was, too, the determination not to submit any demand for a waiver or postponement of convertibility which might subject Britain to fresh Congressional debate. As Dalton wrote, 'we decided to keep our word and face the consequences'.[1] As a precaution Britain drew out $300 million from the International Monetary Fund, virtually the entire amount it was then entitled to draw in any one year. The experiment lasted six weeks. In the last two weeks a demand for convertibility developed which made immediate suspension inevitable. Vinson's successor at the US Treasury, Snyder, with whom Dalton had already established friendly relations[2] was most understanding and co-operative. Convertibility was suspended on 20 August 1947.

This understanding and co-operativeness did not seep through to British opinion, which reacted to the crisis with angry and bitter attacks on the United States in general and on the terms of the Financial Agreement in particular. Injured pride and disappointed nationalism are not good counsellors. The attack was led in Parliament by the combination of radical Left and imperialist Right which

1. Dalton, op. cit., 254.
2. They had met at the annual meeting of the International Monetary Fund in Washington in September–October 1946, and Dalton had done his level best then to win Snyder's friendship (*Dalton Diaries*, entry of 30 September 1946 ff.).

had headed the original opposition to the agreement. But the width of press comment made it clear that they spoke for much larger segments of opinion in Britain. *The Economist*, by no means a left-wing or even pro-Labour journal, wrote:

The fault for the present crisis is far more America's than Britain's. . . . American opinion should be warned that over here in Great Britain one has the feeling of being driven into a corner by a complex of American actions and inconsistencies which in combination are quite intolerable. Not many people in this country believe the Communist thesis that it is the deliberate and conscious aim of American policy to ruin Britain and everything that Britain stands for in the world. *But the evidence can certainly be read that way.* And if every time that aid is extended, conditions are attached which make it impossible for Britain ever to escape the necessity of going back for still more aid *to be obtained with still more self-abasement* and on still more crippling terms, then the result will certainly be what the Communists predict.

The *New Statesman* (23 August 1947) put this more strongly for the Left:

British people would prefer to go hungry and work out their own salvation, rather than live on American charity with such strings attached.[1]

Luckily for the future of Anglo-American relations a more adult mood obtained in Washington, at least in Administration circles.

The introduction of the Marshall Plan brought a marked change into the problem with which this paper is concerned. The failure of Britain to achieve the hoped-for recovery for which the loan had been intended had given rise to considerable private misgivings in Administration circles as to the capabilities of the Labour Government. It was almost a matter of doctrine in American cabinet and diplomatic circles that the administrative ability necessary to cope with the problems the British Labour Government were coping with could only be developed in large-scale capitalist enterprises, and that kind of ability was of course not to be found in the Cabinet or the administration. On 22 July 1946, in the course of a visit to London, Forrestal, the US Secretary of Defence recorded Averil Harriman, then Ambassador in London, as saying:

the chief deficiency of the Labour Government is lack of knowledge in the broad practical fields of administration and management. Have probably

1. Both cited from Gardner, op. cit., p. 338–9 (italics supplied by D. C. W.).

bitten off more than they can chew with nationalization of the steel industry.[1]

Again in April 1947, the same witness records General Marshall, then Secretary of State, as saying that the British were trying a great experiment 'without very much management skill either in government or out of it'.[2] In Forrestal's own view the Labour Government was more or less overwhelmed by the scale and depth of its problems. The 'convertibility' crisis drove Harriman to even graver doubts, which were echoed by Snyder, Marshall and Lovett, the Assistant Secretary of State.[3] In their views there had not only been a marked deterioration in the quality of British governmental administrative ability, but the Labour Government had become so obsessed by the struggle for survival against the pressure of their doctrinaire Left that severe doubts were expressed by Harriman and Lovett as to whether any more American aid should be given to underwriting their stability. The lack of warning with which the convertibility crisis had struck Britain was particularly resented, Lovett saying that the Labour Government had behaved with a 'recklessness' almost bordering on 'anarchy', and even expressing doubts whether a British collapse would mean disaster for the American position in Europe.

Such doubts were inevitably echoed in the public press. The *New York Times*, failing to distinguish between internal and external recovery, argued that the crisis represented the 'failure of British productive effort under Socialism' (though British recovery had proceeded far farther and far faster than had that of the other European states), and posed the classic question 'Is production – is post-war recovery – perhaps incompatible with Socialism?'[4] And where the normally Anglophil *New York Times* expressed doubts, isolationists and Anglophobes, and the financial press heralded the immediate disappearance of the hated British socialism.

By this time the Marshall Plan had already been launched. It took its origin in the communication to Washington at the end of February 1947 of the British decision to withdraw troops and aid from Greece and Turkey, because of the impossibility of continuing to finance their

1. *The Forrestal Diaries* (1952), 186–8.
2. Ibid., 262.
3. Ibid., 292, 293, 296, 330.
4. Gardner, op. cit., 343–4, citing *New York Times* of 31 July and 11 August 1947.

presence there out of Britain's dwindling external balance of payments. This had given rise to the American decision to step in and take over Britain's responsibilities in that area, the so-called 'Truman doctrine', and to the back-stairs decision to direct any future American aid towards a general co-operative recovery programme in Europe rather than in loans or grants to individual countries. Care was taken by Acheson to 'leak' this decision to press sources in close touch with the British Embassy in Washington and the Foreign Secretary, so that when Marshall's speech of 5 June 1947, the third and most important in this process of diplomacy by oratory which marked a major revolution in American foreign policy, took place, Bevin was forewarned and could take up Marshall's proposals at once with his European colleagues.

The course taken by American and British foreign policy over the previous two years thus culminated finally in the Marshall Plan, a set of proposals which introduced a new instrument of policy, unprecedented in its scope, into the general armoury of devices employed in the conduct of foreign affairs in the twentieth-century world.[1] It is worth noting, in view of the theme of this essay, that the original draft of President Truman's speech delivered on 12 March, embodying the 'Truman doctrine', included a passage to the effect that 'there had been a world-wide trend away from the system of free enterprise toward state controlled economies, ... the disappearance of free enterprise in other nations would threaten our economy and our democracy'. This passage was removed after Acheson had pointed out that the Labour Government's policy in England of 'asserting greater state control over the economy and narrowing the area of free enterprise' had been carried through by democratic processes, and had not impaired 'the free institutions and basic freedoms of the British people', or made Britain's continued survival as a free and independent nation any less important for the security of the United States.[2]

More important than this, though, is the extraordinary lack of contact between the British and American administrations revealed

1. There are precedents for international aid to a single country in the aid programmes of the League of Nations to Austria in the 1920s and in the proposals which surrounded the Rajchman mission of the League to China in 1933; but aid from one nation to an organized group of nations was something new.

2. Joseph M. Jones, *The Fifteen Weeks* (New York, 1955), 156–7.

by the development of British and American policy. Proposals to put American aid to Europe on a new footing (and especially aid to Greece and Turkey) had been discussed within the United States administration since the summer of 1946. The Secretariat of this co-ordinating committee of the State, Navy and War Departments undertook in April 1947 a study of the policy, procedure and costs of American assistance to foreign countries, and recommended that aid programmes should be co-ordinated so as to take advantage of the possibilities of material assistance on a regional basis, priority to be given to the democracies of Western Europe, and the economic division of the State Department suggested American aid for a co-ordinated European recovery programme. On his return from the Moscow Conference of Foreign Ministers in April 1947, convinced by Stalin's comment that compromise would come 'after the exhaustion of both sides in the dispute' that the Soviets were stalling in the hope of an economic débâcle in Western Europe, General Marshall, then American Secretary of State, set up a group under George Kennan to think over the problems of American aid to Europe. At the same time Will Clayton, returning from a European trip, proposed a new programme of aid based on a European economic federation to be worked out by the Europeans themselves. Kennan's report formed the basis of Marshall's speech of 5 June 1947.[1]

On at least three occasions in this process there was occasion for Anglo-American conversations. On 5 October 1946 Dalton and Clayton had a lengthy discussion on 'a number of European financial points'. Yet according to Dalton's record the outcome was to end UNRRA aid to Europe, to agree that further 'doles' should be confined to Italy, Austria and Greece, and that all aid to Germany should stop after 1948.[2] This came, it is true, at the end of the *annus mirabilis* of British recovery, the year which ended in the catastrophic winter of 1946–47.[3] But the whole tone of the conversation accords not at all with the ideas already being mooted in US administration circles. The second occasion came at the end of November 1946 when

1. This account is based essentially on W. C. Mallalieu, 'The origins of the Marshall Plan; A study in policy formulation and national leadership', LXXIII, *Political Science Quarterly*, no.4 (December 1958), which is based on the Clayton Papers. See also Garwood, *Will Clayton*, 14.

2. *Dalton Diaries*, entry of 5 October 1946.

3. It was on his return from Washington that Dr Dalton announced that the British export drive had succeeded 'beyond expectation and beyond estimate', and that he had 'a song in his heart'.

the British administration was already discussing the question of the continuance of British military aid for Greece and Turkey on the assumption that 'financial aid for Greece and Turkey is forthcoming from the United States on the economic side', and proposing talks between Bevin and James Byrnes, the American Secretary of State, then meeting for a Foreign Ministers' Conference in Paris.[1]

Despite these discussions, the British notification to the American government in early March 1947 that they could no longer afford to provide aid to Greece and Turkey seems to have come as a total surprise to Washington, showing the complete failure of communication between the two capitals. Even then, the processes of consultation show no sign of having been improved. Although the State Department proposed informal discussions with the British Ambassador in Washington in May 1947,[2] no echo of these seem to have reached the British Cabinet.

Despite Dr Dalton's brave words and the boasting of the press, the British Cabinet had since November 1946 begun to contemplate with varying degrees of realism the prospect of the American loan running out in two years, without a proper balance of trade having been established with the dollar-holding countries. The lead in this was taken by Cripps and Dalton, with Attlee, who had gone so far as to propose in February 1946 the total abandonment of the Middle East for a fall-back position in Central Africa, swinging in behind them. In January 1947 Dalton was driven to direct a note to Attlee complaining of the failure of other ministers to take the export problem seriously. Unless Britain could build up exports much faster than at present, and hold them at a new high level, he argued, Britain would have no remedies in two years' time when the dollar loans were exhausted, except to borrow more abroad – 'and where from, and at what level?' The occasion of this broadside was a bitter argument in Cabinet over the strength of the armed forces and the need to transfer men from the armed forces to the productive labour force in Britain, in which Dalton had run into the direct opposition of the Foreign Secretary, the Minister of Defence and the Chiefs of Staff.[3]

Three overseas commitments were particularly worrying to the Treasury, those to Greece and Turkey, the drain of dollars to cover

1. *Dalton Papers*, memorandum of 28 November 1946; *Diaries*, entry of 29 November 1946.
2. Mallalieu, loc. cit.
3. The letter is quoted in Dalton, op. cit., 194–8.

the gap between Germany's export earnings and her bill for imports, mainly food, and Palestine. In March 1947 the rate of withdrawal of the American loan had so quickened as to advance to February 1948 the date of its exhaustion. A 30 per cent rise in American wholesale prices did a good deal to increase the rate of withdrawal, as did the falling off of the export drive as a result of the crisis of February–March 1947.[1] This led directly to the decision to withdraw from Greece and Turkey, and to the message to President Truman, which triggered off the Truman doctrine.

His success with this led Dalton to press again for further withdrawals, especially the taking over by the United States of the dollar cuts of feeding the British and American zones in Germany. But his proposal, made at the beginning of May,[2] showed no awareness of the way in which American thoughts were turning, though it did foreshadow consultations with other countries, especially France, on the developing world dollar shortage. Marshall's speech was welcomed in the Foreign Office, Bevin deciding at once to take it at its face value and jumping at once into consultation with the French, out of which came the conference of July in Paris. Yet there was still no real guidance from Washington. On 13 June the 'Big Five', Dalton, Cripps, Bevin, Morrison and Attlee, met and agreed on the need to goad the United States into further action. Dalton's note[3] agrees that 'Marshall gives the impression of wanting to do something big', but he put no reliance on Congress at all. Clayton's visit to London at the end of June stirred Dalton to write 'Clayton has no plan'.[4] The Paris conference gave Bevin 'courage and hope',[5] but the loan was running out much faster than things were moving. Thus it was that the convertibility crisis, the lowest point in Anglo-American relations, came after Marshall's speech, and was followed, while the European Committee working in Paris with brilliance and speed put together a draft scheme to take to Washington in reply to Marshall's proposals, by a bitter crisis among the Big Five themselves, with Cripps and Dalton trying to win Morrison over to replacing Attlee, as Prime Minister, by Bevin.

It is not surprising, therefore, that the first reactions of the British

1. The letter is quoted in Dalton, op. cit., 220–1.
2. *Dalton Papers*, memorandum of 2 May 1947.
3. *Dalton Diaries*, entry of 13 June 1947.
4. Ibid., entry of 27 June 1947.
5. Ibid., entry of 4 July 1947.

Left to the Marshall proposals were coloured by the suspicions of the convertibility crisis.[1] Thereafter the universalism of the Marshall Plan, the Soviet pressure on Poland and Czechoslovakia to abandon their desires to participate in it, the onset of the Berlin crisis[2] and most of all the *coup d'état* in Czechoslovakia with the putative murder of the much-loved Jan Masaryk, swung all but the fellow-travelling section of the British Left into all-out support of the Marshall Plan and the American administration, which was seen, especially after Truman's victory in the 1948 Presidential elections and the launching of the 'Fair Deal', as pursuing a parallel path towards a state of democratic and egalitarian welfare socialism.[3] With this change in the attitude of the non-fellow-travelling Left the Labour leadership was easily able to deal with the authors of the 1948 telegram to the Italian Socialist leader, Nenni, and to expel the hard-core of fellow-travellers together with the maverick Zilliacus in 1949.

It was thus that Anglo-American relations were able to survive a degree of anti-socialist expression in 1948, far greater than that which had accompanied the Congressional Hearings and debates of 1946 on the Anglo-American Financial Agreement, without any real impact being made on the British Labour party whatever. Yet the range and degree of doubts expressed at the Senate Hearings on the European Recovery Programme[4] in 1948, and the importance of those giving voice to them, were much greater than in 1946. The National Association of Manufacturers, for example, demanded that a condition of American aid should be that no more nationalization programmes be initiated,[5] and made blanket allegations as to the uses to which American aid had been put, much more offensive in their directness than those which had caused the British Cabinet to take offence in 1946, without any echo breaking through to embarrass that Cabinet in its relations with its own party.

1. *Tribune* called them 'the Washington Trap' (22 August 1947). Leon Epstein, 'The British Labour Left and US Foreign Policy', *American Political Science Review*, XIV, no.4, (December 1951).

2. Aneurin Bevan allegedly wished to break a way through to Berlin by force (Joseph and Stewart Alsop, *The Reporters' Trade* (1958), 85).

3. The evidence has been set out in detail in Epstein, article cited in fn. 1 above; Epstein, *Britain – Uneasy Ally*, 45–50, 109–11, 144; M. A. Fitzsimons (see fn. 3 above, p. 61).

4. US Senate, Committee on Foreign Relations, *Hearings on the European Recovery Programme*, 80th Congress, 2nd Session.

5. Ibid., 813–14.

Not that the continued utterance of such opinions did not give the Cabinet continued cause for anxiety. But the anxiety lay entirely as to the effect the utterance of such views might have in the United States on the readiness to give aid. Every care was taken, particularly by Sir Stafford Cripps, who succeeded Dalton at the Exchequer in the autumn of 1947 and carried the whole weight of directing Britain's recovery on his shoulders from then until his retirement and death. The policy he followed was to take every opportunity of putting Britain's need for Marshall Aid as clearly as possible before American opinion, while making it clear that the goal of British recovery was ultimate independence. It is not too much to say that the annual *Economic Surveys* and the vast majority of public statements he made in the years 1948–49 were intentionally aimed at American rather than British opinion. Innumerable press conferences were held (especially during his visit to the United States in September 1948 for the meetings of the I.M.F. and World Bank), and special arrangements were made to see that they received as full coverage as possible in the United States press.[1] A particularly bad moment was caused him in February 1949 when Christopher Mayhew suggested at Lake Success that Britain's economic recovery was complete, prompting American comment that no more Marshall Aid need be forthcoming. Despite Cripps' immediate statement denying this and the backing of Paul Hoffman, the head of E.R.P., the availability of new aid remained in doubt until the moment the new Congressional appropriation for Britain was actually made.[2]

That Cripps was well advised in his anxieties may be seen in Ambassador Lewis Douglas' comment in November 1948 that he was concerned by the 'continued underwriting by the United States of British Labour's political objectives' and opinion that Labour policies would 'inhibit' real economic recovery in Britain.[3] The basic criticism was now inclined to be framed less in ideological terms than to be disguised in the language of economics, as, for example, in the repeated assertion that the necessary disinflation was being frustrated by increased social welfare expenditures, nationalization, excessive taxation, the continuance of direct controls and the 'unwillingness or inability of the Labour Government to apply the necessary pressures

1. See Colin Cooke, *Life of Richard Stafford Cripps*, (1957), 266, 381. Also private information.
2. Cooke, op. cit., 383–4.
3. *Forrestal Diaries*, 488.

77

on labour and business to bring down export costs'.[1] Care on both sides of the Atlantic was needed to control the resurgence of this feeling in the United States to a point where it would not threaten the renewed Anglo-American co-operation which the Marshall Plan had brought with it, and the austere figure of Cripps himself (one difficult to associate with the idea of cosseting or 'featherbedding' anyone) came to stand as a guarantee of renewed British effort, if not of achievement.

This factor can be seen at its clearest when the 'devaluation crisis' of August 1949 is considered. The crisis seems to have developed as a result of a widespread conviction that the need for an expansion of British exports would necessitate devaluation sooner or later. In June 1949 at the Brussels meeting of the E.R.P. nations, Belgium had proposed that the drawing rights of Marshall Plan debtor countries should be convertible into dollars freely convertible within the European zone – a proposal which had implied that European countries trading with Britain could claim dollars in settlement of their balances with Britain. This proposal Cripps was alone in resisting, as the American delegation, especially Hoffman, saw in it a proposal which would conduce to general European recovery. At the subsequent meeting at Paris in July, Cripps was forced to offer compromise proposals which were taken up in direct Anglo-American conversations in mid-July in London between Cripps and Snyder. There then developed both in Europe and in the United States a formidable attack on British policies accusing the British Government of a rigidly defensive posture in economic matters, springing not from economic necessity but from the desire to defend British socialism. This posture was held directly responsible for the continuing economic weakness of Europe. In August Hoffman went publicly on record about Britain's need to treble her exports to the United States. Heavy speculation against the pound began on the European exchanges, from the conviction that the necessary increase in British exports could only be achieved by a considerable measure of devaluation, so heavy that on 18 September, after having given advance warning of his step in Washington to the American administration and the I.M.F., Cripps was forced to announce just such a step.[2]

1. See John H. Williams, 'The British Crisis. Problem in Economic Statesmanship', *Foreign Affairs*, xxviii, no.1 (October 1949); also Roy Harrod, 'Hands and Fists Across the Sea', *Foreign Affairs*, xxx, no.1 (October 1951).   2. Cooke, op. cit., 389–90.

Again, one might have expected a recrudescence of the anti-Americanism of the 1946–47 period, the more so as sections of American opinion made no bones of their conviction that the 'socialistic' and welfare policies of Britain were to blame for the need to devalue.[1] But the main burden of British Labour criticism was turned not against America but against European speculation. Labour adherents of the 'conspiracy theory of history' added a new set of figures to their demonologies, what have recently been called the 'malignant gnomes of Zürich'. A great deal of credit for the lack of injury done to Anglo-American relations by the 'devaluation crisis' must rest with the main leaders of the American administration,

. . . those American . . . politicians and officials who were handling their end of the situation. It was useless to attempt to keep the public quiet. Their problem was to convince a sceptical public and vociferous collection of Congressmen from making it impossible for the still small voice of reason to be heard, to convince enough people in North America that all this good American money was not being poured into the waste lands. . . .

Such guidance was not wasted. If Britain had come to believe that the United States was concerned to wreck Britain's Socialist experiment, socialists and non-socialists would have united in a deep resentment. Because the men with power in Washington did not believe that they should interfere with that, they allowed the experiment to be worked out where it should have been worked out – in Britain.[2]

Despite the existence of a considerable doctrinal difference between the public postures and values to which the American and British Governments were committed in the period between the end of the war and the end of Marshall Aid to Britain in December 1950, it is surprising what little effect it has had in general on the course of American aid, despite the activities of busy-bodies such as Baruch with his continuous demand that US aid should only be given to private agencies in Europe. Some of the reasons for this may be sought in the American conviction that a collapse of Britain was not in America's interests, a conviction that grew easily out of American Anglophilia and the impact of the cold war. The self-deception, or alternatively the temporary lapse into realism, of the non-fellow-travelling Left in Britain (it depends on the viewpoint) during the Marshall Plan definitely aided matters too. But the greatest credit

1. W. E. Mallalieu, *British Reconstruction and American Policy* (New York, 1956), 188.
2. Ernest Watkins, *The Cautious Revolution* (New York, 1950), 366–7.

must be given to the realism and sophistication (so greatly in contradiction to the long-standing British mythology) of the American leadership in this period in doing all they could, despite their private misgivings, to avoid gratuitous offence to British susceptibilities. They learnt well and they learnt very quickly. That new causes of Anglo-American friction beyond their control arose between British Left and American 'conservatism' was the fault not of any new ideological upsurge in either country, so much as of a disturbance in the internal balance inside the Labour party, which it has still not entirely overcome, and the impact of the Korean War and McCarthyism in the United States. Both can be seen as in part the product of disappointed short-term hopes, and the impatience with long-term, continuous, open-ended political processes to which both British and American radicalism are by nature peculiarly vulnerable.

PART II

The Influencing of Opinion

Britain, the United States and Japan in 1934

AT the beginning of the year 1934 the British Cabinet faced a new and terrible dilemma in the formulation of their foreign policy. Since 1922 their main efforts had been directed to ironing out the international dissensions and disputes which had survived the 1914–18 war or found their origin in the years of the Peace Settlement, as an essential corollary to the rebuilding of the economic and financial position Britain had occupied in the prewar world. Thus in successive steps Britain had worked for the tranquillization of Europe through the readmission of Germany to the ranks of the Great Powers. She had done her best to satisfy France's demands for security in Europe, or as much as her economic and financial preoccupations would allow. She had accepted a settlement of the War Debts and Reparations issues which threw very considerable burdens on her international balance of payments, and accepted a deflationary economic policy at home which contributed greatly to her economic stagnation and domestic labour troubles as the price of the return of the pound to the prewar gold standard. In the Far East she had accepted a settlement much closer to that demanded by the United States than that recommended by the Admiralty, as the price of good Anglo-American relations and to avoid the strain on relations within the Commonwealth that a contrary policy would have imposed.[1] Thereafter she had plunged into the confusion of the World Disarmament Conference with the double aim of ending the Franco-Italian disharmony which the London Naval Conference of 1930 had displayed, and of attempting to negotiate a satisfactory settlement of Germany's demands for an abrogation of the limitations on her sovereignty in matters of national defence imposed on her by Part IV of the Treaty of Versailles.

By 1933 this policy seemed near to shipwreck. In November 1931 the Japanese military had run amok in Manchuria, to be followed in

---

1. Essay 7 below; Raymond O'Connor, *Perilous Equilibrium* (Kansas, 1962).

February 1932 by the Japanese Navy in the attack on Shanghai, an attack which had been accompanied by rumours of a Japanese plan to attack the still-unfinished naval base at Singapore on which Britain's whole defence position in the Far East rested.[1] The Japanese cabinet responsible for the signature of the London Naval Treaty of 1930 had fallen, to be replaced by one much more amenable to the demands of the Japanese ultra-nationalists,[2] and the Naval High Command was being systematically purged of all those senior officers who had supported them. The two admirals most opposed to any restrictions on Japan's naval armaments, Admirals Kanzi Kato and Suetsugu, were firmly in the saddle and conducting a rigorous campaign against any renewal of the disarmament treaties. In January 1933 Japan withdrew from the League of Nations. Most ominously, talk was beginning in Japan about the coming 'international crisis of 1935–36' when the naval disarmament treaties were to expire, and in the winter of 1933 a group of Navy and civilian officials was set up in anticipation of meeting it.

In February 1933 the British Chiefs of Staff had reacted to the Japanese withdrawal from the League of Nations by raising the problem of defence in the Pacific in a memorandum to the Cabinet. The existing conditions of the Singapore base, they reported, made it impossible for the main strength of the British fleet to go to the Far East in the event of trouble with Japan.

The whole of our territory in the Far East as well as the coast-line of India and the Dominions and our vast trade and shipping is open to attack.

Although there was no reason to impute aggressive intentions to Japan, their reports continued, Japan had shown herself disquietingly adept at surprise attacks, and the state of Britain's defences in the Far East must be a constant temptation to the more aggressive elements in Japan.[3]

In the summer of 1933, however, the revival of German power under Adolf Hitler, the signs of secret German rearmament, especially in the air, and the violent German pressure on Austria provided Britain's defence planners with a source of anxieties much

1. See Essay 7 below; Major-General S. Woodburn Kirby, *The War in the Far East* (1957), I, 11; Basil Collier, *Defence of the United Kingdom* (1957), 24.

2. See R. W. Storry, *The Double Patriots* (1957), 96–154.

3. F. L. Wood, *The New Zealand People at War: Political and External Affairs* (Wellington, 1958), 60–1.

nearer home. These anxieties were greatly strengthened in October 1933 when Hitler's Germany followed the Japanese example by leaving both the League of Nations and the World Disarmament Conference. The matter led the Chiefs of Staff, long worried by the effects of the Government's policy of economy on the state of Britain's defences, to issue the gravest of warnings in their annual report to the Committee of Imperial Defence:

The accumulation of deficiencies . . . is very heavy, and if we are to be ready for grave emergencies a steady increase in certain of our estimates over a number of years is essential.

The report concluded with the flat assertion that, with their existing strength and armaments, Britain's armed forces could no longer be responsible for national and imperial defence.[1]

It was at this stage that the two most senior permanent civil servants, Sir Robert Vansittart and Sir Warren Fisher, intervened. Both were men obsessed, to put not too fine a point on it, with the peril to Britain represented by Germany. Their animus against Germany stemmed less from a hatred of Nazism as such than from a quasi-racialist conviction, not uncommon in their generation, of the peculiar and continuing wickedness of Germany, her unreliability and the uncompromising challenge to Western civilization she represented. Both were prepared to compromise if need be with an aggressive Italy or Japan; with Germany there could be no compromise. Of the two, Sir Warren Fisher, Permanent Under-Secretary of the Treasury, was the more formidable proposition. In 1919 he had succeeded, shortly after his appointment as Permanent Under-Secretary, in obtaining the recognition of his post as Head of the whole Civil Service. By 1933 his influence within the Civil Service was paramount, and his influence on the formulation of policy within the network of committees through which the Cabinet received advice was second only to that of Sir Maurice Hankey, who had occupied the twin positions of Secretary to the Cabinet and to the Committee of Imperial Defence since 1916. Fisher's position was reinforced by the fact that in Neville Chamberlain, Chancellor of the Exchequer, he had as his Cabinet chief the ablest and most forceful personality in the National Government.

In October 1933 a special sub-committee of the Committee of

1. Kirby, op. cit., 12; Admiral of the Fleet Lord Chatfield, *It Might Happen Again* (1947), 78–80.

Imperial Defence was set up at the sub-ministerial level under the title of the Defence Requirements Sub-Committee. It comprised the three Chiefs of Staff, Fisher, Vansittart and Sir Maurice Hankey as its Chairman. The terms of reference of the sub-committee included the assessment that for the moment the chief danger to Britain lay in the Far East.[1] But in its report which was placed before the Cabinet and the Committee of Imperial Defence in February 1934, the DRC, one suspects under the urging of Vansittart and Fisher, came round to the view that the 'ultimate potential enemy' was Germany.[2] Against Germany, 'we have time, but not too much time, to make preparations', their report commented, basing itself on the belief that Germany would not be ready before 1942.[3]

On Japan, the report commented that the danger from Japan was nearer than that from Germany; the precise meaning of this assessment, given that the choice of preventive action against Japan was ruled out by the state of Britain's military and naval resources, let alone the improbability of obtaining public support for a preventive war, was clearly that ways should be found to avoid a direct conflict with Japan, while Britain's defences were built up against Germany.

The report faced the Cabinet with a very considerable dilemma. Since 1929 the basis of British disarmament policy had been the closest co-operation possible with the United States, especially in the naval field. The structure of treaties they had co-operated in creating was now threatened by Japanese action. In addition, both had very considerable interests in the Far East which were threatened by Japanese expansion. Until the receipt of this report the obvious course had seemed to be that of co-operation with the United States, a co-operation limited, it is true, by a certain degree of mis-understanding at times, but the political side of the DRC's report seemed to call for a reconsideration of this policy in favour of an approach to Japan. The naval side of the report made the dilemma still more acute. The Chiefs of Staff, in fact, seem to have taken little note of the views of their political advisers. The Admiralty asked for funds over the following five years to modernize the five battleships of the Queen Elizabeth class, for the restoration of the naval bases abroad to something approaching a state of readiness, the expansion of the Fleet Air Arm,

1. Collier, op. cit., 25.
2. Ibid., 26.
3. W. K. Hancock and M. M. Gowing, *The British War Economy* (1949), 64.

and, most important, a restoration of the target for Britain's cruiser strength to the figure of seventy approved in 1925, and abandoned in 1929 in the face of American unwillingness to accept a figure so much beyond their own capacity to match.[1] Their main aim was clearly an increase in the rate of British naval construction sufficient to make British paper superiority over Japan a reality. To achieve this aim it required either an acquiescence in the abandonment of the structure of disarmament treaties or the obtaining of American agreement to an upward revision of Britain's cruiser strength, and a new set of proposals for the naval disarmament conference due to meet not later than the end of 1935 under the terms of the Washington and London Naval Treaties. Thus the political side of the DRC's report seemed to imply a *rapprochement* with Japan, while the naval side necessitated a continuation of the old policy of Anglo-American co-operation. In the current state of American and Japanese opinion the two were mutually incompatible.

The instincts of the majority of the Cabinet, especially of the Prime Minister, Ramsay MacDonald, and of the Admiralty, lay in favour of a continuation of the policy of co-operation with the United States. This policy had already been renewed in March 1934, before the DRC report was given full Cabinet consideration, when the principal American negotiator on disarmament matters, Norman H. Davis, passed through London. On 6 March Davis reported to the President that the British were most desirous to reach agreement with the United States because of the salutary effect this would have on Japan, whose activities were most disturbing to them. The Singapore base would not be ready until 1937. Until then British policy would be to reach a common understanding with the United States as to how to meet Japan's demands

and even to go further, if we are disposed to do so, for the maintenance of peace and the protection of our respective rights and interests.

In the more detailed memorandum of his talk with the Prime Minister which took place on 2 March, Davis reported MacDonald as outlining proposals to express to the Japanese Ambassador in London the disquiet felt by the British Government as to the nature of Japan's naval claims, which Britain regarded as 'unjustifiable'.

1. M. M. Postan, *British War Production* (1952), 24; Commander P. K. Kemp, *Key to Victory: The Triumph of British Sea-Power* (Boston, 1957), 20–1.

Davis recorded himself as holding out to MacDonald the prospect of an arrangement by which American ships might use British bases in the Pacific as part of an agreement on the tonnage of future battleship construction.[1] Davis added, however, that the Conservative leader, Stanley Baldwin, and some others in the Cabinet were fearful that any Anglo-American arrangement against Japan might be upset by the US Senate, and were reluctant to upset Japan's susceptibilities until they knew where they stood. They insisted on talks with the Americans at this stage being conducted in secrecy. In a private letter of the same date to the President, Norman Davis added that the Prime Minister and the Foreign Secretary, Sir John Simon, had been under strong attack within the Coalition, but that they had succeeded in riding out the storm.[2]

Davis' report of MacDonald's remarks to him of the need for Anglo-American co-operation were almost immediately confirmed by the American Ambassador in London, Robert Bingham, reporting on a conversation with the First Lord of the Admiralty, Sir Bolton Eyres-Monsell:

Almost immediately he said to me that he thought our general situation, especially our Japanese situation, made it highly desirable for both countries to co-operate in dealing with the whole naval situation, and that we could handle the Japanese situation satisfactorily if we handled it together.[3]

The conversations continued in April on Davis's return from Europe. Ramsay MacDonald referred Davis to the two British technical experts on naval disarmament, Mr Craigie of the Foreign Office, and Admiral Sir Charles Little, head of the Admiralty's Plans Division. Davis had conversations on 11 April with Craigie and Vansittart, and on the following day with Craigie and Little. Craigie showed himself anxious that the Americans should not demand any further reductions in the level established in the Washington and London Naval Treaties, but both he and Admiral Little agreed that there was no reason to recognize Japan's claims to be allowed parity with the United States and Britain.[4] Craigie said that he felt Japan would probably give in at the end. Bingham had further conversations with the British Foreign Secretary, Sir John Simon, with

1. *US National Archives: State Department records*, 500.A15. A4/2515.
2. *Franklin D. Roosevelt Papers*, PSF III, London Naval Conference, 1934–36.
3. Bingham to Roosevelt, 8 March 1934, ibid.
4. Davis' memoranda of 11 and 12 April 1934, *Norman H. Davis Papers*, Box 9.

Eyres-Monsell and with Admiral Sir Roger Keyes, one of the only two Admirals of the Fleet, all of whom spoke of the need for co-operation with the United States against Japan.[1]

In the letter in which Bingham reported on his conversation with Sir John Simon, however, he noted a warning from the British Foreign Secretary of a new element in the situation. Angered by League of Nations action designed to strengthen the financial position of the Chiang Kai-shek Government, the spokesman of the Japanese Foreign Office, Mr Amau, warned very strongly against alien intervention in what Japan regarded as her special sphere of influence. Simon warned Bingham that the situation in his view was

very grave indeed, and that undoubtedly great pressure would be brought to bear upon the British government by British financial interests if the Japanese attempted to carry out their plan. . . .

The British Government, in fact, reacted very strongly to the Japanese action, delivering a protest in Tokyo couched in very strong language.[2] At the same time, however, the British Ambassador in Washington, reading the instructions to the British Embassy in Tokyo to William Phillipps, the Under-Secretary of State, expressed his Government's opposition 'to any concerted action'.[3]

It was under these circumstances that the Cabinet found themselves confronted with the necessity of considering not only the DRC report but also the need to draw up a new set of proposals to be put before the forthcoming naval conference. On 2 May Bingham reported on the emergence of an

important group of opinion [which] . . . believes that until the menace of Japanese policy is actually more pressing, and events in the Far East overshadowed the threats inherent in the European situation, Britain should oppose too obvious Anglo-American co-operation against Japan . . . this element would prefer to abandon the idea of a subsequent conference than to attempt by Anglo-American coercion to force Japan into a ratio agreement that would arouse national resentment there.[4]

The American Ambassador was well served by his informants. He had already noticed a phrase in Sir John Simon's statement in the

1. Bingham to Roosevelt, 23 April 1934, *Roosevelt Papers*, PSF III, London Naval Conference, 1934–36.
2. The Japanese record is in *International Military Tribunal for the Far East*, Transcript, vol.67, 29,579–86.
3. Phillipps Memorandum, *Roosevelt Papers*, PPF I, Diplomatic Correspondence Great Britain, Box 7.
4. Bingham to Davis, *Foreign Relations of the United States, 1934*, 1,232–3.

House of Commons on 30 April on the Amau declaration, a phrase that referred to Japan's special rights 'recognized by other powers but not shared by them'. On 7 May he forwarded a memorandum drawn up by the Counsellor of the American Embassy, commenting that an element traditionally friendly to Japan

is opposed to antagonizing her as (1) this would lead to Japanese action against Britain's trade in China, (2) would strengthen the militarist element in Japan and might lead to an issue at a time when the Singapore base . . . is almost two years from completion. (3) It would have to be calculated on co-operation with the United States. . . . The British Government is determined to run no risks in the Far East at the moment and to concentrate all the efforts in trying to keep the peace in Europe and to rehabilitate its economic life. . . .[1]

In a letter to the President dated the next day, Bingham recorded a conversation with Vansittart which follows so closely what we know of the political side of the DRC report as to make it worth recording.

Sir Robert said that he thought the danger now was in Europe and from Germany; that the Germans were not only arming generally but were building a large number of heavy bombing planes. . . . I gathered from what he said that the British considered the Russian and the Chinese (and obviously the American) attitude in the Far Eastern situation would deter the Japanese from taking any immediate action. However he realized that the Japanese had never abandoned for a moment their 21 Demands . . . and he had no doubt that they would not only put these demands in force but add other ones in the event of an outbreak of war in Europe. Meanwhile he saw no immediate danger in the Far Eastern situation and believed that any disturbance there was unlikely unless and until Germany precipitated war in Europe.[2]

In the Cabinet's discussions, the dominating factor was finance. The pre-eminent need, so they decided, was to build up Britain's air defences against Germany. Their decision on the DRC report was to cut the total figure of expenditure proposed by the three Service representatives by one-third, the bulk of which cuts fell on the Army, and to force the Royal Air Force to devote itself to building up Fighter Command. If the pre-eminent need was to develop Britain's air force against Germany, wrote Neville Chamberlain, the Chancellor

1. Bingham to Hull, *F.R.U.S., 1934*, III, 165 ff.
2. *Roosevelt Papers*, PSF I, Diplomatic Correspondence Great Britain, Box 7.

of the Exchequer, 'we certainly cannot afford at the same time to rebuild our battle fleet',[1] and again

this all works out as a result of the proposition that we cannot provide simultaneously for hostilities with Japan and Germany and that the latter is the problem to which we must now address ourselves.[2]

He devoted himself, therefore, to composing a long memorandum advocating the need for a *rapprochement* with Japan.[3]

From that point on the chancelleries of the world began to whisper with reports of an Anglo-Japanese *rapprochement*.[4] These rumours did not do justice to the dilemmas of the British Government. Whatever might be demanded about the replacement of Britain's battleship fleet – which was no more obsolete than that of Japan – the Admiralty were determined to have their seventy cruisers. For a time there seems to have been discussion of the possibility of abandoning any attempt at further naval limitation and working simply for a fleet adequate to meet Britain's responsibilities in European and Far Eastern waters; but the possible effect on American opinion, let alone that on public opinion in Britain still firmly wedded to the mystique of disarmament, made this a political impossibility. Given the need for a new disarmament treaty, the need to obtain American approval of Britain's increased cruiser figures and the hope that the Japanese civilian elements might reassert themselves against the hotheads of the Navy, conversations with the United States became a necessity.

The first round of these conversations took place in London in June and July 1934. They were singularly unsuccessful. Despite all the British warnings, the state of Britain's naval needs and the change in her strategic position had not registered in Washington at all. Britain's demand for seventy cruisers left the American delegation frankly appalled – the more so as they had come with instructions from Roosevelt to press for a reduction of one-third in the general level of naval armaments, a singularly unrealistic suggestion under the circumstances, which makes one wonder whether he had read Davis'

1. Keith Feiling, *The Life of Neville Chamberlain* (1946), 258.
2. Ibid., 253, diary entry of 6 June 1934.
3. Iain Macleod, *Neville Chamberlain* (1960), 178.
4. See *F.R.U.S., 1934*, I, 238–9; ibid., III, 189–93; *German Naval Archives*, Intelligence reports of 28 May 1934, 7790/E561218–19; Moffatt to Davis, 28 May 1934, *Davis Papers*, Box 12; *German Naval Archives*, German Naval Attaché report of 1 June 1934, 7790/E561221.

and Bingham's reports and letters. The British demand revived all the US Navy's old suspicions that the only guiding principle of British naval policy was to deny the United States parity at sea. The talks broke up in an atmosphere of subdued bitterness. The British proposal for a contractual agreement on resistance to Japan was turned down by the United States as out of the question – while MacDonald stuck firmly but courteously to his guns in the face of a direct appeal from Roosevelt.[1] It was agreed, however, that there should be a second round of talks in October.

During the summer the pro-Japanese group in the Cabinet seems to have returned to the attack. The outcome of the June talks had, after all, accorded very closely with their pessimistic diagnosis of American policy. No sign of understanding of Britain's dilemmas had been shown. America's own disarmament proposals bore no relation to the realities of the situation, and seemed to have been drawn up without any reference to British representations or interests. At the same time there were signs that the Japanese cabinet were resisting the outrageous financial demands involved in their navy's proposed construction programme.[2] In August there was a revival of the May rumours of an Anglo-Japanese *rapprochement*.[3] In September, a mission of the Federation of British Industries visited Japan and Manchuria, and there was talk of an Anglo-Japanese trade agreement.[4] At the same time the evidence of Hitler's aggressive intentions multiplied. British intelligence sources were well aware of the illegal rearmament of Germany in the air; and at the end of July the murder of the Austrian Chancellor, Dollfuss, by a group of Nazi killers

1. The course of the talks may be followed in *F.R.U.S., 1934*, I.

2. See Grew to Hull, 13 September 1934, *F.R.U.S., 1934*, I, 307; the same to the same, 17 October 1934, *F.R.U.S., 1934*, I, 309–10.

3. Davis to Roosevelt, 20 August 1934, *Roosevelt Papers*, PPF 33, Norman H. Davis; J. Pierrepont Moffatt to Davis, *Davis Papers*, Box 41.

4. Particular stir was caused by a speech made in Tokyo by a member of the British Trade Commission, Sir Charles Seligman, in which he spoke of the close relationship between Britain and Japan approaching the status of an alliance. This was accompanied by rumours of an Anglo-Japanese understanding on the division of China into spheres of influence (*German Naval Archives*, German Naval Attaché in London to Berlin, 26 October 1934, 7790/E561471); the Foreign Office in London seized the opportunity to issue a denial of these reports worded in the strongest terms, which was widely featured in the British press on 26 October (Davis to Hull, 26 October 1934, *General Board of the US Navy*, Telegrams, October–December).

attempting to stage a *coup d'état* in Vienna caused a thrill of horror to run through Europe. In September Norman Davis reported information from Lord Lothian that at least two Tory ministers were reluctantly convinced that war with Germany was inevitable in three years, and therefore felt that British policy had to be assured that there would be no trouble in the Far East.[1]

The leaders of the pro-Japanese group continued to be the same, Warren Fisher and Neville Chamberlain. The main advocates of as close Anglo-American co-operation as possible were MacDonald, Sir John Simon and the Admiralty. The arguments, however, were more closely balanced than the distribution of opinion in the Cabinet and among senior civil servants would suggest. The lack of any tangible support from the United States made it easy for those who favoured the reaching of a compromise with Japan to accuse the pro-Americans of preferring sentiment to realities.[2] The memory of 1919, of the many unilateral actions of the American Senate in the early 1920s, were constant factors on their side.[3] The British Embassy in Washington could not but have reported on the growth of isolationism in the United States.

Under the circumstances, there was every inducement for both sides to listen to the advice of those who argued that the Japanese were really concerned to avoid a new public humiliation, and would accept some new set of proposals which did not involve a public restatement of Japan's inferior position at sea. What was important in the view of these would-be mediators was to treat Japan gently, to avoid any overt pressure or the appearance of an Anglo-American line-up against her.[4] When the second round of talks began in the last week of October, the British negotiators decided to conduct bilateral talks with the Japanese and the Americans separately and, as Simon told Norman Davis, to 'wait until the Japanese showed their hand'.[5]

1. *J. Pierrepont Moffatt Diary*, 27 September 1934.

2. See, for example, Vansittart's criticism of MacDonald's reliance on America, *The Mist Procession*, 403, 466, 467–8.

3. See, for example, Lothian to Colonel House, 20 November 1934, *House Correspondence: Lord Lothian*, Drawer 9, Folder 29.

4. See Davis to Roosevelt, 6 November 1934, *Davis Papers*, Box 41; *Roosevelt Papers*, PSF III, London Naval Conference, 1934–36.

5. Davis to Hull, 19 October 1934, *General Board of the US Navy*, Telegrams, Preliminary Naval Conversations, October–December 1934; Davis to Roosevelt, 23 October 1934, *Davis Papers*, Box 51; *Roosevelt Papers*, PSF III, London Naval Conference, 1934–36.

The decision was understandable but unfortunate. Such a procedure led inevitably to Britain appearing to play the United States off against Japan for her own interests. The appearance became even greater when the Japanese position became known, and it was seen to be completely irreconcilable with that of the American delegation. The US delegation, who had expected nothing else, felt that the next move should have been the co-ordination of British and American pressure on Japan to make her modify her position. In the British delegation, however, such a proposal at once raised again fears that matters could not be confined to the purely diplomatic plane, as they had been in 1922 and 1930; that the Japanese delegation could not again be put in a position where to accept an Anglo-American agreement would be to admit diplomatic defeat; that the Japanese would withdraw, all hope of a treaty structure would fall to the ground and Britain would be faced with a position where her interests in the Far East could only be defended by force or the threat of force – a force which, despite MacDonald's brave words about sacrificing all the Government's plans for social security, roads, etc., to construct a fleet capable of restraining both Japan and Germany,[1] the bulk of the Cabinet felt to be beyond Britain's strength.

The British delegation preferred to continue to play things carefully and to avoid any direct pressure on the Japanese.[2] Despite their shock at the first Anglo-Japanese meeting of 23 October, further Anglo-Japanese meetings followed on 26 October, 3 November and 7 November. Other talks were held in private at the technical and the diplomatic level in the hope of hammering out agreement on technical details.[3] The delays were accepted with reasonable patience by the leaders of the American delegation in London, but in Washington suspicion seethed,[4] as the debate within the British Cabinet and administration continued without apparent resolution. These suspicions broke out into public when the British proposals to be put to the Japanese on 7 November were leaked to the press and published in the *Daily Herald* that morning, and taken up in *The Observer* and

1. See Noel Field's memorandum of the Anglo-American conversation of 29 October 1934, *Davis Papers*, Box 36.
2. Davis to Roosevelt, 31 October 1934, *Davis Papers*, Box 51.
3. *German Naval Archives*, German Naval Attaché report, 9 November 1934, 7790/E561505–8; Davis to Hull, 9 November 1934, *F.R.U.S., 1934*, I, 326.
4. Roosevelt to Davis, 9 November 1934, *Davis Papers*, Box 51; Moffatt memorandum of 10 November 1934, *Moffatt Papers*.

The Times on 8 and 9 November.[1] On 11 November Roosevelt called in Wilmot Lewis, the great *Times* correspondent in Washington, a law unto himself even where his editorial superiors were concerned,[2] and gave him a personal interview, in which he warned the British Government most severely against abandoning co-operation with the United States for the hope of an agreement with Japan. Lewis' report of this interview appeared in *The Times* the next morning, 12 November, rewritten by arrangement between *The Times* and the Foreign Office so as to remove much of its original acerbity. Even in its bowdlerized form it was not well received by MacDonald, but he felt it necessary to issue, the next day, a formal categorical denial that any secret agreements existed between England and Japan on particular economic matters in connection with the naval talks. Despite this, however, the British negotiators still wished to avoid an overt break,[3] and in fact came forward with new proposals.[4]

It was at this stage that the back-stage battle came to its climax. The crucial influence was exerted by an alliance between *The Times* and *Observer* newspapers, General Smuts, and the group around the *Round Table*, especially Lord Lothian. Lothian was very much aware of the strains which naval issues could exert on Anglo-American relations as he had been much concerned by the earlier acerbities which this issue had raised between the two countries in the years 1927–29. He had, in fact, taken part in a back-stair attempt to smooth them out by private pressure on his contacts and friends in the Foreign Office and the Cabinet. He originally intervened in the 1934 negotiations during the Anglo-American talks in the summer, with a proposal revived from those earlier years. On that occasion he was warned off the course in a private letter from his old associate in the Cabinet Secretariat, Sir Maurice Hankey.[5]

1. German Naval Attaché report, 9 November 1934, loc. cit.
2. See the highly entertaining picture of him in Claud Cockburn, *In Time of Trouble* (1956), 187–94, 209, 211.
3. Davis to Hull, 12 November 1934, *General Board of the US Navy*, Telegrams, October–December 1934; *German Naval Archives*, German Naval Attaché report, 14 November 1934, 7790/E561521–3; the same, 17 November 1934, 7790/E561554–6.
4. Davis to Hull, 13 November 1934, *F.R.U.S.*, *1934*, I, 328–30; the same to the same, 14 November 1934, ibid., 331–2.
5. Hankey to Lothian, 7 July 1934, *Lothian Papers*, General Correspondence. Lothian's proposals were first made in an address at Chatham House on 5 June 1934 (the Marquess of Lothian, 'The Place of Britain in the Collective System', XIII, *International Affairs*, no.5 (September 1934).)

The warning only seemed to apply to the precise proposals Lothian was proposing to advance. It did not prevent him from continuing to keep his hand on the course of negotiations.[1] He had been a close friend of Norman Davis since they had first met at the Paris Peace Conference. Much of Davis' information as to the state of the debate within the British Cabinet came from Lothian who was very much in Baldwin's confidence. In October Lothian had visited the United States and had had a lengthy conversation with President Roosevelt, one in which he did his best to impress Britain's dilemmas on the President, and learnt how little the American administration were open to the British proposals.[2]

Lothian's group shared the American anxieties as the last week in October and the first in November brought continuing rumours of Anglo-Japanese agreements. With his inside sources of information he must have known that the rumours were as yet without foundation, but he was also well aware of the strength of the pro-Japanese group. None of them were particularly close to him, and the civil servants must have detested the amateur meddling which in their eyes his intervention represented. This group had strong support in Parliament also, and in October they were, in Davis' words at least, 'the only ones with a definite view as to the solution of the problem'.[3] On 12 November Lothian wrote to MacDonald asking him for an interview so as to report on the view of Roosevelt's intentions he had formed as a result of his October meeting.[4]

At this stage, however, General Smuts decided to intervene. On 13 November he delivered himself of a powerful address at a dinner arranged by the Royal Institute of International Affairs,[5] at the Savoy Hotel, London, an address the text of which, so the Editor of *The*

1. He sent Sir John Simon a memorandum on the naval question in August 1934 (*Lothian Papers*, General Correspondence).
2. Memorandum of 11 October 1934, *Lothian Papers*, File 6.
3. Davis to Hull, 13 November 1934, loc. cit.
4. Lothian to MacDonald, *Lothian Papers*, General Correspondence.
5. General J. C. Smuts, 'The Present International Outlook', xiv, *International Affairs*, no. 1 (January–February 1935). The vital section of his speech read as follows: 'While therefore our Far Eastern policy should, I submit, be based on friendship with all and exclusive alliances or understanding with none, the ultimate objectives of that policy should continue to conform with that general American orientation which has distinguished it since our Association with the United States in the Great War. . . . Any other course would mean building our Commonwealth policy on quicksands, and placing the future of this group at the mercy of incalculable hazards. . . .'

Times told the German Naval Attaché,[1] was discussed in the Foreign Office before it was delivered, which was given a good deal of publicity (in direct breach of the normal practice at that Institute), and which was taken up in the editorial columns of *The Times* as well as in its news columns the next day.[2] On 14 November Smuts wrote to Lothian of a dinner at which he and Lloyd George, now secure in his role of elder statesman, had planned to stage a debate on the occasion of the King's speech 'to be led in a non-party spirit by Lloyd George so as to elicit from the Government their real policy'.[3] The day of Smuts' dinner there had been a meeting between representatives of the Dominions and Sir John Simon who had assured them that no matters outside the scope of the naval question were being made the occasion for a bargain with either Japan or the United States.[4]

Lothian's part in this follow-up to Smuts' speech came in next Sunday's *Observer*, the issue of 18 November 1934, to which he contributed a centre page on the Japanese crisis. In his letter of 16 November to J. L. Garvin, its editor, accompanying the typescript of the article, he commented on Smuts' concern:

As he put it, he found the pro-Japanese and anti-American element all over the place, 'like a snake in the grass'.[5]

His view was confirmed by Davis who reported the same day that

That group within the British Cabinet who are particularly fearful of the European situation from which Great Britain cannot detach herself and

1. Report of 14 November 1934, loc. cit.

2. The file on this dinner preserved in the Royal Institute of International Affairs, shows that *The Times* was given an advance copy of the speech by arrangement between Lord Lothian and Geoffrey Dawson, the Editor. A pamphlet reprinting the text of the speech and *The Times* editorial had sold 37,867 copies by January 1935. The speech itself was widely reported in the United States and read into the *Congressional Record* (6 February 1935, 1668 ff.) by Senator Pope of Idaho. The entire Cabinet were invited, including MacDonald and Sir John Simon, who cried off at the last moment. No Cabinet member in fact attended. I am grateful to the Director of the Royal Institute of International Affairs for allowing me to consult these papers.

3. Smuts to Lothian, 14 November 1934, *Lothian Papers*, General Correspondence.

4. German Naval Attaché report of 14 November 1934, loc. cit.; Davis to Roosevelt, 27 November 1934, *Davis Papers*, Box 51; *Roosevelt Papers*, PSF III, London Naval Conference, 1934–36.

5. Lothian to J. L. Garvin, 16 November 1934, *Lothian Papers*, General Correspondence.

who feel it is of vital importance in some way to bind and limit Japan by Agreement are at present largely controlling the course of negotiations.[1]

Lothian's article was followed by an almost immediate easing of the situation. On 21 November Davis was able to report that the opposition of the pro-Japanese group was weakening. Baldwin told him that he was strongly impressed by Davis' view that the Japanese should be given time to 'go home and think it over'.[2] Neville Chamberlain, according to his information, 'hitherto the leader of the group in favour of a conciliatory policy towards Japan, had come to the conclusion that . . . the Japanese are bluffing, and that their bluff should be called'.[3] This information presumably came from Lothian himself as a result of a lunch arranged by Simon between Lothian and Chamberlain. On this occasion Chamberlain told Lothian

that he was now convinced that Japan could not be trusted, that she was perhaps bluffing and that England and the United States must at the proper time take a common stand and call the bluff. He thought however that it was better to avoid a rupture just now for fear that we would drive Japan in desperation to make an alliance with Germany.[4]

Lothian himself certainly felt that the worst was over, writing to various friends that the 'pro-Japanese movement' had been killed as a result of the work which 'Smuts and some others had done'.[5] His view of the role of his and Smuts' efforts was shared by others, most notably by Sir Harold Butler,[6] William Phillipps, the American Under-Secretary of State in the State Department (to whom Lothian had sent a copy of his *Observer* article),[7] and above all, by the British Ambassador in Washington, Sir Ronald Lindsay.[8]

Not that the movement to treat Japan easily was altogether defeated – only the notion of a separate deal. The main British anxieties continued, especially that of a link between Germany and Japan.[9]

1. Davis to Hull, 16 November 1934, *F.R.U.S., 1934,* I, 351–3.
2. The same to the same, 21 November 1934, *F.R.U.S., 1934,* I, 356–8.
3. The same to the same, 21 November 1934, *F.R.U.S., 1934,* I, 358–9.
4. Davis to Roosevelt, 27 November 1934, loc. cit.
5. Lothian to J. W. Dafoe, 27 November 1934; the same to H. V. Hodson, 29 November 1934, *Lothian Papers,* General Correspondence.
6. Butler to Smuts, 1 December 1934, copy in *Lothian Papers,* General Correspondence.
7. Phillipps to Lothian, 3 December 1934, ibid.
8. Lindsay to Lothian, 7 December 1934, ibid.
9. Davis to Roosevelt, 14 December 1934, *Davis Papers,* Box 51; *Roosevelt Papers,* PSF III, London Naval Conference, 1934–36.

The final word was contained in a letter from Smuts, now returned to South Africa, to Lothian:

I should say the pro-Japanese movement must be in a bad way by this time . . . judging from cuttings and letters that have reached me, my Chatham House speech has served the purpose for which it was intended. . . . It is not only Asia but Europe that should be tackled. We *must* prevent a Japanese-German combination which will be fatal. And this can only be done by ceasing to treat Germany as a pariah in Europe.[1]

The logic seemed, therefore, to lead inescapably to a policy of attempting to appease Hitler's Germany.

1. Smuts to Lothian, 14 December 1934, *Lothian Papers*, General Correspondence.

Sir Warren Fisher and British
Rearmament against Germany

IN the post-1939 debate over Britain's policy of appeasement against Germany attention focused very early on the role of the Permanent Under-Secretaries of the Treasury, Sir Warren Fisher and his successor, Sir Horace Wilson. Both were alleged to have been full-blooded supporters of appeasement; and both were alleged to have interfered in the distribution of Foreign Office reports to the Cabinet and in the general management of British foreign policy so as to prevent the Cabinet from receiving reports which did not support their common thesis, and to hold back on the official ladder of promotion those who did not share their views. This paper is not concerned with the case against Sir Horace Wilson;[1] since, unlike some of Wilson's sterner academic critics, the author does not feel confident that the background to his activities has been sufficiently established, nor that the motives of those of his critics who claimed to speak with inside knowledge are altogether unrelated to the memories of contemporary controversies. Sir Horace Wilson himself has chosen to keep his silence – a matter which the contemporary historian must regret since what evidence there is points rather against him. But in the case of Sir Warren Fisher, there is now a sufficiency of evidence not only to call into question the case made against him, but to establish a reliable counter-hypothesis to the one advanced by his detractors.

The first public attack on Sir Warren Fisher was advanced by Lord Perth, the former British Ambassador in Rome, in a debate in the House of Lords in February 1942. The gist of Lord Perth's case[2] was that Fisher, who occupied the position of permanent Under-Secretary of the Treasury and Head of the Civil Service from 1919 to 1938, exercised pressure in 'those inter-departmental discussions which so often precede the deliberations of ministers' to prevent views contrary to his own going forward to the ministerial level,

1. For a recent statement see Martin Gilbert and R. W. Gott, *The Appeasers* (1963).
2. 125, *Hansard's Parl. Deb., H. of L.*, cols 224–32.

especially in matters of rearmament against Germany, that he interfered in the circulation of Foreign Office reports, and that a superstition had arisen that 'if people made too strong a fight with the Treasury for the policy of their Departments they would not perhaps be quite so lucky in the next turn for promotion'. Lord Perth's accusations were implicitly denied by Lord Hankey,[1] and explicitly by Lord Tyrrell,[2] Permanent Under-Secretary in the Foreign Office in the late 1920s, and Lord Mottistone.[3] But this did not prevent the growth of a school of thought[4] which sought to lay at Sir Warren Fisher's door the main responsibility for the policy of appeasing Germany, and of seeking to further this policy by illegitimate intervention into the running of the Foreign Office, which then by definition was part of the Home Civil Service. The attack came largely from a section of the diplomatic service,[5] and it may be noticed that the Eden reforms of 1943[6] explicitly separated the Foreign Service from the Home Civil Service, whether as a result of a general uneasiness in the Service or more detailed experience is not clear. The most detailed strictures on Sir Warren Fisher's record made by a former member of the Foreign Service, Sir Walford Selby, were denied officially in the strongest terms after their appearance in print.[7] It was noticed that during the period in which Sir Warren Fisher's activities were at their height, both Lord Perth and Sir Walford Selby were out of the country, and could have had little first-hand experience of relations between the Treasury and the Foreign Office;[8] while Ashton-Gwatkin had been mainly involved with Fisher over a prolonged controversy about whether the Foreign Office should have an Economic Section of its own, or whether such matters were better handled by the inter-

1. 125, *Hansard's Parl. Ded., H. of L.*, cols 268–9. Lord Hankey did, however, accuse Fisher of excessive interference with Britain's efforts in the rearmament field.

2. Ibid., col.275.

3. Ibid., col.297.

4. F. Ashton-Gwatkin, *The British Foreign Service*, (Syracuse, 1950), 26–7; Lord Murray of Elibank, *Reflections on Some Aspects of British Foreign Policy between the Wars* (Edinburgh, 1946), *passim*; G. Legge-Bourke, *Master of the Offices* (1949), *passim*; Sir Walford Selby, *Diplomatic Twilight* (1953), *passim*.

5. Ashton-Gwatkin and Selby were both former members of the Foreign Service.

6. Cmd.6420 (1943), *Proposals for the reform of the Foreign Service.*

7. 516, *Hansard's Parl. Deb., H. of C.*, cols 151–2.

8. Selby served in Vienna and Lisbon.

departmental agency, the Department of Overseas Trade. It was also noticed that Lord Vansittart, the hero of the anti-appeasers, who was Permanent Under-Secretary in the Foreign Office from 1930–38, failed to support Fisher's critics in any way.

These allegations have recently found fresh voice in the first volume of Lord Avon's memoirs,[1] in so detailed and circumstantial a form that they must be given their due weight. There is, however, another side to the story. The facts are that, whatever Sir Warren Fisher's motives were for what he did, he was by no means pro-German, and had no faith whatever in the possibility of a long-term accommodation with Germany. He was, in fact, as virulently and obsessively anti-German as Vansittart himself. It is true that he did intervene persistently and successfully in matters of defence policy and on questions of rearmament; on matters of foreign policy, how-ever (as the previous essay has shown in one special case), his inter-ventions were fewer and a good deal less successful. In intervening in, and largely dictating the course of British policy on defence and re-armament, he of course profoundly influenced the limits of action of any Foreign Secretary or Cabinet. And as a result of his close co-operation with Neville Chamberlain at the Treasury during the latter's tenure of the Exchequer, he retained a very close link with him after he assumed the Premiership. In view of what is known of Chamberlain's use of advice from those he trusted it may be assumed that Fisher retained considerable influence over him as a result of this.[2]

Four main motives seem to have inspired Sir Warren Fisher in advocating the particular policy in matters of rearmament and foreign relations he succeeded in so large a degree in urging upon his political overlords. The first of these was his conviction that the only enemy Britain had really to fear was Germany. The second was his belief that as a result of the technological development of air warfare Britain was vulnerable to German pressure in a way quite without historical precedent. The third was a profound disagreement with the policy of deterrence advocated by the Air Ministry and the figures and intelligence assessments they used to back this. The fourth was his obsession with personal quality as a factor in government, and

1. Earl of Avon, *Facing the Dictators* (1962), 319–20, 447–8, 521. His predecessor, Sir Samuel Hoare, denied any interference from Fisher (Viscount Templewood, *Nine Troubled Years* (1954), 137).

2. Much of what follows is based on private information.

his conviction that in the 1930s Britain was desperately poor in such
quality among her professional military and civil advisers.

During the 1930s Sir Warren Fisher was to put the whole of his
tremendous vigour and personality into the furtherance of Britain's
rearmament efforts, becoming, in the words of one of his protégés, a
'kind of unofficial Minister of Defence – alas without portfolio'.[1] He
was to show himself determined to retain Treasury control of the
rearmament drive, since only through such financial control could he
ensure that it took the course he desired, and that it did not fall into
the hands of the Service advisers whom he regarded with contempt
as men unable to rise beyond the imbued assumptions and doctrines
of their own Services. He had some justification for this view.
Although the Chiefs of Staff of the three Services had been formed
into a sub-committee of the Committee of Imperial Defence as early
as 1924 and enjoined to evolve a common strategic viewpoint above
and beyond the views of their respective Services,[2] the experiment
had not hitherto been a success largely because of the total failure of the
three Chiefs of Staff to obtain a meeting of minds on the place of the
Air Force in modern warfare,[3] and their preference for taking the
strategic view most likely to buttress the needs of their own Service
in the annual battle with the Treasury over the Service estimates in
an age of economy and the Ten-Year Rule.

Sir Warren Fisher himself had played no very great part in this
battle. He had naturally backed his Chancellor, Winston Churchill,
in the famous Cabinet crisis of 1925 over Britain's cruiser programme,
but he had never shown himself an outright advocate of economy
for economy's sake.[4] The brunt of this particular battle was, in fact,
borne by others, and even though Fisher was to disagree with the
Admiralty in the mid-1930s, they never earned from him the enmity
and hostility he reserved for the Air Staff, and the then First Sea
Lord in fact pays a generous tribute to him in his memoirs.[5] It was

1. P. J. Grigg, *Prejudice and Judgement* (1948), 53.
2. The directive is printed in W. S. Chalmers, *Life and Letters of David, Earl Beatty* (1951), 380, 474–5.
3. See D. C. Watt, 'The Air Force View of History', *The Quarterly Review*, October 1962.
4. Oral information from the late Sir Donald Fergusson, private secretary to successive Chancellors of the Exchequer, 1919–36. Fisher spent much of his time in this period on his responsibilities as Head of the Civil Service.
5. Lord Chatfield, *It Might Happen Again* (1947), 79; oral evidence leads me to believe that Fisher if anything rather resented Chatfield's

only with the advent to power in Germany of Hitler, and the evidence which mounted during the spring and summer of 1933 of illegal German rearmament and of German subversion in Austria, that Fisher took up the issue of Britain's preparedness for war.

Before embarking on this, however, it is clear that Sir Warren Fisher himself needs a further introduction. He has been described by one of his juniors, who was to follow in his footsteps as Permanent Under-Secretary of the Treasury as

a man of enormous dynamic energy, quick to make up his mind, and with a great capacity to get things carried through to their conclusion . . . fearless and restless in disposition and rather impatient . . . given to quick enthusiasms, both for people and for causes. . . .[1]

His early career certainly bore that out. Educated at Winchester and Hertford College, Oxford, where his contemporaries remembered him chiefly for his refusal to take part in any undergraduate activities likely to impede him in obtaining a sufficiently high place in the Civil Service entrance examinations, he made it his major work so to reform the Civil Service as to make of it a single efficient entity, a unified machine in which advancement came by merit, whose standards of conduct were of the highest and whose administrative capabilities would not be impeded by jealousies or red tape.[2] He believed firmly in informality[3] and the cultivation of close contacts between the senior figures of the administration. He held equally firmly to the need for cross-promotion between departments, and for selection in filling the highest administrative posts from the whole Civil Service. He was enthusiastic about those in whom he detected ability, and given to the most sweepingly condemnatory remarks about those in whom he did not; much of the controversy which still surrounds his name stems from the enemies he made by the unguarded nature of his comments on the capabilities of those he 'held in no high repute'.[4]

support. He certainly came to resent Chatfield's later criticisms of the Treasury, and resigned from a committee of which he and Chatfield were members, after a speech critical of the Treasury made by Chatfield in the House of Lords, on 7 March 1945.

1. Lord Bridges, *The Treasury* (1964), 171.

2. His work and career in the Civil Service are admirably, if succinctly, summarized by Sir H. Hamilton, 'Sir W. Fisher and the Public Service', xxix, *Public Administration*, (Spring 1951).

3. A senior political figure of the 1920s commented to the author in tones of the deepest disgust: 'Fisher! He ruined the Civil Service! Got everyone on Christian name terms'. See also Bridges, op. cit., 171.

4. Ibid., 175; private information.

Only the briefest of records from his own pen of these years is in the public domain. It is so characteristic of the man as to be worth quoting in detail: after the 1914–18 war, he wrote in 1948,

We converted ourselves to military impotence. To have disarmed so drastically in the two or three years after the war was not unnatural though possibly not wise. But the Government of 1924 to 1929 had no excuse for further reducing our armed forces to a skeleton, as by then it was known that the Weimar Republic (so called) was in process of reconstructing a disguised army on a truly formidable scale. This British government's tragic action formed unfortunately a model for subsequent Governments; and though in 1936 a façade of rearmament was announced by the then Government, it was ludicrously insubstantial. . . .

And then look abroad. In 1922 [*sic*], we abruptly tore up our alliance, dated back to 1902, with the Japanese; and not content with getting them on the raw by thus mortally affronting their *amour-propre*, we rubbed vinegar into the wound by forcing them to pretend to agreement to a battle-fleet less than one-third of the combined American and British forces. And we fondly imagined that the Japanese, who are not remarkable for playing the game at any time, would wholeheartedly play the game in these circumstances! In that same year we only avoided a war with Turkey because the Dominions quite flatly and most rightly refused to join in. . . . Skipping a dozen years, in 1935 we addressed moral platitudes to the Italians about the integrity of Abyssinia without any advantage to the latter and merely driving Italy into Germany's arms; and in 1936 we addressed questionnaire after questionnaire to the Germans about their military re-occupation of the Rhineland.

When the Spanish Civil War broke out we deceived ourselves with a non-intervention pact which nobody but us observed. And in 1938 we partitioned Czechoslovakia.

This brief sketch omits many things, including our fatuous performance or non-performance about Manchuria. But the moral for the future is plain. . . .

. . . Had the British Empire, the United States and France squarely faced the facts in unison, the horrors which started up with the rape of Manchuria, followed by the outrage on Abyssinia, the all-out attack on China, the seizure of Austria and Czechoslovakia and culminating in the years from September 1939, could have been prevented; and therefore none of these countries can disclaim or escape a heavy measure of responsibility.[1]

1. Sir Warren Fisher, 'The Beginnings of Civil Defence', xxvi, *Public Administration*, (Winter 1948).

Sir Warren continues to make it clear that he played his part in attempting to get the British Government to take the German challenge seriously, and that he managed to do a certain amount behind ministerial backs to get Civil Defence measures advanced 'by circumstance and guile' despite ministerial indifference. In the field of rearmament against what he persisted in calling 'the Prussians', he had to work through more orthodox channels.

In September 1933 he returned from a long illness, and suggested that a special sub-committee of the Committee of Imperial Defence should be set up consisting of the official heads of the four Crown Services, together with official representatives of the Foreign Office and the Committee of Imperial Defence to review Britain's defence requirements. As the annual Chiefs of Staff report had stated categorically that Britain's armed forces, given their existing strength and armaments, could no longer be responsible for Britain's national and imperial defence,[1] and had called for 'a steady increase in certain of our Estimates over a number of years',[2] and as a deficit was no longer expected in Government expenditure[3] by the end of the current financial year, the Committee of Imperial Defence agreed that such a sub-committee should be set up. The Defence Requirements Sub-Committee began its meetings in November 1933, and although it took as its point of departure a recent dictum from the CID that for the moment the chief danger lay in the Far East,[4] Fisher and Vansittart between them were able to convince their colleagues that the ultimate potential enemy, 'certain to become within a few years a serious menace to Britain',[5] was Germany.

The DRC's report revealed that its civilian members, Fisher and Vansittart, were dominated by their fear of a 'knock-out blow from the air' at the very outset of the war.[6] They called attention to a probable demand for at least twenty-five squadrons for the defence of Britain's ports at home and abroad, and both the civilians asked for an addition of twenty-five extra air squadrons to the existing strength of

1. Chatfield, op. cit., 78–80.
2. Major-General S. Woodburn Kirby, *The War in the Far East* (1957), I, 12.
3. Neville Chamberlain to Hilda Chamberlain, October 1933; Iain Macleod, *Neville Chamberlain* (1960), 177.
4. Basil Collier, *Defence of the United Kingdom* (1957), 25–6.
5. Memorandum by Sir Robert Vansittart, *Documents on British Foreign Policy, 1919–39*, Second Series, vol.VI, document no.363.
6. Collier, op. cit., 26–7.

the RAF.[1] But they found it impossible at that stage to carry the Chief of Air Staff, Sir Adrian Ellington, with them. The civilian element were, in fact, unable to win any support from the Air Staff representative for their views. As a result Fisher came to believe the proposals for improving Britain's defences in the air to be quite incommensurate with the scope of the danger. In its place he found a preoccupation with the Army which he regarded as altogether outdated. The Chiefs of Staff assumed, in fact automatically, that a British Expeditionary Force would be sent to the Continent to aid France, as in 1914. They recommended that in the first instance it should consist of four infantry divisions, one cavalry division, two anti-aircraft brigades, one tank brigade and an air component to be sent within one month of the outbreak of hostilities.[2] In all, their combined programme to repair Britain's deficiencies amounted to about £71 million spread over five years, additional to the standard estimates, of which about 50 per cent was to be spent on the Army.

The terms of the Service recommendations clearly showed no sign whatever of any genuine strategic thought about Britain's defence position and the kind of war she might have to fight. Fisher found this totally unacceptable, and made it his business to see Neville Chamberlain privately and urge the drastic alteration of the DRC's recommendation. In July 1934 the Cabinet cut the total figure by one-third, halved the Army's proposed figure, agreed to postpone for several years the replacement of Britain's obsolescent capital ships and to allot a vastly increased sum to the building up of the air defence of Great Britain.[3] Chamberlain and Fisher as a result did their best to secure a modification of Britain's policy in the Far East and in matters of naval disarmament to reach an accommodation with the Japanese, but (as related in Essay 4 above) were unsuccessful.

The Chiefs of Staff were far from happy about this report, refusing to accept that Britain and her Empire could be made 'safe and secure by the unilateral rearmament of one service only'.[4] As a result of their protests the DRC was reconstituted and told to report on the full measures needed to increase the country's defences in all three Services without regard to their financial requirements. In the meantime,

1. Lord Vansittart, *The Mist Procession* (1958), 443.
2. Collier, op. cit., 26–7.
3. Macleod, *Chamberlain*, 168; Keith Feiling, *The Life of Neville Chamberlain* (1946), 258; Collier, op. cit., 27; P. K. Kemp, *Key to Victory, The Triumph of British Sea-Power in World War II* (Boston, 1957), 20–1.
4. Chatfield, op. cit., 83.

a reluctant Cabinet, faced with a mounting toll of by-elections lost on the issue of disarmament, were beginning to face the need to awaken the country to the need to rearm in the year in which a general election would probably have to be held. The outcome of their debates was the decision to hold a full-dress debate on defence as such, and to issue as prior preparation for this a lengthy White paper. This, in fact, only represented a transfer to the field of defence policy as a whole of a practice introduced for the Navy Estimates in 1919 by Lord Beatty. Fisher, however, took a major share in the role of urging the Government to follow this course, which represented a major innovation in British constitutional practice.[1] For the first time defence policy was to be considered as a whole and debated as a whole in the British parliament. Moreover, Fisher made it his business to secure the insertion in this White paper of passages putting the blame for the need to rearm squarely on Germany's shoulders.[2]

At the same time the Cabinet, feeling the need to exert closer civilian control over the Services, instituted a Ministerial equivalent to the DRC, the Sub-Committee on Defence Policy and Requirements, chaired by the Lord President of the Council, Stanley Baldwin, and including the Chancellor of the Exchequer, Neville Chamberlain, the Foreign Secretary, Sir John Simon, with the three Service Ministers, Viscount Hailsham (War), Sir Bolton Eyres-Monsell (Admiralty) and Lord Londonderry (Air).[3] A great deal of the new committee's time was almost immediately taken up with the Abyssinian crisis. The DRC reported twice, in July and November 1935. It reported that Germany's weakness at sea could be expected to impel her into an all-out attack 'on a tremendous scale' in the early

1. The reference in G. M. Young, *Stanley Baldwin* (1952), 191, indicates Fisher's role in this.

2. Young (ibid., 193–4) prints a letter from an anonymous civil servant (in fact, from Fisher), complaining about attempts in Cabinet to water down the terms of the White Paper so as to make it palatable to Germany. See also ibid., 199.

3. In June Ramsay MacDonald became Lord President of the Council; Sir Samuel Hoare replaced Simon as Foreign Secretary; Lord Halifax became Minister for War; and Sir Philip Cunliffe-Lister (later Lord Swinton) became Air Minister. In November 1935 Duff Cooper succeeded Halifax as Minister for War. See J. D. Scott and R. Hughes, *The Administration of British War Production* (1955), 61; W. K. Hancock and M. M. Gowing, *Britain's War Economy* (1949), 63–5; Cmd. 5107 (1936), *Statement Relating to Defence*; 309, *Hansard's Parl. Deb., H. of C.*, col.654.

days of the war.[1] The fear was expressed that such an attack might well be so continuous and concentrated, and on such a scale, that a few weeks of it might so undermine civilian morale as to render it difficult for the Government to continue the war.[2] In 1914, by contrast, the worst that could have been expected was a sea-borne raid which the Navy could quickly contain and control. In 1935 Britain's defence planners had to add to this the risk of air attack of great and possibly unknown strength.

At the same time the DRC stepped up the size of its projected British Expeditionary Force to five regular divisions and twelve territorial divisions. At sea, it recommended a two-power standard adequate to put in Far Eastern waters a fleet large enough to act as a deterrent to the Japanese as well as to maintain in home waters a force able to meet the requirements against Germany. This again was to prove too much for Fisher, but in the meantime there were three serious problems to be settled first. One was Abyssinia, on which Fisher and Vansittart were again of one mind. In July 1935 Fisher was to support those who argued for a compromise with Italy.[3] He does not seem, however, to have been involved in the disaster of the Hoare–Laval proposals which not only caused Hoare's resignation, but gravely weakened Vansittart's effectiveness as an influence on policy. He was deeply involved in the second of his problems, the London Naval Conference, where he was a member of the British delegation, ironing out differences between the Navy's approach and that of the Foreign Office naval expert, Sir Robert Craigie,[4] and doing his bit behind the scenes in the vain effort to prevent the Japanese from walking out of the conference.

More important than this, however, was the question of the organization of defence. Parliamentary pressure had been building up for some time for the setting-up of a full-dress Ministry of Supply which should organize and co-ordinate all Britain's efforts to rearm. This was something to which both Lord Hankey, as joint Secretary to the Cabinet and the CID, and Sir Warren Fisher may be presumed to have been bitterly opposed. Hankey opposed it because no Ministry of Supply could be properly in action unless decisions had already been reached on the kind of war for which to prepare. Otherwise the

1. Hancock and Gowing, op. cit., 65.
2. M. M. Postan, *British War Production* (1952), 22–5.
3. See his own remarks of 1948 cited above.
4. Admiral Sir William James, *The Sky was always Blue* (1951), 185.

Minister would find himself, as Fisher was doing, dictating British strategy as the only means of preparing a logically constructed rearmament effort. All Fisher's actions suggest that he was determined to retain this task in Treasury hands in view of what he felt to be the total lack of top-rank ability at the top of the three Services. It seems probable that the idea of a Ministerial appointment to chair the sub-committee of the Principal Supply Officers, to which should be added the Chiefs of Staff and a Treasury representative,[1] was either Fisher's or Hankey's. In any case, one was necessary to bring the detailed recommendations of the Chiefs of Staff, as contained in the second and third DRC reports, into some kind of order.

The obvious choice for this post was not Churchill, as the outsiders argued, but Neville Chamberlain. He had been the main force in the Ministerial Sub-Committee on Defence Policy, and had outlined the modifications in the DRC report which he (and Fisher) desired.

I am pretty satisfied [he wrote in his diary on 9 February 1936] that, if only we can keep out of war for a few years, we shall have an air-force of such striking power that no one will care to run risks with it. I cannot believe that the next war, if it ever comes, will be like the last one, and I believe that our resources will be more profitably employed in the air and on the sea, than in building up great armies.[2]

The post was offered first to his brother, Austen Chamberlain; then both Swinton and Hoare were discussed, the one to be ruled out because he was in the Lords, the other by the jealous objections of his successor in the Foreign Office. Eventually the choice fell on the unhappy Sir Thomas Inskip.[3] His appointment was accompanied by the issue of a Treasury Minute,[4] drafted by Fisher and attached to the Defence White Paper,[5] ensuring the continued central control of the Treasury over matters of defence and setting up a Treasury Inter-Services Committee bringing together representatives of the three Services under the chairmanship of a Treasury official as part of the necessary machinery.

The new minister's first job was to preside over a Committee of Enquiry on the future of the capital ship.[6] His second was to sort out

1. Lord Ismay, *Memoirs* (1960), 76.
2. Feiling, op. cit., 313–14.
3. Macleod, op. cit., 192–3.
4. Cmd. 5114 (1936).
5. Cmd. 5109 (1936).
6. Cmd. 5301 (1936).

a major dispute between the Chiefs of Staff and the Cabinet and Treasury. In April 1936 the Cabinet had set up a Ministerial Defence Plans (Policy) Committee to examine the defence plans of the Chief of Staff in the light of government policy. The DRC report and the Chiefs of Staff had picked the latter half of 1939 as the most probable date for the outbreak of a war with Germany (a remarkable piece of prophecy). On this basis the Chiefs of Staff had produced a scheme for a balanced development of all three arms, to cost £1,760 million to £1,811 million over five years. This was added to in the summer of 1936, when depressed by the failure of all efforts to get Japan into the 1936 London Naval Treaty network, the Admiralty felt bound to prepare an augmented two-power standard to enable Britain to place a fleet of eight capital ships at Singapore and to maintain in home waters a fleet capable of meeting the requirements of a simultaneous naval war with Germany. By 1937 they wanted an additional six capital ships, ten aircraft carriers, fifty cruisers and proportionate increases in smaller craft.[1] The new committee's reaction had been to propose a cut in the Army and a build-up of the air defence of Great Britain, especially in its anti-aircraft component. The matter was referred to Sir Thomas Inskip. He ruled that the British defence effort should involve four objectives, the protection of the United Kingdom, the provision and maintenance of forces to defend Britain's territory overseas, the preservation of merchant shipping for our imports and co-operation in the defence of Allied territory. In view of Britain's financial difficulties and the need to maintain financial stability, this fourth objective would have to be dropped.[2] With this the idea of an expeditionary force was virtually dead.[3]

The thinking behind this decision is well illustrated by a note of 25 October 1936 in Neville Chamberlain's diaries:

... we have not the man-power to produce the necessary munitions for ourselves, and perhaps, if the USA stood out, for our Allies, to man the enlarged Navy, the new Air Force and a million man army. .... We should aim at an Army of four divisions plus one mobile division ... for overseas work. Territorials should be kept to AA work.[4]

Fisher shared these views, if indeed he did not originate them. Indeed, during most of the period of Inskip's activity as Minister for

1. Kemp, op. cit., 22–41; Postan, op. cit., 25.
2. Kemp, op. cit., 23–4.
3. Hancock and Gowing, op. cit., 66–7.
4. Cited in Feiling, op. cit., 314–15.

the Co-ordination of Defence, he seems to have acted virtually as Inskip's permanent under-secretary. In his view the maximum war standard of the Army should have been about 600,000 men. He had never encouraged an expansion of the Army's regular and territorial elements on a scale equivalent to that of a continental conscript army or of that developed by Britain in the First World War. He did not believe the British people would ever consent to be conscripted again for a European war and he did not believe this would be the best use for Britain's man-power. Rather she should devote her man-power and industrial capacity to the new and probably decisive air arm, which would need proportionately much less in terms of arms and munitions than an army. The ban put by the United States Senate on the export of munitions in her neutrality legislation, and the prohibition against states in default on their First World War debts being allowed to raise credit in the United States, only reinforced him in his views.

In the spring of 1937 Chamberlain presented his last budget before taking over the Premiership from Stanley Baldwin. Its main feature was concealed from all but expert view; the Treasury had decided, again in the cause of financial stability, that no more than £1,500 million could be spent on defence over the next five years. The job of rationing the Services was again handed to the unfortunate Minister for Co-ordination of Defence. In June the three Services were told to review their armament proposals.[1] Once again the first casualty was the Army. The Territorial divisions were only to be given training equipment, except for the two AA divisions.[2] This time the fight was a longer one where the other services were concerned. The Admiralty, spurred on by the Japanese attack on China in July 1937, returned to their demand for a genuine two-power standard.[3] The Air Ministry having produced scheme after scheme of bomber production warned that 'parity' with Germany was virtually unobtainable.[4] The Foreign Secretary called for 'some more deliberate national effort'.[5] And the Secretary of State for Air pleaded for abandonment of the doctrine that the rearmament programme should not interfere with the normal processes of trade.[6]

1. Sir John Slessor, *The Central Blue* (1956), 157.
2. R. J. Minney (ed.), *The Private Papers of Hore-Belisha* (1960), 35.
3. Postan, op. cit., 26.
4. Slessor, op. cit., 158–9.
5. Hancock and Gowing, op. cit., 70.
6. Ibid., 70.

In December 1937, Inskip reported to the Cabinet on the allocation of finance. The Admiralty should not incur expenditure beyond the DRC standard. The principal task of the Army should be its imperial defence commitments. The RAF should concentrate on increases in its metropolitan forces, i.e. on Fighter Command, and slow up its rate of bomber expansion.[1] Again Inskip was following the course Fisher laid down. In Fisher's view, the total nature of modern war made success in it dependent not only upon the effective use of national resources but on their care and maintenance. The Treasury, in this view, became a kind of additional Service department. Finance was the fourth arm of war. Without economic stability, which meant the continued capacity to obtain supplies from abroad and the best use of Britain's man-power and industrial resources, Britain's defeat was inevitable.

He was at this time engaged in backing Hore-Belisha's desperate attempts to clean up the War Office, and produce a staff capable of pronouncing on strategic problems, and understanding and executing the Government's policy. The development of AA Command and the Government's decision to devote a substantial proportion of the Army's limited budget to it, as part of the Army's contribution to the air defence of Great Britain, were running into increasing opposition from the CIGS and the Army Council. In December 1937 matters came to a final head. Backed by advice from Lord Weir, the former Secretary of State for Air, a well-known engineer and government adviser on air rearmament, Hore-Belisha sacked the entire Army Council. As his new CIGS he chose Lord Gort, passing over both Ironside and Dill, with Sir Ronald Adams as deputy CIGS. As Master-General of Ordnance to advance the AA defence of Britain he brought in Vice-Admiral Sir Harold Brown, to the Army's eternal shame.[2]

With this Hore-Belisha went on, in February 1938, to outline the role of the British Army in war:

the strategical concept – Defence against air attack at home. Coastal defence and the whole question of our Commitments abroad – in Gibraltar, Malta, Egypt and Palestine, reinforcements for Singapore, a garrison for the Anglo-Iranian oil-fields – all are of immense importance. Then there are Kenya and Ceylon, Hong Kong and Malaya, the Sudan. . . .

1. Scott and Hughes, op. cit., 67; Postan, op. cit., 26; Slessor, op. cit., 160.
2. Minney, op. cit., 65–75.

but no word of a continental expeditionary force. Fisher's ideas are reproduced, together with those of Inskip.

In March 1938, however, Hitler marched into Austria. All that summer the Czech crisis rumbled and thundered. The Cabinet threw caution to the winds and reconsidered the clause forbidding interference with normal trade.[1] Reluctantly, two divisions were offered the French in the event of war with Germany,[2] but fortified by the insistence of the Chiefs of Staff that war could not be risked that year,[3] the Cabinet bent its efforts to finding a way out of the Czech–German imbroglio. Fisher's main worry since 1934 was beginning to come true. Long a friend and follower of Lord Trenchard, he had absorbed his friend's belief in the war-winning power of air attack, without accepting its corollary that only a bomber force capable of deterring political enemies could protect Britain against this. For this reason, he had always pressed the Air Staff to expand Fighter Command, and he had urged the Army to concentrate on the air defence of Great Britain. Now intelligence statistics of German aircraft production showed them to be far beyond Britain's output. For the first time in centuries Britain lay open to the attack of a foreign power, open, defenceless and at her mercy.

Thus it was that in the days immediately following Munich he apparently did not share in the general euphoria, but did his utmost to urge increased efforts in the British rearmament programme. He laid especial emphasis on the need to expand in the air, to build an air force substantial enough to give Germany pause. The 1939 Defence White Paper,[4] with its lengthy account of the expansion of Britain's defences against air attack, bears the unmistakable stamp of his ideas. And in 1939 the production of British aircraft began for the first time to come within an appreciable distance of that of Germany.

Shortly, thereafter, he retired. The strategy he advocated had ceased to be politically feasible. In April 1939 conscription was reintroduced, and Britain again committed to a continental war in Flanders on the French left wing, from which only the miracle of

1. Kemp, op. cit., 25; Hancock and Gowing, op. cit., 70.
2. The effect of the 1938 budget had been to eliminate all provision for the Territorial Army. Nominally five Regular Divisions should be available for overseas service, but in fact only two were available in 1938. Hancock and Gowing, op. cit., 67; Minney, op. cit., 138.
3. Kemp, op. cit., 26.
4. Cmd. 5944 (1939). Statement relating to Defence.

Dunkirk could rescue her. In the Battle of Britain the pilots of Fighter Command lived much more up to his estimate of their capabilities than those of the Air Staff, whose strategic bombing offensive was shown for some time to lack the range or the technical accuracy to make it effective. Nevertheless, up to 1938 British strategic planning had effectively followed the paths he suggested for it. It had failed to attain the necessary state of readiness in time to forestall Hitler in 1938, and Britain had found herself, in his view, faced with the situation he had always dreaded.

One is left to speculate at the reasons for his intervention in May 1937 with J. P. L. Thomas on the latter's appointment as Eden's Parliamentary Private Secretary.[1] Thomas records Fisher and Wilson expressing their dissatisfaction with Vansittart and his obstruction of all efforts 'to make friendly contact with the dictator states'. The suggestion is clearly implied that Fisher and Wilson favoured such 'friendly contacts'. Wilson may well have done, but in the strategic views known to be held by Fisher there is no evidence of anything but fear of, and hatred for, Germany. It may be that Fisher shared, or even originated, Chamberlain's desire to avoid difficult situations until Britain was strong again. As to approaches to Italy or Japan, Fisher and Vansittart were agreed as to the desirability of this in 1934 and 1935; and there is no evidence that Vansittart changed his mind as to the primary importance of avoiding trouble with those two countries after 1935, and Fisher certainly did not. The suggestion that Fisher expected anything to come from a policy of appeasing Germany is clearly not borne out by what is known of his views on what strategy Britain should pursue.

There the matter must perhaps rest till fifty years have unwound their weary way and the archives are opened. What is clear is that, apart from Vansittart and Hankey, Fisher was and felt himself to be a titan among minnows. Despising the Chiefs of Staff, he chose to use his central position and his access to the heir apparent in the Conservative party, Neville Chamberlain, to impose upon them a unity of strategy which they were unable or unwilling or had not the capability to achieve. He was aided by the palpable failure of the Services to evolve a genuine inter-Service point of view. His record in the 1930s is, perhaps, the outstanding illustration of how influence can be used within the foreign-policy-making élite to lead in the

1. Earl of Avon, *Facing the Dictators*, 447.

formulation of policy, where those formally responsible are, as so often, divided and ineffective. The moral must be for the Service Chiefs that if they cannot agree on a policy and educate their civilian masters into understanding the reasons behind it, they risk having imposed on them a united policy which is offensive to all of them and justified by arguments of a civilian rather than a strategic nature.

Influence from Without: German Influence on British Opinion, 1933–38, and the Attempts to Counter it

THE two previous essays in this section have examined cases in which influence was exerted on opinion in the British foreign-policy-making élite from within that élite itself. In Essay 4 the debate over British policy towards Japan in 1934 was used to illustrate how a division of opinion within the élite could be resolved by a judicious use of publicity, even though the initiative in that use came from someone on the fringes of the élite, from Lord Lothian. The second case, that of the debate over British defence policy in the years 1933–38, provided an example of an opposite sort, that of the degree of influence which a single individual in a key position can exert without ever coming into the open at all. In both cases, of course, the opportunity for the use of influence came because the majority of those upon whom influence was exerted and who were responsible for taking the ultimate decisions, were undecided or indeterminate in their own views. Indeed, as is so often the case, they had to be convinced not only of the need to take one course rather than another, but also of the need to take any course at all.

The case to be considered in this essay differs from its two predecessors in two respects. Firstly, it is one in which the initiative came from outside the élite, indeed from outside Britain as such. Secondly, it illustrates the importance of long-term campaigns to influence the language, attitudes and concepts within which debate on the relevant issues takes place.[1] The most important and significant work in predisposing opinion within the British foreign-policy-making élite towards accepting the foreign policy of Nazi Germany had, in fact, been done before Hitler came to power and by agencies which were far from Nazi in character.

1. For another illustration of this see D. C. Watt, 'Some reflections on Austrian Foreign Policy, 1945–55', *International Relations*, I, no.6 (October 1956).

This may at first seem rather to overstate the case. But the statement rests on the assumption that for the bulk of the élite, the issues raised by Nazi Germany turned not upon its internal policy, its totalitarianism, its suppression of political parties, its anti-Semitism, its enlistment of terror as a weapon of government or its embodiment of the *Führerprinzip*. The issue was simply one of whether Nazi German foreign policy was a threat to peace or whether it could be contained and opposed without war. The reasons for this narrowing of the issues and this failure to see that those who made terror a weapon of domestic state policy would use it to the same effect in their external relations,[1] the failure to see that while a small-scale totalitarian state can be contained, Nazi Germany could not, the failure to heed the warnings of those who saw more clearly,[2] are reasons inherent in the intellectual weakness of British liberalism as expressed in its educational system and in its preference for the study of political theorists rather than ideological systems, and have nothing to do with this essay as such.

It is now apparent that within the Foreign Office, the three armed Services, the Civil Service and the Cabinet there were few illusions at any time about the nature of the threat to peace constituted by Hitler. From the reports of the Defence Requirements Sub-Committee of 1933–34, from the exhortations of Lord Vansittart and from the increasing knowledge we now have of Chamberlain's private views, it is clear that the idea that there was any blindness to the peril or desire to divert it on to other targets, against the Soviet Union for example, a view still maintained in some circles, is quite mistaken. It is rather that those responsible for the ultimate decisions could not be convinced of the unavoidable nature of the coming conflict with Nazi Germany. They could see a threat, but not a certainty.[3] They could see a peril of war, but not the impossibility of evading it. It was on this point that the perpetual flow of periphrastic memoranda with which Sir Robert Vansittart bombarded them failed to carry ultimate conviction. And it was here that, troubled, perplexed and

---

1. See the brilliant study by Dr Brigitte Granzow, *A Mirror of Nazism* (1964).

2. As, for example, the reports of Sir Horace Rumbold, the British Ambassador in Berlin, or the warnings of Sir Robert Vansittart.

3. It is worth pointing out that their sternest critics at that time and later also thought war could have been avoided – but by taking a sterner, more determined line at the outset.

above all undecided, they listened to the voices of those within their own circles who maintained an alternative view, that a policy of judicious and controlled concessions, designed to remove the grievances and injustices on which Nazi chauvinism throve, would draw its teeth and make it tolerable as a neighbour on the European continent.

There is by now a considerable body of literature on the group of men associated with the policy of appeasement.[1] Not all of it is very scholarly, and the bulk of it is highly polemical. Apart from members of the Cabinet, of the administration and the Foreign Service, attention has been most focused on the activities of the quality press, particularly *The Times*[2] and *The Observer* and their editors, Dawson and J. L. Garvin, on the influential group connected with the *Round Table*, most notably Lord Lothian,[3] and on a number of Conservative back-benchers, MPs such as Colonel Moore, Victor Cazalet, Lord Londonderry and others.[4] Others have seized on the so-called 'Cliveden Set', centred on the family home of Lord and Lady Astor at Cliveden Manor, which was alleged to have great influence on Chamberlain.[5]

What is significant about these latter groups is that they had their own sources of information on Nazi Germany, and that both they and much of their audience were predisposed to listen to German justifications of Nazi foreign policy. Some were certainly also predisposed to welcome or support aspects of Nazi internal policy. But the point of this essay and the point at which they won and found sympathetic hearing from those in positions of power and responsibility was, as remarked above, in their defence of Nazi foreign policy, especially while that policy could be identified with one aiming at the revision of the 1919 Peace Settlement. In approaching them and attempting to influence opinion in Britain in favour of Nazi

1. See, for example, Sir Lewis Namier, *Diplomatic Prelude* (1948); Martin Gilbert and R. W. Gott, *The Appeasers* (1963).
2. *The History of 'The Times'*, vol.IV, part II; Sir Evelyn Wrench, *Geoffrey Dawson and our Times* (1955).
3. J. R. M. Butler, *Lord Lothian (Philip Kerr), 1882–1940* (1960).
4. See Simon Haxell, *Tory MP* (1939); Cato (Pseud.), *Guilty Men* (1940).
5. See especially Claud Cockburn, *In Time of Trouble* (1956); Maurice Collis, *Nancy Astor,* (1960); Michael Astor, *Tribal Feeling* (1963); Ivan Maiski, *Who helped Hitler?* (1964); Communist Party of Great Britain, *Hitler's Friends in Britain; Sidelights on the Cliveden Set* (March 1938).

Germany's foreign policy, their German contacts were capitalizing on British revulsion against and criticism of the Treaty of Versailles.[1]

This revulsion arose long before German attempts to exploit it. It found its first voice in the publication of Lord Keynes' *Economic Consequences of the Peace*, a brilliantly destructive tract exemplifying at once both the worst and the best qualities of the British liberal intellectual tradition. The Germans began their attempts to develop and capitalize on this feeling in Britain and in the world with the setting-up within the German Foreign Ministry in the 1920s of a *Kriegsschuldreferat*, a 'War Guilt Section', devoted to the dissemination of high-level propaganda and the encouragement of historical research into the origins of the war of 1914,[2] and the justice or otherwise of that clause in the Treaty of Versailles which imputed to them the responsibility for beginning it. An unofficial agency, however, is always much more successful in this kind of work than an official one, and German official circles therefore smiled favourably upon the setting up in February 1922 of the independent *Wirtschaft-politische Gesellschaft* under the direction of a certain Dr Margarete Gärtner.[3]

Dr Gärtner was the daughter of a Silesian electrical engineer, and educated at a commercial school. She had first been involved in German propaganda activities before the First World War as statistical assistant and secretary to Professor Dr Ernst von Halle of Berlin, who was employed by the German Admiralty to prepare a memorandum on German maritime interests, to make the Naval Budget more plausible to the Reichstag. Thereafter she had worked as a temporary civil servant for a time, and then as a private secretary to the State Secretary in the German Colonial Office. During the 1914–18 war she was a member of the official German foreign propaganda agency, the so-called *Zentralstelle für Auslandsdienst*, first set up by the German Admiralty, and then transferred to the German Foreign Ministry.

After the German débâcle in 1918, this organization was disbanded, and Dr Gärtner turned to the countering of French-inspired separa-

1. See R. B. MacCallum, *Public Opinion and the Last Peace* (1943).
2. Combined with a certain judicious suppression of evidence which might have tended to throw dust on their propaganda.
3. What follows is based on her autobiography, *Botschafterin des Guten Willens* (Bonn, 1955).

tist propaganda in the Rhineland, in another organization, the *Reichszentrale für Heimatsdienst*, which came directly under the Reichs Chancellor. Through this there developed the idea of using the women's organizations in the Rhineland as an instrument of propaganda abroad against the French use of African troops in the occupation of their zone in the Rhineland. A new organization, the *Rheinische Frauenliga*, was set up, on which sat representatives of all the existing women's organizations. After taking over the direction of this organization, Dr Gärtner was used by Krupps, the German armaments and steel firm, to accompany English journalists sent over on the initiative of Vickers-Armstrong, their British counterpart, to cover conditions in the occupied Rhineland. Krupps had made the use of Vickers-Armstrong's influence to secure a more favourable reportage of conditions in Germany in the British press a condition of the reopening of the prewar relations between themselves and Vickers-Armstrong, proposed by the British firm.

Her experience gave Dr Gärtner the idea of setting up a permanent body designed, by the organization of study tours, the aiding of research and the provision of introductions, etc., to spread knowledge of and understanding for the German case against the territorial provisions of Versailles. With tacit official approval she therefore founded the *Wirtschaftspolitische Gesellschaft* independent of the German Government, with a standing council of reputable names, and financed by grants from Rhineland heavy industry. From 1922 onwards, she was its director and guiding spirit. By 1933 she had succeeded in building links with both political parties in Britain, with the British press and with most of the other organizations in Britain active in this hey-day of the promotion of international good-will and understanding. She had built up excellent contacts with the Empire Parliamentary Association, with the International League of Women, with the now defunct All-People's Association, an organization founded by Sir Evelyn Wrench, then editor of the *Spectator*, in an attempt to repeat on a world basis the success of the English-Speaking Union he had founded during 1914–18. On the left of British politics she worked closely with the Union of Democratic Control, one of whose guiding spirits, E. D. Morel, she had met in 1921 and whom she had furnished with much of the material for his campaign against French occupation policy in the Rhineland. She had been instrumental in providing material for a number of British authors working on the aftermath of Versailles, and had built up connections with British publishers.[1] From 1928 her organization maintained a press representative in London, and in 1929 she was involved in the foundation of the Anglo-German Association in London under the joint presidency of Lord Reading, a former Lord Chancellor, and Wilhelm von Cuno, a former Reichs Chancellor.

The skill with which Dr Gärtner and others penetrated the outer non-official circles of the foreign-policy-making élite in Britain seems to have been partly a product of native snobbism, partly of instinct, partly of the deep interest taken in that period by German Conservative circles in what they took to be the élitist nature of British society.[2] By 1933 she had laid a groundwork of British contacts and understanding for the German revisionist case against Versailles which only a few public figures would have challenged.

This was just as well. The first impact of the Nazi régime on British opinion was disastrous. In the summer of 1933 the German Foreign Minister, Baron von Neurath, himself a former German Ambassador in London, visited London for the World Economic Conference. His experience of British opinion led him to write to Hitler and President von Hindenburg that Anglo-German relations had hit an all-time low.[3] He was soon to be proven wrong. The lowest point was reached a year later after Germany had left the League of Nations and the Disarmament Conference; been irretrievably associated with the assassination of the Austrian Chancellor, Dollfuss, in the course of an attempted *coup d'état* in Vienna; defaulted in transfer payments on all her international financial obligations, both private and public; and seen the 'purge' of the left wing of the Nazi party and a number of prominent non-Nazis including the former Chancellor, General von Schleicher, by Hitler and the SS in circumstances bloody, indefensibly non-legal, sexually revolting and smacking generally of Chicago-style gang-warfare.

Six months later all this seemed forgotten. A rather shaky Anglo-German entente had been established, which was to last on an in-

1. She was instrumental in securing publication in England of the German Foreign Minister Gustav von Stresemann's speeches.
2. It was in this period that Dr Kurt Hahn, a former colleague of hers in the *Zentralstelle für Auslandsdienst*, tried to introduce the British public school system into Germany, with the foundation of his famous school at Salem. He moved, in the Nazi period, to Britain and founded Gordonstoun; the Duke of Edinburgh was among his pupils.
3. International Military Tribunal, Nuremberg, *Trial of the Major War Criminals*, XL, 465–71, documents Neurath–11 and –12.

creasingly tenuous basis until March 1939. Dr Gärtner was associated with the re-establishment of this entente. It took its origin, however, in a series of unofficial initiatives from the British side. It was aided by Hitler's concurrent decision to court British favour by playing the trump of offering to Britain an agreement on naval disarmament.[1]

These initiatives came largely from a new group of men who had hitherto played little or no part in the active fostering of Anglo-German relations, although some of its members had been associated with Germany before. Their interest was governed less by the interest in Germany as such which had proved the strongest weapon at the disposal of Dr Gärtner and her colleagues, than by a basic humanitarian, if not Christian, interest in the avoidance of war. There were, it is true, a considerable number of individuals interested in discovering the nature of the new régime in Germany, ranging from journalists and commentators to would-be imitators of Hitler such as Lieutenant-Colonel Graham Seton Hutchinson, or Lord Lymington with his curiously named 'British Mistery'. Lord Rothermere, then in full support of Sir Oswald Mosley, exchanged letters with Hitler in December 1933,[2] having used the former German Crown Prince and the Hungarian-born Countess Stephanie von Hohenlohe[3] as his intermediaries. But they were comparatively unimportant by comparison with the would-be defenders of peace.

The German Embassy, of course, continued the work, obligatory on any embassy but peculiarly difficult in the circumstances of 1933, of providing introductions in Germany for important unofficial visitors, and of doing its best to secure a favourable press coverage of German affairs.[4] But it was getting increasingly difficult for the Embassy to secure the kind of British initiative for a détente that Germany desired, as their official channels to the Foreign Office came

1. See D. C. Watt, 'The Anglo-German Naval Agreement of 1935: an interim judgement', *Journal of Modern History*, xxvii, no.2 (June 1956).

2. Copies of these with an explanatory memorandum were preserved in the *German Reich Chancellery Archives* now on photostat in the Foreign Office Library (C 86/f 001469, 472, 001293/1–296, 001292–3).

3. On Stephanie von Hohenlohe see the guarded reference in Sir Lewis Namier, *Europe in Decay* (1950), 217 and n.

4. A letter from a member of the German Embassy staff to the head of the Foreign Ministry press department, of 15 December 1933, reports the use of Sir Roderick Jones, head of Reuters, as an intermediary to secure a moderation of the *Manchester Guardian*'s 'anti-German tone', *German Foreign Ministry Archives* (7609/E544907–15).

increasingly to be used for protests against the arrest of British subjects in Germany, or against attacks on Germany in the British press and public opinion.

In this situation the way was open for development of a new kind of intermediary not so much of German as of British origin. A small group of men, some Quakers, some pacifists, some Christian Scientists[1] and some plain opportunists, came forward with the aim of repairing the breach and attempting to prevent what they feared was a steady drift of Anglo-German relations towards war. The most prominent were two Quakers, Corder Catchpool[2] and Charles Roden Buxton, MP;[3] a Christian Pacifist, Clifford Allen, Lord Allen of Hurtwood;[4] a Christian Scientist, Philip Kerr, Lord Lothian, and two others, Philip Conwell-Evans and Charles Spencer. These men made it their business to ease the path of German policy and to avoid a direct conflict between British and German policy until it was absolutely unavoidable. With the best intentions in the world they thus became the unpaid servants of German and Nazi foreign policy.

The first and most significant move came in the last days of 1933,[5] when a number of men partly of Quaker origin or connections, partly Labour party, and partly connected with the Royal Institute of International Affairs, constituted themselves into a group with the aim of working systematically for a better understanding of Nazi Germany in Britain, in the words of their German intermediary,

by a comprehensive instruction of British public opinion and also by the exercise of influence on the British government in thorough-going accordance with British political practice.[6]

1. For what follows see D. C. Watt, 'Christian Essay in Appeasement', *Wiener Library Bulletin*, XIV, no.2 (1960).

2. W. Corder Catchpool (1883–1952). Worked among German P.W.s in Britain 1914–18, then in Germany on relief work 1918–19. Head of Quaker office in Berlin 1920–36. See W. R. Hughes, *Indomitable Friend* (1956).

3. Charles Roden Buxton, Parliamentary adviser to Labour party on Foreign Affairs until 1939; Victoria de Bunsen, *Charles Roden Buxton, A Memoir* (1948). His brother was Lord Noel-Buxton, Labour peer; Mose Anderson, *Noel-Buxton, A Life* (1952).

4. Arthur Marwick, *Clifford Allen, The Open Conspirator* (Edinburgh, 1964).

5. Marwick, *Clifford Allen*, 159, post-dates the formation of this group by a year.

6. *German Reichs Chancellery Records*, Dr Fritz Berber to Dr Lammers, 12 January 1934, (1506/371242–6).

The intermediary they chose was a certain Dr Fritz Berber, then connected with the German equivalent of the Royal Institute, who was to develop in his later years into one of Ribbentrop's most effective propagandists. In the course of a visit Berber made to London at their request in the first week of January 1934, they spent a whole day explaining their aims to him and discerning the best methods of achieving them. They defined their aims, according to Dr Berber (and there could not be a better definition of the policy which has come to be called 'appeasement') as to secure a clear and decisive British policy,

in the direction of securing German equality of rights, the formal and material abandonment of the Treaty of Versailles and the erection of a new system of states in Europe.

This group called itself the 'Anglo-German Group'. Its chairman was Lord Allen of Hurtwood himself – it included Lord Noel-Buxton, Charles Roden Buxton, St John Catchpool (also a Quaker), W. Arnold Forster of the League of Nations Union, Carl Heath, another prominent Quaker,[1] Sir Walter Layton, proprietor at this date of both the *News Chronicle* and *The Economist*,[2] Vernon Bartlett, foreign editor of the *News Chronicle*[3] (which was, incidentally, connected with the well-known Quaker chocolate manufacturing family of Cadbury), General Sir Neill Malcolm and John Wheeler-Bennett of the Royal Institute of International Affairs,[4] G. P. Gooch, the historian, former Liberal MP and co-editor of the official British publication, *British Documents on the Origins of the War*,[5] Philip Noel-Baker, Vivyan Adams, MP, and Robert Law, MP, H. G. Alexander and R. Wilson Harris,[6] editor of the *Spectator*.[7]

1. F. J. Tritten, *Carl Heath, Apostle of Peace* (1951).
2. This was a little more than piquant to German ears as Sir Walter Layton had been refused access to all German ministries in September 1933 as a result of an article in *The Economist* on the Hitler Terror. *German Foreign Ministry Archives*, letter of 11 September 1933, Dieckhoff, German Foreign Ministry, to Reichs Chancellery (5740/H031087–8).
3. Vernon Bartlett was the author of an early sympathetic study of the Nazi system, *Nazi Germany Explained* (1933), and had previously been Secretary of the League of Nations Union.
4. John Wheeler-Bennett and many others in this group soon switched to steady opposition to any idea of appeasement.
5. G. P. Gooch, *Under Six Reigns* (1958).
6. R. Wilson Harris, *Life so Far* (1954).
7. On the whole group see Marwick, op. cit., 159–60.

There are two other interesting points about this group which characterize its actions and place in contemporary British intellectual life. Many of its members stem from the National Peace Council, which although founded in 1905, and moribund for much of the 1920s, had undergone a sudden renaissance since its wildly successful conference at Oxford in July 1933. Its membership included not only pacifists by conviction but a whole range of men for whom the problem of war was limited entirely to that of the 1914–18 war, and who were convinced that the international political system which preceded that war was 'utterly wrongheaded' and the war itself a desperate mistake.[1]

Members of this group had merged together with others from the League of Nations Union and the liberal centre, seduced by the two fashionable doctrines of the 1930s, scientific planning and anti-politics, into the group known first as 'Liberty and Democratic leadership', which published its first manifesto in February 1934, and then as the 'Next Five Years Group', inaugurated in February 1935 in a meeting at the Oxford Union. Their manifesto, published as *The Next Five Years* (1935), included a section dealing with international relations, which makes it fairly clear that Allen's approach to Hitler and the Anglo-German group must be seen as a manifestation on the international scene of the basic philosophy of the 'Next Five Years Group'.[2]

Nothing came of this group's activity for a little, and the events of the summer of 1934[3] put all ideas of developing their plans out of court for a while. Lord Allen, however, returned to the idea in November 1934, and an invitation was issued to him at the instance of the German Foreign Ministry by Dr Berber early in December 1934. It was arranged that he should meet Hitler, especially as the German Embassy in London believed, on what evidence is not clear, that his close friendship with Prime Minister Ramsay MacDonald meant that he was travelling to Germany with some kind of unofficial

1. This paragraph and that following are based on Arthur Marwick, 'Middle Opinion in the Thirties, Planning, Progress and Political Agreement', *English Historical Review*, LXXIX, no.311 (April 1964).
2. See the remarks on the need for equality of treatment of Germany within a collective security system (*The Next Five Years*, 253–5).
3. Dr Gärtner gives a graphic description of the effects of the Roehm purge and Dollfuss' murder on her work (Gärtner, op. cit., 285–93).

brief from the Prime Minister and would certainly report to him in detail on the visit.[1]

It was at this point that Lord Lothian entered the scene, apparently at the instigation of Conwell-Evans. Despite the fact that he held the position of Secretary to the Rhodes Trust he does not seem to have shown much interest in Germany before Hitler's advent to power or to have visited the country. It was only when Germany became a 'European problem' that his interest in Germany was aroused. His proposal to visit Germany was not notified to the Germans until 17 January 1935, and, despite his connections with the Royal Institute of International Affairs, members of whose Council and research staff were involved at least in the early stages of Lord Allen's visit, his visit seems to have been arranged without any connection with that of Lord Allen. The telegram from the German Embassy in London heralding his visit mentioned that Sir John Simon had asked him to report on its outcome.[2] Lothian, like Allen, was given the full treatment, interviews with Hitler, Blomberg, Ribbentrop, and the full assurance of Hitler's goodwill towards Britain, will for peace, desire to settle all outstanding issues between the two countries, including the conclusion of a Naval Agreement designed to recognize Britain's supremacy at sea.[3] It was in the course of a conversation with General von Blomberg, the German Defence Minister, Ribbentrop and Albrecht Haushofer, son of the famous German geo-politician, that Lord Lothian enquired 'Would you think a visit by Simon to Berlin useful?'[4]

On his return to London he reported to Simon that he believed Germany was prepared to pay the price of an assured peace, by, for example, the renunciation of Alsace-Lorraine and the Treaty with Poland. Hitler would agree not to interfere with Austria by force if

1. Marwick's biography sheds no light on this point, although it does cite Allen's memorandum on his visit, setting down his personal impressions of Hitler as a 'revolutionary' who 'looks upon politics as a kind of religion' and 'believes in it with an honesty and determination which it is folly either to disguise or caricature' (Marwick, op. cit., 160–2).

2. *German Foreign Ministry Archives*, German Embassy telegram, 17 January 1935 (9102/E640390–1).

3. For Lord Allen's interview see *Documents on German Foreign Policy, 1918–45*, Series C, vol.III, document no.463. For Lord Lothian's record of his interview see Butler, *Lord Lothian*, App.III.

4. *German Foreign Ministry Archives*, unsigned German memorandum of 30 January 1935 (7467/H181848–51/2).

others did not. It was contrary to Nazi principles to incorporate non-Germans (!). There was, in his view, a chance of a political settlement which would keep the peace for ten years, provided there was a frank discussion between Great Britain and Germany. He therefore recommended that Simon visit Germany and talk to Hitler himself.[1] The visit of Sir John Simon and Anthony Eden to Germany in March and the signature of the Anglo-German Naval Agreement followed, despite Germany's unilateral denunciation of the restrictions on her armaments imposed by the Versailles Treaty, within the next six months.

This was followed by the organization of a series of visits from all kinds of prominent personalities to Germany. In the summer of 1935 an official visit by a delegation of the British Legion, the British ex-servicemen's organization,[2] was arranged by Corder Catchpool, and given a send-off by the Prince of Wales, who had already on 12 April expressed himself to the German Ambassador, according to the latter's report, as convinced that war was no longer a means of solving political questions and as critical of the British Foreign Office's 'one-sided attitude' towards Germany.[3] On 5 June 1935, at the opening of the Convocation of the Church of England, the Archbishop of Canterbury announced that

Statesman-like realism requires that the position which Germany has in fact won should be accepted. . . . The true way is to regard what Hitler said as sincere.

On 1 July of that same year Lord Allen of Hurtwood in a letter to *The Times* spoke of the 'errors of Versailles' and the 'striking unanimity' with which British opinion stood behind the efforts of the British Government 'to extend the hand of friendship towards Germany'.[4]

Dr Gärtner herself was not idle during this period. It was through her that Philip Conwell-Evans, formerly Lord Noel-Buxton's private secretary during the latter's tenure of office under the second Labour Government, 1929–31, and lecturer at the University of Koenigsberg since 1932, was drawn into the work of furthering an Anglo-German understanding. She had collaborated with Conwell-Evans in trans-

1. Butler, op. cit., 203–94.
2. Graham Wootton, *The Official History of the British Legion* (1956).
3. *German Foreign Ministry Archives*, Ambassador von Hoesch to the German Foreign Ministry, 12 April 1935 (1506/371333–5).
4. *The Times*, 1 July 1935.

lating into German the list of questions which Lord Lothian proposed to put to Hitler, largely in vain, as Hitler spent the whole interview in a non-stop monologue, or so Conwell-Evans told her. In April 1935 she had written a pamphlet on German frontier problems for the New Fabian Bureau, and throughout much of the year she had been working on her British parliamentary contacts, especially Colonel Moore and Captain Victor Cazalet, to obtain their intervention in Parliament on the issue of Lithuanian action against the leaders of the German minority in March; with some success as Colonel Josiah Wedgewood, MP,[1] was led to follow one of Colonel Moore's questions with the supplementary question

Is the Secretary of State aware that this and similar questions about Memel have been hawked among members of this House by German agents![2]

Colonel Moore and Corder Catchpool together were instrumental in securing the services of Sir Alexander Lawrence, the well-known British QC, to represent the 126 arrested leaders of the German minority in Memel at their subsequent trial.

Enough has, perhaps, been said to show the extreme importance of this group of intermediaries in the organization of visits, and the influencing of prominent personalities of all political complexions into visits to Germany where the 'full works', the carefully stage-managed propaganda occasions and the equally carefully selected groups of sympathetic non-Nazi German conservatives, could be shown to and introduced to the visitors in circumstances which made the asking of awkward questions and the drawing of inconvenient comparisons almost impossible. Philip Conwell-Evans was extremely active in this, and Ribbentrop, once appointed to succeed the German Ambassador in London on the latter's death in 1936, threw himself into similar activities with a whole-hearted vulgarity, which does not seem to have made him any the less successful, greatly though it grated on the susceptibilities of Dr Gärtner and her friends in the German Foreign Ministry. He was able to organize visits by George Lansbury, the ex-leader of the Labour party, by Lloyd George, and even, after the abdication, by the Duke of Windsor and his new Duchess.[3]

1. C. V. Wedgewood, *The Last of the Radicals, Josiah Wedgewood, MP* (1951).
2. 299, *Hansard's Parl. Deb.*, H. of C., cols 804–5. See also ibid., vol.297, cols 322–3.
3. The Duke of Windsor, *A King's Story* (1951); the Duchess of Windsor, *The Heart has its Reasons* (1951).

There were others active. Perhaps the most notable was a certain Charles Spencer, who in May 1936 succeeded in organizing a visit by a number of Labour MPs which included Arthur Greenwood and two other Labour Privy Councillors, Tom Johnstone and Tom Kennedy, Ben Smith, one of the Labour Party Whips and four other Labour MPs. They were not received by Hitler but were shown the German compulsory Labour Corps, the *Reichsarbeitsdienst* camps, and otherwise given the full treatment by Dr Gärtner's organization with the help of a subsidy from the German Foreign Ministry.[1] A subsequent report from the German Embassy in London purported to observe that Greenwood had ceased publicly to attack Germany since his visit.[2]

It is not the intention of this essay to cover the subsequent history of Anglo-German relations or the later activities either of the more respectable of the 'appeasers' or of the less reputable pro-German organizations such as 'the Link' into which a number of the Conservative right were lured or snared in the last years before the war. Despite the picture painted of these men by writers of the left in British politics,[3] these latter groups were largely without influence in the circles where the ultimate recommendations were made and decisions taken. To do this would require a book in itself. For the purpose of this essay is to call attention to the peculiar success of the German nationalist propagandists, especially Dr Gärtner, in enlisting in support of their case against Versailles a large number of prominent political and intellectual leaders of British opinion, and to link up after 1933 with those who went on from the conviction of the basic justice of that case to argue that a policy of working with Hitler's aims rather than against him was the only way of avoiding war. The British Government itself took rather longer to be convinced of this argument, if indeed it ever accepted it. But in the spring of 1937, as argued elsewhere, the new Chamberlain Government seems to have reached a decision to attempt a last series of efforts to remove any possible *casus belli* in Europe, at least until Britain's armed strength was great and glorious enough itself to act as a deterrent. It is at this point that the previous activities of the German propagandists and

1. Curiously Dr Gärtner does not mention this visit in her memoirs, though she had first met Greenwood in 1923. *German Foreign Ministry Archives*: memorandum, 9 May 1936 (5730/E415719–20); German Embassy report, 9 May 1936 (5730/E415721–3).

2. Ibid., German Embassy report of 12 September 1936 (1437/363571–2).

3. See the sources cited in fn. 5 above, p. 119.

their intermediaries became so important, since they had already won for the new policy the necessary support among the British élite. After 1935 those intermediaries gained greatly in effectiveness in that they could work for German aims without being suspect in the way even an 'official' personality like Dr Gärtner could never hope to evade.

What of the counter-campaign? It must not be thought that there was no counter-campaign. There seem, in fact, to have been four main branches of this, entirely or almost entirely disparate from one another. The first was that waged inside the administration by Sir Robert Vansittart and others, notably Sir Warren Fisher. To them, at least in part, is owed the fact that the British Government never entirely swallowed the pro-German case. They were gravely handicapped by the suspicion with which the professional diplomatist and the Foreign Office had come to be regarded in 'liberal' circles,[1] by Vansittart's débâcle in the Hoare–Laval plan which brought down his minister, by the strained relations which always obtained between Vansittart and Anthony Eden, Hoare's successor, and by the disastrous appointment, of the blame for which Vansittart cannot himself be acquitted, of Sir Nevile Henderson as Ambassador to Germany in the summer of 1937.

The second was that waged within Parliament by a maverick group of MPs of whom Winston Churchill was the most senior, although the younger members of the group seem to have preferred to look for leadership elsewhere. Churchill himself was much in contact with members of the élite, of which he remained always a recognized member.[2] He lacked, however, any reputation for balance and judgment, and was greatly hated on many sides. Twice he destroyed the influence and position he had gradually built up, once by his intemperate opposition to the India Act of 1934–35, once by his romantic backing of Edward VIII in the Abdication Crisis. Churchill's role was to act throughout this period as the quasi-leader of the Conservative opposition to the Liberal wing of the National Government which maintained itself in power between its formation in November 1931 and Chamberlain's resignation in May 1940.

1. A suspicion which Neville Chamberlain felt particularly deeply.
2. His contact with Vansittart and Clive Wigram of the section of the Foreign Office responsible for Anglo-German relations is most important. On Wigram, see W. S. Churchill, *The Second World War*, 1 (1947); Valentine Lawford, *Bound for Diplomacy* (1963); and Sir John Wheeler-Bennett, *John Anderson, Viscount Waverley* (1962).

The third campaign was that waged within the Labour party on the issue of rearmament and collective security. Its leaders were Ernest Bevin[1] and Hugh Dalton,[2] and despite the claims advanced by the latter in his memoirs it cannot be claimed that they had secured more than a qualified victory by August 1939.[3] They were greatly hampered by the innate pacifism of much of the party, even after the resignation of George Lansbury[4] after Bevin's brutal attack on him at the 1935 Party Conference; but a bigger obstacle was the constant need to fight off the attempts of their left and the fellow-travellers of the Communist party to engulf them in a Popular Front on the French or Spanish model.[5]

The last was that waged behind the scenes by the international cover-organizations of the Comintern centred around Willi Muenzenberg in Paris. During the summer of 1933 they published the *Brown Book of the Nazi Terror*, and staged the 'counter trial' on the Reichstag fire in London.[6] They led the organization of a boycott of German goods that summer and took great care to counter any move in a pro-German direction on the public level. In August 1935 for example they arranged their own 'unofficial' visit of British ex-servicemen in answer to the visit of the British Legion's delegation and secured considerable press coverage for the meetings addressed by the 'unofficial delegation' on its return. They led public protest against the Nuremberg Laws which translated Nazi racialism and anti-Semitism into law in the autumn of 1935, even managing to secure Attlee's presence on the platform shortly after he had succeeded Lansbury as leader of the Labour party. Their most successful weapon was the mimeographed weekly *The Week*, edited by Claud Cockburn,[7] subsequently editor of the Communist *Daily Worker*, whose circulation among the innermost circles of those concerned the world over with international matters marks perhaps the high-water mark of Communist penetration into the élites of the Western world. Their essential aim, however, was not so much to influence the policy of

1. Alan Bullock, *The Life and Times of Ernest Bevin* (1960).
2. Hugh Dalton, *The Fateful Years* (1957).
3. W. R. Tucker, *The Attitude of the British Labour Party to European and Collective Security Problems, 1920–39* (Geneva, 1950).
4. R. Postgate, *The Life of George Lansbury* (1951).
5. See Colin Cooke, *The Life of Richard Stafford Cripps* (1957).
6. See the laborious reconstruction of this in Fritz Tobias, *Der Reichstagbrand, Legende und Wirklichkeit* (Rastatt, 1962).
7. Cockburn, op. cit. We still lack a decent study of this journal.

the élite as to replace it or at least greatly to alter its composition. They were greatly aided by the extraordinary position of confidence built up with organs of the British press by the Soviet Ambassador, Ivan Maiski, which enabled him on a number of occasions to pursue a policy of intervention in British internal politics which would have led to the immediate expulsion of any other diplomat.[1]

The only attempt made to tie together the various campaigns against Hitler, was that organized in 1935 by an emigré German of no particular political complexion, Eugen Spier.[2] It comprehended members of the Conservative opposition such as Commander Locker-Lampson, Duncan Sandys, Churchill himself and the Duchess of Atholl, Independent, Liberal and Labour MPs such as Sir Arthur Salter, Seymour Cocks, Philip Noel-Baker, Emrys Evans and Dingle Foot, Wilson Harris of the *Spectator* and Kingsley Martin, editor of the *New Statesman*, Lord Cecil of Chelwood, Sir Walter Layton,[3] Philip Guedalla, the historian, Professor Gilbert Murray, Lady Violet Bonham-Carter and Sir Archibald Sinclair, leader of the Liberal Party.

The aim of this grouping, to which the name 'Focus' was given, was to attempt to get some of its members into office, to secure Government approval of its recommendations and alternatively to build up a public ground-swell of feeling strong enough to force the British Government into active opposition to Hitler. It was thus designed to follow roughly the same combination of aims, though in an opposite direction, as the Allen of Hurtwood group in January 1934. But its membership lacked the ultimate contact with British Cabinet circles that Allen had had while Ramsay MacDonald was in office, and that Lothian had via Geoffrey Dawson's friendship with Neville Chamberlain. Their only real contact, besides Churchill himself, was through Sir Austen Chamberlain, the former Foreign Secretary, now in 1936 the elder statesman *par excellence* of the Conservative party. Their efforts were dissipated in the organization of public meetings, which were inadequately reported in the press,

---

1. See Sir Llewellyn Woodward, *British Foreign Policy in the Second World War* (1962) xxv, 198–9. On Maiski see also his own memoirs, op. cit., and George Bilainkin, *Maiski, Ten Years Ambassador* (1944).

2. Eugen Spier, *Focus* (1963).

3. The attentive reader will have noted several others who had previously sponsored Lord Allen of Hurtwood's activities in 1934. Lord Allen himself appeared on the platform at its first major public meeting.

if they were noticed at all.[1] This can, in part, be ascribed to the failure of their more important associates, except for Churchill, to lend them their oratorical presence after the first big public meeting in December 1936 in London at the Albert Hall. The bulk of their members were men prominent enough, but outside the current foreign-policy-making élite or at best on its fringes. The group was thus ill-placed for the task of penetrating the administration, and insufficiently armed to exert the public pressure which might have induced the Government to take notice of their contentions. Their major role perhaps was to disseminate information from sources close to the German opposition to Hitler[2] on the pace of German rearmament and the development of Hitler's plans against Austria and Czechoslovakia. To counter the long-term work of the German nationalist propagandists they needed time and access to the organs of publicity which was denied to them.

To sum up: the work of winning support for the policy of a revision of Versailles, undertaken by German official and demi-official organizations from 1922 onwards, was very much eased, and could possibly not have succeeded at all without the positive rejection of the Versailles Treaty by large sections of British opinion, and the consequent revulsion against French efforts to enforce it in the years 1919–23. On this basis the various German agencies, of which the *Wirtschaftpolitische Gesellschaft* was by far the most active, was able to build up among British élite circles a steady reservoir of conviction of the folly of the Versailles Treaty and the need for its revision in Germany's favour. On Hitler's return to power they were able to continue, their work only being upset by the revelation of Hitler's own methods given the world in the summer of 1934. With that exception Hitler's policies did not differ from those they had advocated, save in his methods and in the contempt he displayed for foreign criticism of those methods.

1. Spier blames this on the control exercised, on the one hand, by Dawson, through *The Times* and, on the other hand, by the press lords, Rothermere and Beaverbrook. But it is odd that no reports were carried by the *Daily Telegraph*, the *Manchester Guardian*, the *News Chronicle* or the *Daily Herald*, all of whom were to some degree at least, anti-appeasement. The role of the press and of the numerous individuals who tried to "tell the truth" about Germany should not be overlooked.

2. Spier was in contact with Karl Goerdeler, the former Lord Mayor of Leipzig, one of the leaders of the 1944 conspiracy against Hitler. See G. Ritter, *Carl Goerdeler und die deutsche Widerstands-Bewegung* (Stuttgart, 1954).

Nevertheless, the obvious threat of war contained in Hitler's more aggressive pursuit of revisionist aims led to the entry into the game of a new group of intermediaries whose contacts were such as greatly to ease the task of the German agencies, and who were able to provide a set of justifications for the policy of appeasement which in public fitted into the existing pattern of prejudice and were more than adequate to counter in private the arguments of the opposite school. Their campaign succeeded because it worked with and was aimed at the existing power-structure of the foreign-policy-making élite. Their opponents were forced willy-nilly to attempt to disturb or even to overthrow its leading members. Perhaps the most surprising thing about the 'Focus' campaign is their failure to contact any Cabinet members other than Eden. Duff Cooper and the other doubters on appeasement, Hore-Belisha for example, whose Jewishness should have made him a sensitive target, do not appear to have been considered at all. No attempt was made to organize a cabal within the Cabinet against the Chamberlain–Halifax–Simon–Hoare–Inskip grouping which dominated it. Spier's list of names came from the alternative élites. And those who fought within the élite were defeated one by one and resigned or were promoted into desuetude.

PART III

The Impact of the Commonwealth

Imperial Defence Policy and Imperial Foreign Policy, 1911–39: The Substance and the Shadow

ANY student of British foreign policy between the wars must begin by being struck by the fact that the vast bulk of comment on that policy has been couched in terms that either deny the importance of the development of consultation with the Commonwealth, or more commonly ignore this consultation altogether.[1] The student who attempts to fill this gap begins, of course, by running his head on what seems at first sight a total absence of documentation. But perseverance in study reveals two factors of importance: first, the psychological vulnerability of members of all governments to representations from the Dominions; and secondly, that one and the same organ advised both British and Dominions Governments on the strategical factors underlying their position in the world, namely, the Committee of Imperial Defence, with, since 1924, the Chiefs of Staff Sub-Committee. And what seems to be a curious paradox emerges. The political membership of the CID also dominated Cabinet discussion and formulation of British foreign policy. Yet in matters of foreign policy they spoke for Britain alone (unless otherwise authorized by Dominion Governments); in matters of defence, in matters of that ultimate sanction of force which is, in domestic and foreign affairs alike, the *ultima ratio regum*, they acted for, and were responsible for the defence of the Commonwealth as a whole.

Attention had been called to this paradox indirectly by Sir Edward Grey before the First World War, although he approached the

---

1. These strictures are not intended to cover works specifically intended to deal with problems of Commonwealth as opposed to British foreign policy, such as P. N. S. Mansergh, *Commonwealth Affairs, Problems of External Policy 1931–39* (1952); Gwendolen Carter, *The British Commonwealth and World Security* (Toronto, 1947); W. Y. Elliott and H. Duncan Hall (ed.), *The British Commonwealth at War* (New York, 1943); J. D. B. Miller, *The Commonwealth and the World* (1958); though there are differences of emphasis between these works and the approach adopted in this paper.

matter from the opposite angle, that of the existence of separate Dominions, armies and naval forces.[1] Speaking to the 113th meeting of the Committee of Imperial Defence at which the Dominions delegates to the Imperial Conference of 1911 were present he said:

It is possible to have separate fleets in a united Empire but it is not possible to have separate fleets in a united Empire without having a common foreign policy, – the creation of separate fleets has made it essential that the foreign policy of the Empire should be a common policy.[2]

At the time his words fitted accurately enough into the anxieties of his listeners. The main aim of the Conference in the eyes of its conveners, or at least of one of them, was achieved: Dominion aid, moral, material and financial for the mother country staggering under the weight of the increased armament expenditure made necessary by the menace of Germany, was secured;[3] the Pacific Dominions increased their naval expenditure still further, and the very next year, impressed by the evidence put before him during his attendance at meetings of the Committee of Imperial Defence, the Canadian Premier, Sir Robert Borden, introduced into the Canadian Parliament a bill providing for the construction on Canada's account of three dreadnoughts to be presented to the Royal Navy.[4] In the event his bill was defeated in the Canadian Senate; but the actual onset of war in 1914 found the Dominions more or less at one with Britain on the policy which had involved Britain in the war and the defence policy with which she entered it.

The machinery by which this comparative unanimity had been achieved was two-fold. Colonial and Imperial Conferences had, in fact, met at biennial intervals in 1907, 1909 and 1911; on each occasion problems of defence and foreign policy had been reviewed in detail.

1. See Arthur J. Marder, *From the Dreadnought to Scapa Flow* (1961), vol.1; Donald C. Gordon, 'The Admiralty and Dominions Navies, 1902–14', *Journal of Modern History*, 33 (1961); Brian Tunstall, 'Imperial Defence, 1900–14', *Cambridge History of the British Empire*, III (1959).

2. G. P. Gooch and Harold Temperley, *British Documents on the Origins of the War, 1898–1914*, VI, App.V.

3. Already in 1902, during the Colonial Conference of that year, Joseph Chamberlain had spoken in somewhat highly coloured language of the 'Weary Titan' struggling under the 'too vast orb of its fate'. On the impressions left on the minds of Dominion Premiers see Lord Hankey, *The Supreme Command, 1914–18* (1961), I, 129.

4. Gordon, loc. cit.; Gilbert M. Tucker, 'The Naval Policy of Sir Robert Borden, *Canadian Historical Review*, XXVIII, no.1 (1948).

The Admiralty and the Imperial General Staff had provided advice on military and naval problems, and the whole field of defence policy had been thrashed out at Cabinet level in Britain through the machinery of the Committee of Imperial Defence. The 1907 Colonial Conference had provided for meetings of imperial conferences every four years, and had established an Imperial Conference Secretariat, while at the 1911 Conference the delegates had agreed that representatives of the Dominions Governments could be invited to attend meetings of the Committee of Imperial Defence when questions of defence which affected the overseas Dominions were under consideration. They had agreed also that Committees of Defence, patterned on the CID should be established in each Dominion; and between 1911 and 1914 Canadian, New Zealand, Newfoundland and South African representatives attended meetings of the Committee of Imperial Defence, which had come to assume the role of the key co-ordinating force in imperial affairs – 'a forum first for shared information and later an undefined but united share of defence policy making'.[1]

Three themes which stand out in these years were to dominate postwar developments, each a different aspect of the same central problem. First, there was the conflict between the home defence anxieties of the individual Dominions and the equally clear truth that a defeat of Britain meant, as Grey pointed out in 1911, that each Dominion would be left on its own; that the major threat to the Dominions came from Europe. Secondly, there was the problem of the organization of imperial defence, in which Dominions nationalism and the isolationism of the non-English speaking peoples in Canada and South Africa pulled one way, and the Admiralty, the Committee of Imperial Defence and neo-imperialist ambition pulled the other. Thirdly, there was the brute fact that every major move towards the Dominions made in Britain was made because of the disparities between Britain's defence commitments and obligations and Britain's own resources. The Empire before 1914, the Commonwealth after 1931 were equally dominated by Dominion dependence on Britain and independence of one another, a cluster of bilateral alliances, rather than an interlocking multilateral alliance. Without Britain there was neither rhyme nor reason in the Commonwealth. The

1. Franklyn Arthur Johnson, *Defence by Committee, the British Committee of Imperial Defence 1880–1959* (1960), 121. See also Hankey, *The Supreme Command*, I, 124–36.

principal threats to the Commonwealth came from European challenges to Britain. And Britain herself was decreasingly able to handle them or to measure up to them on her own.

In the meantime, behind the operation of the machinery developed by 1914, there lay a fairly determined body of opinion in Britain, voicing itself at one stage through the theorists of the *Round Table*, and at others in the quiet extension of the pattern of consultation by the secretariat of the CID, especially as developed by Lord Hankey, which was set on developing the Commonwealth into a quasi-federal organization with common economic, common defence and common foreign policies. A great deal of steady and sophisticated thinking, a great deal of quiet, persistent lobbying and a gradual permeation of the higher civil service,[1] all very much heightened by the events and pressures of the war, led in 1917 to the next stage, the summoning of the Imperial War Conference and the establishment of the Imperial War Cabinet. Again the motives impelling the British Cabinet to take these steps were as much dictated by British needs as by neo-imperialism. The original prompting came from Lord Milner.[2] But Lloyd George's letter to the Colonial Secretary, Walter Long, of 12 December 1916, puts the matter in terms of naked want:

I am convinced that we should take the Dominions into our counsel in much larger measure. . . . As we must receive even more substantial support from them before we can pull through, it is important that they should be made to feel that they have a share in our Councils as well as in our burdens.[3]

But the Premiers of three of the Dominions came to London determined to attack the Admiralty and the Foreign Office for ignoring their position in the Pacific in 1914 and to make certain that machinery should be devised to prevent a recurrence of this situation. The two New Zealand representatives devoted the fourth and fifth days to a

1. See Hans E. Bärtschli, *Die Entwicklung vom imperialistischen Reichsgedanken zur modernen Idee des Commonwealth im Lebenswerk Lord Balfours* (Berne, 1957), 125–31, 136–8.

2. Hankey, *The Supreme Command*, II, 657. That the motives underlying this move included the desire to take advantage of the moment of crisis to advance further towards the imperial super-state is suggested by a memorandum in Austen Chamberlain's papers which analyses the characters and attitudes of the Dominion representatives scheduled to attend the Conference, from the point of view of their views and openness to Imperial considerations.

3. David Lloyd George, *War Memoirs* (1933–36), IV, 1733.

detailed criticism of the Admiralty for ignoring the prewar agreements with Australia and New Zealand and leaving the South Pacific almost undefended before the German Pacific squadron in 1914. They ended by presenting a resolution calling upon the Admiralty to work out a scheme of naval defence for the Empire as soon as the war was over. A resolution of equal force was presented by Sir Robert Borden, the Canadian Premier, which spoke of the Dominions' 'right to an adequate voice in foreign policy and in foreign relations' in calling for 'effective arrangements for continuous consultation in all important matters of common Imperial concern'.[1] It was agreed that the Imperial War Cabinet should meet annually or more often if possible. Borden's approach was essentially governed by his conviction, first voiced in 1910, that co-operation in imperial defence should carry with it the right to an effective voice in determining the foreign policy of the Empire. And alone of Dominion premiers before 1914 he had agreed to the Canadian High Commissioner being a regular member of the CID, and had appointed Perley simultaneously as Minister without Portfolio and High Commissioner in London.[2]

The position attained in 1917–18 was to last formally until the Imperial Conference of 1923. It marks the high tide of the pan-Imperial movement in the Dominions. Beneath the surface signs of its weakness were evident in two directions. First, an imperial foreign policy could only be carried out on a basis of continuous consultation. This Borden, William Hughes of Australia, Massey of New Zealand and Smuts of South Africa readily realized was in itself technically difficult except where a British Empire delegation attended an international conference. It raised great difficulties in spheres where a basic difference of approach between the Dominions became apparent. And it depended on there being one recognizable source of advice and action at the head of the conduct of British foreign policy, and one, moreover, prepared to consult and take notice of consultations with the Dominions. Secondly, the conduct of a single imperial defence policy was comparatively simple where there was unity of purpose between the Dominions and the home country, with

1. *Public Archives of Canada, Sir George Foster Papers*, File 75; *Imperial War Conference 1917, Minutes of Proceedings*, etc., Cmd. 8566 (1917); see also Sir Robert Borden, *Memoirs* (Toronto, 1938), II, 693–6; M. Ollivier (ed.), *The Colonial and Imperial Conferences from 1887–1937* (Ottawa, 1954), II, III.

2. Hankey, op. cit., I, 134; Tucker, loc. cit.

priority for expenditure on imperial defence, and unity of command. None of these survived the end of the war. To achieve agreement on an imperial defence policy came to necessitate as careful a set of compromises as did agreement on an imperial foreign policy.

To take the theme of foreign policy first. At Versailles a good deal of care was taken to maintain a unified policy as between the Dominions and Britain. The demands of the Australian Prime Minister, Hughes, were backed by Britain, even where they conflicted directly with American ideals as set forth by President Wilson.[1] Smuts and Borden played a considerable part in hammering out much of the Peace Treaty and the Covenant of the League of Nations, incidentally providing Wilson's Republican critics with a good deal of ammunition by their insistence on separate votes in the League for the Dominions ('6 votes for the British Empire').[2] These developments have been admirably summed up in a recent study:

The strategic circumstances of the First World War had produced a major revolution in the diplomatic relations of the English-speaking world. The self-governing Dominions with Great Britain had taken on a joint responsibility for foreign policy. Joint responsibility of governments required unanimous agreement. The British Government knew that the experiment with the Imperial War Cabinet and the continued Dominions aid in the war could founder on the abyss of disunity. Consequently it became peculiarly sensitive to Dominions' demands. Hidden behind each Dominion's demands lay a threat fraught with dire consequences for the Empire's survival. Where earlier in the history of the Empire Great Britain could sacrifice Dominion interests to the needs of British foreign policy, now Britain was compelled to heed Dominions' advice and take up their causes, even if these were not what the British government itself would have desired.[3]

1. Hughes had considerable support inside the British Cabinet from those who disliked the Fourteen Points, and resented the way the Allies had been compelled to allow the conclusions of an armistice with Germany on this basis without prior consultation. See *Public Archives of Canada*, Sir Robert Borden Papers, minutes of Imperial War Cabinet, meetings of 30 and 31 December 1918. (The minutes of the first meeting are also to be found in Colonel House's papers, Sterling Library, Yale.) On the Peace Conference, see Seth W. Tillmann, *Anglo-American Relations at the Paris Peace Conference* (Princeton, 1961); Harold Nelson, *Land and Power* (1964).

2. This was one of the few items on which Lord Grey was not allowed to offer any compromise in his mission to the United States in the last few months of 1919 (*Documents on British Foreign Policy, 1919–39*, 1st series, vol.v, chapter 2, *passim*).

3. Neville Kingsley Meaney, 'American Attitudes towards the British

But once the Conference was over, the Treaty signed and the British Empire delegation dispersed, differences rapidly began to develop between the various Dominions and Britain, Canada and South Africa particularly moving back into an isolationism almost as extreme as that of the United States. Reactions against the final form the peace treaties had taken was fairly uniform both in Britain and among Dominion representatives. Indeed, it was with backing from the British Empire delegation that Lloyd George succeeded in getting the terms on Upper Silesia altered, but failed to secure a revision of those governing the occupation of the Rhineland. But despite their intense dislike of the treaties, necessity forced the British into attempting to operate them, particularly in the Near East. The Dominions felt no such urgency and began very swiftly to lapse back into that curious attitude, half resentment, half automatic assumption of British leadership, which had been so marked a feature of their earlier reaction to Britain's European preoccupations. In Pacific matters, meantime, the growth of American–Japanese hostility and the question of a renewal of the Anglo-Japanese alliance brought to the fore an issue where the Dominions themselves were divided.

To these divisive forces was added one which it lay within British power to remedy, the absence of a clear and single recognizable source of advice and action at the controls of Britain's own foreign policy. The Coalition Cabinet of 1918–22 was one of the ablest, most brilliant and, be it said, least responsible governments Britain has suffered under. But its foreign policy was bitterly divided both on personal and on ideological issues, the only common bonds between Lloyd George, Curzon and Churchill being the detestation of France shared by the first two and of Bolshevism shared by the second two. British constitutional practice has always admitted, moreover, of two interpretations of the powers of the Foreign Secretary. He can be the agent of a Cabinet policy acting as the delegate of a united Cabinet, or he can be the initiator of foreign policy acting in the Cabinet's name but as their representative. Most of the great Foreign Secretaries have held to the second interpretation. But this interpretation is one which it is impossible to reconcile with the conduct of an imperial foreign policy resting on consultation with the Dominions. Thus Lloyd George consulted no one, not even Curzon. And Curzon could not conceive of prior consultation with the

Empire, 1919–22' (unpublished Ph.D. thesis, Duke University, 1959, Library of Congress Microfilm 59–2387), 150.

Dominions other than as an exercise of prerogative to be acted on only if time permitted or Dominion statesmen were unduly importunate.

The issue of the renewal of the Anglo-Japanese alliance and its effect on Imperial-American relations brought the differences between the Dominions into the open. Basically, the division lay between Canada and South Africa for whom good Anglo-American relations and the avoidance of 'entangling alliances' were paramount and Australia (with New Zealand in support) for whom security against Japan in the Pacific was most important. The subsequent clash between Arthur Meighen (who had succeeded Sir Robert Borden as leader of Canada's imperialists) and Hughes paralleled the similar division within the British Cabinet between those who regarded America with distaste and resentment as a factor to be included and reconciled with their calculations, and those for whom American policy was one of the basic principles from which those calculations should start. This latter division had been reconciled in the plan which Curzon and Lloyd George presented to the conference (and which Hughes himself favoured), of coupling the renewal of the alliance with Japan with the summoning of a Pacific conference in which a tripartite relationship with America and Japan should be so far as possible substituted for the alliance as a guarantee of the peace and *status quo*. But Meighen revealed himself as being thoroughly against the renewal of the alliance in any form, and went on to demand that in questions where the interests of one Dominion were 'peculiarly concerned' imperial policy should be shaped by that Dominion. The proposal arose logically out of the attempt to conduct a foreign policy by consultation between separate cabinets responsible to separate electorates. But it was rebuffed in this instance by Lloyd George and Hughes who denied its applicability to Imperial-American relations; and the question Meighen raised of continuous consultation went by default when the American Government won by a hair's breadth the race to call a Pacific Conference.[1]

1. This account is based on the following sources: J. Bartlet Brebner, 'Canada and the Anglo-Japanese Alliance', *Political Science Quarterly*, L (1935); John K. Galbraith, 'The Imperial Conference of 1921 and the Washington Conference', *Canadian Historical Review*, XXIX (1948); William Farmer Whyte, *William Morris Hughes, his Life and Times*, (Sydney, 1957); memoranda in *Public Archives of Canada*, *Arthur Meighen* and *Sir George Foster Papers*; M. G. Fry, 'Anglo-American-Canadian Relations and the Far East, 1918–1922'; (Unpublished Ph.D. Thesis, London University, 1964).

This was, however, a clash within the Empire in which the British Government could to a certain extent play a mediatory role. It fitted, albeit with difficulty, into the general framework of consultation with the Dominions representatives on an agreed line of policy in which the British Foreign Office could act as executive agent for the Empire as a whole. Not that there were not further inconsistencies underlying this theory. For British ministries to act as advisory agents to the Empire as well as to Britain was difficult enough to reconcile with the theory of equality within the Empire between Dominions and mother country. That they should act as executive agents as well (despite the attempts to make the Foreign Service more imperial in its sources of recruitment) was clearly anomalous. But given goodwill, this could be represented as a transitional stage. What was to bring to an end the attempt to evolve machinery for the formulation of an imperial foreign policy based on consultation was the behaviour of the Coalition Cabinet during the Chanak crisis, first in bringing the Empire to the verge of war without a shadow of prior consultation, and secondly in publicly appealing to opinion in the Dominions simultaneously with an approach to their governments.

The Imperial Conference of 1923 thus saw the abandonment of any attempt to formulate a common foreign policy to be executed by the British Foreign Secretary and his agents. The new Canadian Liberal Government under Mackenzie King rebuffed *ab initio* Lord Curzon's claims to have acted on behalf of the Empire as a whole at Lausanne, the more so as they found themselves during the Conference confronted with important telegrams dispatched in their name by Curzon without prior consultation. The agenda again included the item of measures to secure a common foreign policy which had found a place in that of the 1921 Imperial Conference. But the line taken by Mackenzie King, and backed by Smuts, made any further progress towards such an objective impossible. Instead, the Conference was compelled to accept the passage of a series of individual resolutions on individual points of policy, and to devise a formula for the signature of treaties which reserved ratification to the parliaments of the individual members.[1]

Mackenzie King's veto put an end to the efforts to evolve closer

1. This summary is based on Ramsay Cooke, 'J. W. Dafoe at the Imperial Conference of 1923', *Canadian Historical Review*, XLI (1961); R. Macgregor Dawson, *William Lyon Mackenzie King* (Ottawa, 1960), I; Ollivier, *Colonial and Imperial Conferences*, III.

machinery for policy formation though not to the drive of the neo-imperialists for consultation. Their efforts seem, thereafter, to have been forced into new directions. The first of these was the development of the Dominions Office and the High Commissioners as a means of avoiding a repetition of the disastrous Chanak manifesto, in which they rightly saw the cause of the miscarriage of their earlier plans. The second was to face them with the necessity of putting a stop to activities of the Curzonian kind, which they realized were irritating the Dominions into the suspicion that their change in status from colonies who obeyed the central Government to equality as Governments of the Crown was regarded by the British Government as one of form only.[1] The effect of this was to impose on those who formulated British foreign policy the need continuously to consult Dominion representatives, and, where such consultation was impossible, to operate within the limits of what they felt the Dominions would accept. This latter difficulty became larger as Imperial Conferences became less frequent. Three years elapsed between the 1923 and 1926 Conferences; four before the 1930 Conference met and seven before the next (the 1932 Conference was purely economic in its interests).[2] An illustration of these differences can be seen in the attempt to summon a Conference to deal with the Geneva Protocol.[3] And in 1929 Austen Chamberlain commented to Sir Esmé Howard:

The conduct of foreign affairs in present conditions presents indeed an entirely novel problem. In matters of this importance Great Britain can no longer act as the spokesman of the Empire unless with the individual consent of the other governments.[4]

Two factors aided them in their efforts. The annual meetings of the League of Nations Assembly and of the Preparatory Commission to

1. Leo Amery's activities here are of the first importance in view of his personal friendship with Mackenzie King and Smuts.

2. There appears to have been some kind of an unofficial conference on defence matters during the Jubilee Celebrations in May 1935.

3. See Cmd. 2458 (1925), *Protocol for the Pacific Settlement of International Disputes. Correspondence relating to the position of the Dominions*.

4. In 1925 Ramsay MacDonald had called public attention to the difficulty: 'The present system of consultation has two main deficiencies. . . . It renders immediate action extremely difficult. . . . Conclusions reached at and between Imperial Conferences are liable to be reversed through changes in Governments' (Cmd. 2301 (1924–25), *Correspondence with the Governments of the Self-Governing Dominions with regard to consultations on matters of Foreign Policy and General Imperial Interest*, No.1).

the Disarmament Conference provided a regular meeting ground for British and Dominion representatives at a ministerial level. And support of the League of Nations itself provided them with an external frame of reference on which their policies could converge; thus they evolved a regular system of apportioning the initiative on matters before the League among the representatives of various Dominions.

This necessitated avoiding any measures designed to turn the League into more than a permanent international conference. Perhaps the most remarkable agreement on this was achieved in the rejection of the Draft Treaty of Mutual Guarantee and the Geneva Protocol, essentially on the same grounds, that in Smuts' words, they would tend to turn the League into an 'armed alliance to maintain the status quo' in Europe. The members of the Commonwealth came, therefore, to have a vested interest in the maintenance of the League of Nations as an external point of reference around which their differing interests could coalesce. Canada and South Africa could continue the isolationist policies necessitated by their white non-Anglo-Saxon elements. Australia and New Zealand could mask their preoccupation with Pacific problems. Britain, on the other hand, could indulge under Austen Chamberlain her proclivities for leadership in Europe. And the Empire could divide on the obligations assumed at Locarno towards France and Belgium, since these were linked with the League and in any case were designed, it is not too strong to say, to create a set of circumstances in which they would never need in fact to be fulfilled.

This position could only last while the League itself functioned as an instrument to maintain the peace without any major effort being actually called for from its signatories. But before considering the dilemmas which the end of this happy state created for the Commonwealth it would be as well to examine the question of imperial defence. Here the burden lay most heavily on Britain, and the weapon of defence most centrally concerned was the Royal Navy. In 1917, as related above, the Admiralty representative at the Imperial War Conference had been most royally roasted for the Navy's failure to live up to its promises to maintain a reasonable force in the Pacific. And the Conference had passed a resolution calling upon the Admiralty to draw up a plan for imperial defence as a whole once the war was over. The Admiralty in fact anticipated this date, largely, one supposes, because, in late 1917, it had at last acquired a genuine Naval War Staff. The scheme itself was submitted to the Imperial War

Cabinet in an Admiralty memorandum of May 1918.[1] It called for a single Imperial Navy, responsible to an Imperial Naval Authority, whose precise constitutional status was left unclear until the form 'in which it may be ultimately decided to give expression to the desire for closer union' was apparent, but which was to be headed by the First Lord of the Admiralty with a Board on which the naval ministers of the Dominions were to sit at least once a year, and would, it was hoped, be more continuously represented. These proposals were rejected immediately by the Domionion Premiers, Borden taking the lead.[2] Instead, the Admiralty were forced to accept the standardization of Dominion navies and an absence of control over their naval estimates (one of the most important items concealed but implied in the Admiralty scheme). In December 1918 Admiral Jellicoe was dispatched, on the invitation of Dominion premiers, to advise them on naval organization, so as to ensure homogeneity between the practice of the various Dominion navies and the Royal Navy. Jellicoe so far exceeded his instructions as to draw up a major scheme for a British Far Eastern fleet of sixteen capital ships, to be paid for on a contributory basis, either in cash or kind in proportion to their population and the value of their overseas trade.[3]

In the meantime the British Government set up in May 1919 an inter-Service Committee on Imperial Defence Organization, on which the Dominions were by invitation represented, to prepare proposals to be submitted to the Imperial War Cabinet before the Dominion Prime Ministers returned home.[4] The Committee does not seem to have been able to report in time to meet this deadline, but what was presumably the Admiralty's contribution was sent to Jellicoe in November 1919. This called reluctantly for the building up of separate Dominion navies, with separate budgets, etc., but still asked for the creation of an Imperial Naval Council to consider

1. *Public Archives of Canada, Sir Robert Borden Papers.* See also *The Borden Memoirs,* ii, 841–3.

2. The rejection was less categorical than sometimes represented, being couched in terms of its immediate impracticability. The final paragraph read as follows: 'As naval forces come to be developed upon a considerable scale by the Dominions, it may be necessary hereafter to consider the establishment for war purposes of some supreme naval authority upon which each of the Dominions would be adequately represented' (*Borden Papers*).

3. Admiral Sir Frederick Dreyer, *The Sea Heritage* (1955), 240.

4. Brigadier J. H. MacBrien to Sir Robert Borden, 14 July 1919, *Borden Papers.*

matters of policy and for the representation of the Dominions on the Admiralty Naval Staff.[1] Jellicoe's proposals were equally praised and ignored in the Dominions he visited (he did not visit South Africa). Some of his ideas were later incorporated into long-range Admiralty planning, but the bulk of his recommendations as to expenditure and size of fleets, etc., were wildly unreal in the financial circumstances of 1919–20. The Admiralty returned to the charge, however, in 1921. Again they expressed their view that the ideal was a unified navy under a single command with a quota of men and ships supplied by the Dominions, and talked of an 'Empire Fleet' even if Dominions sentiment made it necessary to concentrate on the development and co-ordination of separate Dominions navies. Their main recommendations lay in the need for the Empire of a chain of oil-fuelling stations and the development of Singapore as a naval base.[2] Both of these recommendations were accepted by the Dominions representatives.[3]

The provisions agreed at the Washington Naval Conference and embodied in the Naval Treaty only added force to these recommendations, since British capital ship strength was now rudely limited to a mere fifteen ships in 1936, where the Admiralty could normally have expected an increase in the fleet to something approaching its prewar dominance, once the initial period of financial stringency which followed the war had passed. At the 1923 Imperial Conference, Amery, the new First Lord of the Admiralty, outlined a new imperial strategy to take care of the possibility of a war in the Far East by the development of the Singapore base as a *place d'armes* to which part at least of the battle fleet could be speedily transferred on the imminence of hostilities.[4] He failed, however, to secure Canadian approval, until Smuts' intervention; and the differing support in the Dominions for the Singapore base policy was revealed in 1924 when Ramsay Mac-Donald asked for Dominions' views on the proposal to stop work on the base.[5] The Canadian and South African Governments both approved, while the Pacific Dominions protested violently. The old

1. Admiral Sir Reginald Bacon, *The Life of John Rushworth, Earl Jellicoe* (1936), 425–6.
2. *Austen Chamberlain Papers.*
3. Ollivier, op. cit., ii.
4. L. Amery, *My Political Life*, ii, *War and Peace, 1914–29* (1953), 252–3.
5. Cmd. 2083 (1924), *Correspondence with the Self-governing Dominions and India regarding the Development of the Singapore Naval Base*, nos 1, 3, 12, 13.

policy was resumed when the Conservative Government returned to office in November 1924, and the Pacific Dominions and Colonies in fact contributed very considerably in cash to the development of the base.

For the 1926 Imperial Conference the Admiralty at last came to terms with reality so far as the Dominion navies were concerned. In their view the single collective Empire fleet which would have to exist in war consisted of three categories, the main fleet, detached forces to control lines of communication distinct from the main theatre of operations, and the local defence forces necessary to stave off local enemy pressure. Dominion navies would, they hoped, pass through four phases of development. In the first they would provide local defence forces. In the second they would provide sea-going forces in addition to the local defence forces. In the third, they would take over responsibility for their home station, on which a squadron of the detached forces would be based. In the fourth they would, it was hoped, provide additional units for attachment to the main fleet.[1] From the published resolutions of the 1926 Imperial Conference and Dominion support of Britain's stand on the cruiser question at the ill-fated Three-Power Naval Conference at Geneva the following year, it must be assumed that the Dominion representatives accepted the Admiralty's analysis and proposals. A powerful and unavoidable inducement to them to do this was the refusal by foreign governments (especially the USA), made clear to them at the Imperial Conference,[2] to treat the Dominion navies as separate from the Royal Navy when considering the allocation of quotas for naval construction in the categories of smaller warships in which the Dominion navies were interested. This was peculiarly irksome to the Canadian Government, especially since it would be taken as providing a precedent for the limitation of Dominion military and air forces.[3] The Americans, however, remained adamant, and the Dominions were forced to accept their inclusion in the British quotas established in the London Naval Treaty of 1930. The matter appears to have been raised in private conversations at the 1930 Imperial Conference and

1. *Public Archives of Canada, Arthur Meighen Papers*, Memorandum of 10 May 1926.

2. Meighen Papers.

3. *Canadian Naval Archives*, Governor-General to Secretary of State for Dominions Affairs, 27 June 1927. The author is extremely grateful to the Canadian Naval Authorities and to Mr E. C. Russell, the official Canadian Naval Historian, for permission to quote from these papers.

reluctantly accepted; at any rate Commodore Hose, RCN, was able to make effective use of this fact to defeat in 1933 a cut in the Canadian Naval estimates which would have entailed a virtual disbandment of the Canadian Navy and the sale of its four destroyers to Britain.[1]

In the meantime the arrangements proposed by the Admiralty in 1923 and 1926 for the exchange of ships and officers and the attachment of Dominion officers to the Naval Staff College had developed easily and freely, being duly chronicled every year in the statements accompanying the British Naval Estimates. A further unifying force had come with the establishment of the Imperial Defence College. The Committee of Imperial Defence, now reinforced by the establishment of the Chiefs of Staff Sub-Committee in 1924 and a rapidly increasing network of civilian sub-committees, continued its role as adviser not merely to the British Cabinet but also to the Dominions Governments. At the 1926 Imperial Conference the British Prime Minister, Baldwin, called the attention of the Dominions again to its work, and to the need for Dominions equivalents agreed on in 1911; and a number of Dominions senior officers of all Services attended the Imperial Defence College thereafter.

Thus by 1932, despite the defeat of the Admiralty's schemes for a single Imperial Navy, the Commonwealth amounted for defence purposes virtually to a permanent alliance with armed forces which were at least as integrated as those now comprising NATO's striking forces, with a common centre of advice on defence matters both between the individual armed Services and in the CID as a whole. There was, of course, no compulsion upon the individual governments to take such advice as was given. Yet on all matters of standardization of equipment, training, etc., financial considerations and the virtual lack of domestic armaments industries operated with those of imperial sentiment to hold them on this common course even where the two bilingual Dominions were concerned. All this, coupled with the existence of a world-wide network of bases available to the armed forces of the mother country, operated, as has been pointed out, to make the Commonwealth 'in the matter of sea-power, to some extent an alliance with a certain contractual basis'.[2] Yet this was an alliance

1. *Canadian Naval Archives*, File 4000,100A, Commodore Hose to Canadian Minister of National Defence, Colonel Sutherland, 1 June 1933.

2. H. Duncan Hall, 'The Commonwealth in War and Peace', *The British Commonwealth at War*, ed. W. Y. Elliott and H. Duncan Hall (New York, 1943), 68.

without a common policy and a common enemy, as was to become apparent after 1933, when its varying members began to find themselves faced with differing enemies. In February 1934 the Defence Requirements Sub-Committee set up the previous year on the joint promptings of the Treasury and the Chiefs of Staff Sub-Committee as an organ of the CID reported in strong and pungent terms on the threat from Germany and Japan. The reaction in the Dominions again showed very marked differences. The Canadian Government felt obliged to adopt a policy in public even more cunctatory than that pursued by its American neighbour. The South African Government plunged boldly into a series of ill-considered attempts to mediate between Germany and Britain, meanwhile pressing Britain not to take any action against Germany. The New Zealand Government held out bravely for collective security. The Australian Government, on the other hand, was deeply disturbed by the development of a European threat which might prevent the dispatch of the fleet to the Far East in the face of the increasing bellicosity of Japan. It was, presumably, in part to allay these anxieties and to advise them in the face of this threat that Lord Hankey visited Australia in the summer of 1934;[1] possibly in part to allay any anxieties on the part of the Home Government as to Dominion action in the event of war.

Divided counsels continued to bedevil British ability to evolve an agreed policy to deal with the complete breakdown of European security. Neither South Africa nor Australia were at all happy about the accident which made Italy the first enemy, situated as Italy was across the line along which the transfer of the British fleet to Far Eastern waters should take place. But the obvious inability of the League to prevent the Italian conquest of Abyssinia deprived the whole Commonwealth of the factor which had enabled them to paper over their divisions and avoid the questions that had threatened to disrupt their society between competing nationalisms.

In these circumstances, the last Imperial Conference to meet before the war met under distinctly unhappy auspices. The main motif of the British Government's proposals marked a return to the circumstances of 1911 and 1917, the need for a considerable increase in Dominion contributions to the armaments burden of the Commonwealth as a whole. Particularly were they interested in investigating the possibility of developing native armaments industries in Canada

---

1. Lord Hankey, *Diplomacy by Conference* (1946), 132.

and Australia. To justify the increased expenditure in armaments they embarked upon in 1936, the Commonwealth ministers were given an unvarnished account of Britain's inability to cope with Germany, Japan and Italy together, and of the efforts being made to reach a *modus vivendi* with each of them. They were told of the decision reluctantly made by the Chiefs of Staff that year that Italy had to be counted as a potential enemy. The Chiefs of Staff themselves pointed out that even with France as an ally the naval position would be extremely precarious. But they did their best to assure the Pacific Dominions that even if the Eastern Mediterranean had to be divided the utmost would be done to maintain Britain's position at Singapore. An appeal was made for an increased naval effort from the Dominions.

But behind the scenes there was little unity. The Canadian representative, though sufficiently impressed to undertake, in the course of a forthcoming visit to Germany, to warn Hitler seriously against the idea that the Dominions would not support Britain, continued to maintain that the function of an Imperial Conference was limited to discussion and review. The South African representative delivered a warning as gratuitous as it was unhelpful that South African aid could not be relied on in the event of British involvement in a war originating in a dispute between Germany and Czechoslovakia. The New Zealand delegate appealed for the stationing of a capital ship squadron in the Far East in peacetime, and lectured the Conference on the virtues of simple morality in deciding the course to be followed in international politics. The Australian representative, acting, it is believed, on promptings from Britain, appealed for the preparation of Commonwealth defence plans by mutual arrangement between those members of the Commonwealth who might be interested. In the event only bilateral talks with Britain were held, and the Australian delegate delivered himself of an appeal for a Pacific Security Pact, which the Permanent Under-Secretary to the British Foreign Office told the American Ambassador in London surprised him very much though 'nothing very much would come of it'.[1] As the Australian official historian has commented, the Conference

never ventured beyond the edge of those vital questions which were facing the British Commonwealth and each of its members.[2]

1. *Foreign Relations of the United States, 1937*, III, 102–3, Bingham to Hull, T.292 of 18 May 1937.
2. *Official History of Australia in World War II*, Paul Hasluck, *The Government and the People 1929–41* (Canberra, 1952), 56.

Even the proposal to encourage the development of a native armaments industry in Canada proved on examination to rest on nothing but rather vague cerebration and to be unbacked by any serious intention to place orders on the scale necessary to call such an industry into being. On the general problems facing the Conference, the British Premier was certainly correct in his view that

in no part of the Commonwealth was opinion then ready for a firm commitment against Hitler by force.[1]

It is surely, then, of significance that the two initial moves in Chamberlain's new policy of appeasement, the invitation to Baron von Neurath, the German Foreign Minister, to visit London, and his first private letter to Mussolini, should follow so immediately on the close of the Conference, the more so as all hope of an accommodation with Japan, talks for which had been in progress since October 1936, collapsed with the outbreak of the 'China incident' at the end of July 1937. This is not the place to set out the policies followed towards Germany and Italy thereafter or the parts played by the Dominions in support of them.[2] It is enough to quote again from Duncan Hall, himself no friend of appeasement:

The policy of appeasement was not merely the policy of the Government of Neville Chamberlain. It was a policy shared in varying degrees by all the Dominion Cabinets and persisted in until the fall of Prague in March 1939. It was as near to being a common foreign policy of the whole British Commonwealth as any policy since 1919.[3]

1. This summary is based on: Hasluck, op. cit., 56–72; Major General Kirby and others, *The War in the Far East*, I, 17–18; J. D. Scott and R. Hughes, *The Administration of War Production* (1955), 58–60; H. Duncan Hall, *North American Supply* (1955), 6; Viscount Templewood, *Nine Troubled Years* (1954), 210; C. M. van den Heever, *General J. B. M. Hertzog* (Johannesburg, 1946), 270–1; *Official History of New Zealand in the Second World War 1939–45*, F. L. W. Wood, *The New Zealand People at War; Political and External Affairs* (Wellington, 1958), 48, 50, 54–5, 58, 66–7, 72, 91–2.

2. The special case of Germany is discussed in the essay immediately following. For Italy, especially the role of Australia, see D. C. Watt, 'Gli accordi mediterranei anglo-italiana del 16 aprile 1938', *Rivista di Studi Politici Internazionali*, XXVI (1959). On the last fatuous South African intervention see also D. C. Watt, 'Pirow's mission to Berlin in November 1938', *Wiener Library Bulletin*, XII (1958).

3. Hall, 'The Commonwealth in War and Peace', *The Commonwealth at War*, 13.

In March 1939 Dominion opinion reacted as positively to Hitler's entry into Prague as did that of Britain itself, and was, we are told[1], a factor which determined Chamberlain in his open abandonment of appeasement in his speech of 19 March at Birmingham. Even then, according to the same source, anxiety about French Canadian opinion was a factor in the hesitancy of his approach to Russia.[2] In the event, however, with the exception of Eire the Commonwealth entered the war as a whole, though with nearly as bitter divisions in South Africa as in 1914.

CONCLUSION

Looking back we can see that it was not, as Sir Edward Grey thought, the establishment of separate Dominion armies and navies, but the establishment of separate Dominions whose governments were primarily responsible to their own electorates which threatened the Empire with the alternatives of disruption or the evolution of a common policy in the field of defence or foreign policy alike. Until 1923 the existence of a common European enemy and the dominance of varying degrees of imperialist sentiment in the Dominions achieved this unity, and a habit of consultation developed which made 'imperial' the consultative machinery evolved to solve the problems of civil-military relations in the home country. After the Canadian refusal in 1923 further to countenance the practice by which the executive organs of the mother country acted in foreign policy in the name of the Empire as a whole, part of that unity was disrupted. The common defence policy continued, however, in part because it suited the pockets of the Dominions and the pride of the mother country, in part because foreign countries refused to accept the Commonwealth as anything but a unity in their defence and disarmament calculations. To avoid publicly acknowledging the effects of the Canadian action and facing its implications in the field of defence, the Home Government continued to consult on its own initiative where it could and to act within the scope of what it imagined consultation would approve where it could not. Imperial foreign policy became a matter of the Emperor's clothes; or would have become that, had not an exterior frame of reference, equally unreal in many respects, been provided by the existence of the

1. Keith Feiling, *The Life of Neville Chamberlain* (1946), 400.
2. Ibid., 408.

League of Nations. When the League's failure to cope successfully with the Abyssinian and Rhineland crises revealed the unreality of the League, the British Government tried to return to the atmosphere of 1911; but the lack of a common imperial sentiment and the existence of a threat *more real to the Pacific Dominions than to Britain herself* made this attempt a failure. Britain continued to act as she imagined the Commonwealth would approve until March 1939 awoke the Dominions to the reality of the threat from Europe and recreated the atmosphere of 1911. In the meantime British statesmen had got into the habit themselves of consulting their own individual ouija-boards as to what Dominions sentiment would or would not approve, and the Dominions seemed mainly to prefer this to direct consultation of the kind which might face them with a choice on which their domestic public opinion was itself too unrealistic to prove of effective guidance.[1] Is the position so very much changed today?

1. Though they reserved to themselves the right to complain. As Sir Joseph Ward wrote in 1929 prior to a gentle complaint on inadequate and over-hasty consultation, 'His Majesty's Government in the United Kingdom act in such matters not only on their own behalf but in a very real sense as the agent or trustee of His Majesty's other Governments' (Wood, *The New Zealand People at War*, 16).

The Influence of the Commonwealth on British Foreign Policy: The Case of the Munich Crisis

IN the previous essay the general strategic background to relations between the outlying members of the Commonwealth and Great Britain in the interwar years was examined, and reference was made to the 'psychological vulnerability' of all British governments in this period to representations on matters of British foreign policy from the Dominions Governments. This essay proposes to examine this point with particular reference to British policy towards Czechoslovakia during the crisis months of 1938 which led up to the Munich conference and the dismemberment of Czechoslovakia with British agreement.

The influence of the Dominions in this period has been one of the most neglected of all factors in such examinations of British foreign policy in this period as have been made both in Britain and on the Continent.[1] In part this is due to technical difficulties over the evidence. The policy of publication of official papers followed by the British Government is such that, with rare exceptions, only the correspondence between the Foreign Office and British representatives abroad is considered for publication.[2] None of the communications with the Governments of the respective Dominions on matters of British foreign policy in the 1930s have been published. To this imbalance in the publication of the official records reaching the Cabinet on which the vital decisions in the field of British foreign policy were taken one must add the fact that while ex-members of the Foreign Office and Diplomatic Services have been prodigal

1. The Dominions are not mentioned at all in Sir Lewis Namier, *Diplomatic Prelude* (1948); J. Wheeler-Bennett, *Munich, Prologue to Tragedy* (1948); Boris Celovsky, *Das Münchener Abkommen von 1938* (Stuttgart, 1958); Martin Gilbert and Richard Gott, *The Appeasers* (1963).

2. A rare and useful exception is the correspondence with the Admiralty on British naval weakness in the Far East published in *Documents on British Foreign Policy, 1919–39*, 3rd Series, VIII, App.1.

publishers of memoirs, their opposite numbers in the Dominions (and India) Offices, on the whole, have not. Nor are we at all well supplied for this period with memoirs from statesmen in the Dominions or their representatives in London or elsewhere.[1]

A further difficulty arises when one attempts to assess the British attitudes to the Dominions in this period. There seem to be two sources of confusion. In the first place, the division of function inside the structure of British administration between those concerned with relations with the Commonwealth and those concerned with the conduct of foreign relations reflects a compartmentalization of British thinking, which is in part a hangover from the nineteenth century.[2] 'Foreign relations' cover only those parts of the world from which foreign influence has not been excluded, Europe, the Mediterranean, the Far East. By a kind of assumed Monroe Doctrine, referred to proudly as the Pax Britannica whenever it cannot be avoided, the Commonwealth, India, Africa, Oceania, Australia and New Zealand lie, with Canada, outside this 'foreign' area.[3]

In the second place the old-style imperialists of the Churchill type, who behave sufficiently like the traditional Continental image of a British imperialist to eliminate any further investigation, are usually thoroughly aware of European problems. Since their driving force is anxiety for Britain's position as a world power they concern themselves as European members of the concert of powers with European problems. The unity and loyalty of the Empire they take on the whole for granted. But to accept their attitudes as the only examples of imperialist thinking in British foreign policy is gravely to overestimate their importance. The really significant group, representing what a recent British historian has called the 'new imperialism',[4] has largely escaped observation.

The origins of this group, their aims, philosophy and attitude to the Dominions and to the United States have been examined in earlier essays in this collection.[5] In considering their role in the Munich

1. For some exceptions see the bibliographical Essay 13 below, section II, subsections 6 and 7.

2. Very well reflected in Lord Avon's memoirs, *Facing the Dictators* (1962).

3. It is too early to say what effects the merging of the Commonwealth Relations and Foreign Services implemented in 1964 will have on this state of affairs.

4. The anonymous author of *The History of 'The Times'*, vol.IV, chapter I, *passim*.

5. See above, Essay 2, and Essay 7.

crisis, a number of further points need to be made. In the first place they were of the foreign-policy-making élite, though few of their number held any formal position within the structure of British political or diplomatic organization. They were, in fact, 'irresponsible' in the strict political sense, intellectual free-lances. Secondly, individual members were in close relations of friendship with Baldwin and Chamberlain and other figures in the British Cabinet, and the drawing-rooms of Cliveden, the Common Room of All Souls[1] and other meeting places enabled those friendships to act as vehicles for the transmission of ideas and opinions from other members of the group to those actually responsible for the vital decisions, or absence of decisions, on policy towards Germany. Thirdly, they were on equally friendly terms and in equally close contact with opinion in the Dominions[2] and with the Dominions High Commissioners in London, especially with Vincent Massey of Canada, Bruce of Australia and, on a slightly more awkward basis, with Te Water of South Africa. Fourthly, they controlled or had easy access to the quality press, especially *The Times* and *The Observer*. Fifthly, being 'irresponsible' they could, if needs be, act as go-betweens in international negotiations, 'volunteer diplomats' in Professor Ferrell's phrase cited above. Sixthly, they had so acted on at least two instances, to mollify the strained relations between Britain and America, firstly in the years 1928–29, and secondly to thwart those forces working for an Anglo-Japanese *rapprochement* at the expense of good relations with America in 1934.[3] Lord Lothian and Geoffrey Dawson are the most significant figures in this group in this connection, though Lord Halifax, who succeeded Eden as Foreign Secretary in 1938, could very well be counted one of their number.

Their attitude to European affairs was guided largely by a lack of direct experience to set against their first-hand experience of the Dominions. The only exception to this was the greatest of them, Leo Amery, who exhibits, perhaps to an extent more marked than anyone else, that compartmentalization of thought referred to above. The others took refuge from their ignorance of Europe in a paradox. In Commonwealth affairs their thinking was infinitely more advanced

1. This can of course be grossly exaggerated. But see the sources cited in Essay 6, p. 119, fn. 5; also A. L. Rowse, *All Souls and Appeasement* (1961).
2. The friendships between Dawson and Vincent Massey, and Lothian and Smuts are especially significant here.
3. See Essay 4 above.

than Churchill's romantic Disraelianism. In European affairs, on the other hand, they harked back to the isolationism of Lord Salisbury, under whose restless realism they had seen South Africa saved for the Empire. The Mediterranean, the Middle East, the Far East even, were avenues of Empire whose importance and significance for Britain their imaginations could encompass. Central Europe was another matter. Britain's interest in Turkish control of the Dardanelles was familiar ground. Britain's interest in the maintenance of the independence and well-being of the successor states to the Habsburg monarchy was not. They knew little of central European problems and disliked what they knew; they preferred the policy of *rapprochement* with Germany advocated so ardently in the 1890s by Neville Chamberlain's father, the arch-imperialist Colonial Secretary and crusader for an imperial tariff.

A further obstacle is provided, one suspects, by the fact that even that section of British opinion which is closest to European ways of thinking on international problems, and indeed uses the same vocabulary to discuss them, approaches these problems with minds conditioned by an education which, especially in the early and most formative stage, emphasizes the maritime and extra-European experiences which differentiate British history from that of the great powers of Europe. Identical language will thus conceal differing presuppositions, misleading both European and British alike. Nowhere are these difficulties outlined above more noticeable than in discussions of British foreign policy in the Czechoslovak crisis of 1938. As events conspired to make the position taken by the British Government of paramount importance, the motives of Neville Chamberlain and his entourage are of the first importance. As the crisis developed, Chamberlain's ascendancy over colleagues and critics alike grew and grew, until in the last ten days he acted alone without considering either the representations of his advisers or the divisions, anxieties and hesitations of those he led. Indeed, Professor Mansergh, in the only detailed study of the relations between the individual Dominions and Great Britain during the Munich crisis, concludes that the views of the Dominions only provided Chamberlain with additional reasons for a course on which he had already determined.[1]

1. P. N. S. Mansergh, *Commonwealth Affairs, Problems of External Policy, 1931–39* (1952).

To disagree with so eminent and authoritative a statement is perhaps dangerous. But two considerations, one technical and one analytic, suggest a certain caution before the question to what degree imperial influences operated on the formation of British policy can be dismissed today on these terms. Technically, there is a little more evidence on which to assess British foreign policy in the first two years of Chamberlain's premiership than was available when Professor Mansergh formed this judgment. Analytically, it might be suggested that Professor Mansergh's dictum concerns only the effect which direct representations by Dominions Governments had on British policy; in this it still cannot be challenged. But there is also the question of the influence the knowledge that such representations would be made had on the formation of British policy.

This distinction becomes of particular importance when the character of Neville Chamberlain is considered. The more this is studied, the plainer it seems to appear that his most dominant characteristics were an unshakeable reliance on his own judgment and ruthless single-mindedness in the execution of that judgment. Pliability in the modification rather than the execution of a policy he never possessed. Once his mind was made up on a course of action he pursued it to the bitter end. He was in no sense a deep or original thinker. One looks in vain in the extracts from his diary printed by his biographers[1] for some indication that he thought the principles, on which the measures of policy he discussed there were presumably based, to be in any way relevant. He seems rather to have taken the structure of his ideas from his friends. Brooding on them in solitude, he contributed to them a strength of conviction which imposed itself even over those elements in the situation which conflicted with them.

These traits of character make his close relationship with Dawson and Halifax of great significance. Dawson was far from being Chamberlain's creature as has often been suggested. He was to some extent his 'ideas man'; and he may well have on occasion agreed with Chamberlain to act as the mouth-piece for ideas which he shared with Chamberlain and which they agreed might need ventilating.

The position of Halifax is of even greater importance. Since 1936 he had been displaying signs of wanting to conduct his own foreign policy. In March 1936 he accompanied Eden to Paris to

1. Keith Feiling, *The Life of Neville Chamberlain* (1946); Iain Macleod, *Neville Chamberlain* (1961).

restrain the French from answering Hitler's reoccupation of the Rhineland by the resort to arms. There was a proposal that he should go to Berlin in the summer of 1936 during the abortive negotiations for a Western security pact to replace Locarno. He did, in fact, visit Germany in November 1937 as part of the reformulated policy of appeasement decided on in the summer of 1937 and delayed by von Neurath's cancellation of his visit to London in June and by the encouragement of piracy by Mussolini in the Mediterranean during August. He succeeded Eden as Foreign Minister on Eden's resignation in February 1938. The attitude of the Dominions and India, as expressed at the Imperial Conference in 1937 and during 1938, is one to which it is difficult to believe that he would not be sympathetic.[1]

The attitudes of the individual Dominions to the problems of Europe were at once complex in their origins and simple in their effects. In Canada, Australia and New Zealand, the parties of the Left shared the isolationism and revulsion against the Versailles settlement of their equivalents in America and Britain. While they did not carry their isolationism to the extent America did of withdrawing from the whole structure of the Treaty, they were equally disgusted by the contrast between ideals and power-political realities revealed at the Versailles conference. The League of Nations became for them as for the British Left a protection for their isolationism, a protection, that is, from the power-political realities which they found so difficult to square with their dominant idealism. The Liberal Government in Canada and the Labour Government in New Zealand were particular embodiments of this idea. In Canada and in South Africa the racial attitudes of the French Canadians and the Boers reinforced this isolationism. Field-Marshal Smuts had, indeed, only signed the Treaty under protest, and had played a vital part in encouraging Keynes to write his *Economic Consequences of the Peace*. India was preoccupied with the movement towards independence; and even the most feudal of her native leaders, the Aga Khan, a member of the British Empire delegation to the Versailles conference, shared in this the attitude of the British Left. Australia and Canada were further concerned with Japan's advances in China and the Pacific, especially in view of their laws against Japanese immigration. All these different motives led to the identical conviction that war in Europe was something to be avoided at all

---

1. See the remarks in his memoirs, *Fulness of Days* (1958), 197–8, 205.

costs. This point of view was expressed most forcibly at the Imperial Conference of 1937 by General Hertzog:

I maintain that peace in Europe can be assured today and should be assured if Great Britain approached Germany in the same spirit of friendly co-operation that she has shown France since 1919. I sincerely hope that I shall not be accused of unfriendly feelings towards the British government if I say that the impression so far given by Great Britain's attitude towards Germany is far too much one of cold repelling indifference compared with the warm welcome given to France. . . . If war did come because England continued to associate with France in a policy in respect of central and eastern Europe calculated to threaten Germany's existence through unwillingness to set right the injustices flowing from the Treaty of Versailles, South Africa cannot be expected to take part in the war. . . .[1]

The mention of Czechoslovakia shows, if any indication is needed, that the British Cabinet and the Dominions were already prepared or German demands over the Sudetenland. Halifax informed Hitler that Britain did not regard the *status quo* in Eastern Europe as immutable when he visited Germany in November 1937.[2] From other remarks dropped by Halifax on this occasion, it appears that the British Cabinet would have liked to have seen international talks on a peaceful modification of the *status quo* on Germany's eastern frontiers, and that some kind of initiative on these lines was planned immediately after the Imperial Conference for the visit which von Neurath was to have made to London in June 1937.[3]

There is further evidence to suggest that the failure of the Dominions to respond to the picture of the danger from Germany painted them by Eden and Baldwin at the Imperial Conference in 1937,[4] had a very considerable influence on the policy of seeking a new accommodation with Germany (and Italy) embarked upon by the British Government in the summer of 1937. This lies in the changing attitude of Chamberlain himself to Germany. It is not usually realized that Chamberlain himself was the main force within the Cabinet behind the rearmament programme embarked upon in 1935, so much so that he was Baldwin's first choice for the post of Defence Minister, finally accepted under the curious title of Minister for the Co-ordination of Defence, by Sir Thomas Inskip.[5] His attitude

1. C. M. van den Heever, *General J. B. M. Hertzog* (Johannesburg, 1946), 270–1.
2. *Documents on German Foreign Policy, 1918–45*, Series D, I, no.31.
3. Ibid., Series D, III, nos 281, 287, 291, 293, 298, 346.
4. Avon, *Facing the Dictators*, 444–5.   5. See Essay 5 above.

was governed by a conviction of British weakness and of the menace to world peace represented by Germany. In the Abyssinian crisis of 1935 he was a supporter of sanctions against Italy, for the effect they would have, if successful, on Germany, at least until the obstacles in the way of their successful implementation converted him to the view that the League was an infirm and unreliable vehicle for British policy. His attitude to Germany does not seem to have altered, however, as is shown by his exchange of letters with his opposite number, Henry Morgenthau, Secretary to the US Treasury, in March 1937.[1] The bulk of the letter was drafted in the Foreign Office, but Chamberlain himself added part or the whole of the following passage:

The main source of this fear of war in Europe is to be found in Germany. No other country, not Italy, since she had her hands full with the task of consolidating her Abyssinian conquests, nor Russia, with all her military preparations, certainly not France, England nor any of the smaller powers is for a moment credited with any aggressive designs. But the fierce propaganda continually carried out by the German press and radio under the instructions of Dr Goebbels, the intensity and persistence of German military preparations, together with the many acts of the German government in violation of treaties, cynically justified on the grounds that unilateral action was the quickest way of getting what they wanted, have inspired all her neighbours with a profound uneasiness. Even these islands, which could be reached in less than an hour from German territory by an air force equipped with hundreds of tons of bombs, cannot be exempt from anxiety.

The motive for this aggressiveness on the part of Germany appears to arise from her desire to make herself so strong that no one will venture to withstand whatever demands she may make, whether for European or colonial territory.

With this intention in her heart, she is not likely to agree to any disarmament which would defeat her purpose. The only consideration which would influence her to a contrary decision would be the conviction that her efforts to secure superiority of force were doomed to failure by reason of the superior force, which would meet her if she attempted aggression....[2]

1. For the circumstances of the correspondence see J. M. Blum, *From the Morgenthau Diaries* (Boston, 1959), 458–67.

2. The text of this is taken from the copy forwarded to President Roosevelt by Morgenthau and preserved in the Roosevelt Papers, *PSF I, Diplomatic Correspondence*, GB 1933–38, Box 7. That this passage or parts of it were added by Chamberlain to the Foreign Office draft is stated in Avon, *Facing the Dictators*, 527.

These are not the arguments of a naïve man, easily convertible to pro-German sentiments, but those of one clear as to the danger Germany represented, and determined only to negotiate with Germany for the preservation of peace, as and when Britain and France had reached a position of sufficient strength to be able to rule out any resort to force by Germany. It is clear from the remainder of the letter that he did not feel that that position had as yet been reached, though he thought it to be attainable. It needed only two months at most for this attitude to change, two months in which the most significant international events were the Imperial Conference and his own assumption of office.

From the moment the Anschluss with Austria was successfully achieved, it was clear that a crisis over Czechoslovakia was imminent. The British attitude throughout this crisis remained absolutely unchanged. To the French and the Czechs, emphasis was laid on Britain's determination not to become involved in central European problems by guaranteeing Czechoslovakia's frontiers. In the British view, the conflict lay essentially between the Czech Government and her minorities, the danger being that Hitler's notoriously violent passions might lead him to seize an occasion to intervene and annex the Sudetenland as he had Austria. If he did act in this fashion, neither the Czechs nor their French and Soviet allies could rely on automatic support from Britain. The British were not prepared to fight a war to keep the Sudeten Germans under Czech rule. To the Germans on the other hand, the British emphasized that should Hitler choose the way of the sword rather than negotiation, he could not rely on Britain standing aloof. If he risked war, then he must risk it spreading beyond those immediately involved.

The first public expression of this view came in Chamberlain's speech of 24 March 1938; it was reiterated at the time of the 'weekend crisis' of 21–2 May and again in Sir John Simon's speech at Lanark on 27 August. It is worth noticing that the Canadian High Commissioner in London, Vincent Massey, told Dawson on 21 March, that he thought Canadian opinion would support Chamberlain's policy of restraint;[1] that the Australian Government's reaction

1. Sir Evelyn Wrench, *Geoffrey Dawson and Our Times* (1955), 369. Dawson saw Chamberlain the same day. The view that the invitation to Neurath marks the beginning of the new policy of appeasement is confirmed by a letter from Chamberlain to the American Norman Davis, of 8 July 1937: 'I had hoped that this visit might have led to a clarification of the

to the week-end crisis was to express publicly their hope that Britain's representations to Czechoslovakia would pave the way for a peaceful solution;[1] that on 20 July Halifax rejected a proposal to go beyond Chamberlain's speech of 24 March and disclosed to the French the British plan to send a neutral mediator in the person of Lord Runciman, in these terms:

We should make it plain to Dr Beneš that in no circumstances would we accept a commitment to go beyond the position as stated by the Prime Minister on March 24. Indeed I told the French Ministers . . . that before I had come to Paris I had received a visit from the Aga Khan during which he had stressed the responsibility that lay upon His Majesty's Government to accept no commitments that might land the British Empire in war. The same I said would be the position of South Africa.[2]

When the French chargé d'affaires in London made a similar proposal on 25 August Halifax repeated his objections in almost identical terms:

The position of His Majesty's Government was as defined on March 24 . . . and . . . we cannot go beyond it. Quite apart from the merits, the certain result of any attempt to accept on behalf of this country any more specific commitments would be to evoke violent opposition from several quarters here and also probably in the Dominions which would have an immediate effect exactly contrary to that which a stronger statement might hope to achieve.[3]

The approach of the Nuremberg Party Day and the probability that Hitler would seize the occasion further to inflame German opinion against Czechoslovakia stirred at least two Commonwealth Governments into action. After a lengthy meeting on 1 September, the Australian Government instructed their High Commissioner in London to tell the British Government of the Australian endorsement of Chamberlain's speech of 24 March and Simon's restatement of it

---

position between this country and Germany' (*Norman H. Davis Papers*, Box 8).

    1. Statement by Mr Hughes, Australian Minister for External Affairs, 25 May 1938, *Australia, Parliamentary Debates, House of Representatives*, vol. 155, 1375–6.

    2. *Documents on British Foreign Policy, 1919–39*, 3rd Series, I, no.523. The Memoirs of the Aga Khan do not refer to this incident, but show that his views were in general as Halifax described them (*The Memoirs of the Aga Khan* (1954), 264–5).

    3. *D.B.F.P.*, 3rd Series, II, no.691.

at Lanark, and urged that the Czech Government should be urged to make an immediate public statement of the 'most liberal concessions it could offer'.[1] Menzies, Australia's Attorney-General, visited Germany in July 1938 and came back convinced, as he said later, that 'it would be wrong had Europe drifted into a war in which the merits were distributed'.[2]

The same day, 1 September, the South African Premier, General Hertzog, drafted a statement on the attitude to be adopted by South Africa in the event of Britain becoming involved in a European war arising out of a dispute between Germany and Czechoslovakia. It was equivalent to a statement of neutrality. He showed it first to the Minister of Defence, Pirow, and then to Smuts and the inner cabinet. After a day's consideration Smuts accepted it.[3] The significance of these events was not lost on Britain as a memorandum in the American diplomatic archives shows. On 7 September the British chargé d'affaires in Washington handed over a memorandum on instructions from Halifax, expounding British policy.[4] Enlarging on it, he commented on the basic dilemma which faced British policy makers: if they stayed out of war Germany would have an immense accretion of strength, while if they entered a war brought about by Czech resistance to Germany they would in a peace settlement have to avoid the original mistake of putting the Sudetens under Czech rule:

Furthermore it was becoming clear that the Dominions were isolationist and there would be no sense in fighting a war which would break the British Empire while trying to secure the safety of the United Kingdom.[5]

During the September days the Dominions governments were kept fully informed of the situation both by direct telegrams to the Dominions capitals and by almost daily meetings between the High Commissioners and Malcolm MacDonald, the Secretary of State for the Dominions.[6] The main lead in representations to the British Government was taken by the Australian and South African High

1. Statement by the Australian Prime Minister, Lyons, 28 September 1938, *Australia, Parl. Deb., H. of R.*, vol.157, 306 ff.
2. Ibid., 432.
3. Oswald Pirow, *James Barry Munnik Hertzog* (1958), 226–7.
4. *D.B.F.P.*, 3rd Series, 11, 252.
5. *Foreign Relations of the United States, 1938*, 1, 580–1.
6. See the extracts from Vincent Massey's diary printed in his *What's Past is Prologue* (1964), 257–62.

Commissioners, Bruce[1] and Te Water.[2] The Canadian High Commissioner, Vincent Massey, spoke without instructions from his government,[3] who under the leadership of Mackenzie King deliberately refused to take any line whatever, but there can be little doubt that he spoke for much of Canadian opinion. The Irish High Commissioner, Dulanty, took the same line as his Australian and South African colleagues.[4] The New Zealand High Commissioner chose to spend the whole month of the crisis in Geneva,[4] which can hardly have been without his government's approval. The High Commissioners thoroughly approved Chamberlain's policy, exerting pressure only when it looked as if the British Government were abandoning its hopes of a settlement and resigning itself to conflict. Two out of the four, Vincent Massey and Bruce, were in close contact with Dawson and *The Times*.[5]

The main weight of their representations was exerted after the Godesberg meeting between Hitler and Chamberlain, and the latter's discovery of German intransigence.[6] In the night of 22 September, Vincent Massey, the Canadian High Commissioner, was wakened from sleep by MacDonald's private secretary with a telegram to the Dominions' capitals to the effect that Hitler's 'attitude had been unsatisfactory'. The following day, MacDonald explained that 'Hitler's insistence on moving German troops into the Sudeten area was impossible to accept on the ground that it violates the principle of peaceful negotiations and secondly . . . it unmasks a man of wider and more dangerous ambitions than he admitted even to Chamberlain'. Chamberlain was, however, 'prepared to go a considerable distance to compromise', an attitude of which Massey approved, 'So long as there is no real surrender of principle it is worth taking a very sharp corner to get past this crisis and save civilization as we know it. . . .'

During the following two days, while the Cabinet decided that

1. Bruce poured out his worries to Dawson on 27 September. See Wrench, *Geoffrey Dawson*, 278; Massey, op. cit., 258–9.
2. Te Water resigned his position as High Commissioner in September 1939 from opposition to South African involvement in the Second World War. See also Massey, op. cit., 258–61.
3. Massey, op. cit., 258–60.
4. Ibid., 259–60.
5. *The History of 'The Times'*, vol.IV, 938, 940; Massey, op. cit., 260.
6. The reconstruction which follows is based mainly on Massey's diary, op. cit.

Hitler's terms were unacceptable (25 September), gave assurances of British support to France and allowed Czechoslovakia to mobilize (26 September), the High Commissioners continued their representations to MacDonald. On the 24th, Massey recorded,

all four of the High Commissioners . . . take a view on the basic issue rather different from MacDonald's emphasis. We are all prepared to pay a higher price for peace than he. . . . Bruce . . . feels very strongly that the German proposals *can't* be allowed to be a *casus belli* and says so on behalf of his government. Te Water and Dulanty speak with great vehemence as well. I take the same line.

The following day, Massey expressed his alarm at the tone of the British press:

Can we let war break out – universal war with its appalling consequences – over the method by which the Sudeten territory – already enclosed – is to be actually transferred. It is unthinkable.

His alarm led him to move Dawson to see Halifax, and get Bruce 'to do all he could'. Dawson, in fact, saw the three other High Commissioners either that day or early on the 26th. Bruce delivered 'a helpful message' to Chamberlain on behalf of his government.

On 26 September, the day Sir Horace Wilson was dispatched to Berlin to attempt to get Hitler to moderate the tone of his speech at the Sportpalast and to warn him of British support for France and Czechoslovakia, the High Commissioners met MacDonald in the morning and Chamberlain in the evening. 'All four H.C.s . . . feel that the German proposals should not be allowed to wreck peace.' Chamberlain gave them a full account of his exertions over the previous ten days.

I gathered, he had reluctantly come to the conclusion that Hitler's profession of limited objectives was not sincere and that his ambitions were far wider than the boundaries of the Sudetenland. . . .

27 September was the critical day. That day the Cabinet heard the Dominions' views in detail, together with a telegram from Lyons, the Australian premier. Although Duff Cooper, the most European-minded of the Cabinet, argued strongly against their acceptance, stigmatizing them as unrepresentative of the real feeling in the Dominions,[1] his views were not borne out by the anxieties of the

1. Viscount Norwich, *Old Men Forget* (1955), 239–40.

High Commissioners. That same morning, they tackled MacDonald until 2 a.m. the following morning.

We all made it clear for ourselves (and some spoke for their governments) that there might be a dangerous reaction in the Dominions to a decision to plunge the Empire into war on the issue of how Hitler was to take possession of territory already ceded to him in principle . . . surely the world can't be plunged into the horrors of universal war over a few miles of territory or a few days one way or other in a time-table. That thank God! is I believe Chamberlain's view and that of his Cabinet. . . .[1]

An indication of how correct this assessment of Dominions opinion was for at least one crucial Dominion was given when Hertzog assembled the South African Cabinet on 28 September and put before them the declaration of policy he had prepared three weeks previously. Its text was as follows:

The existing relations between the Union of South Africa and the various belligerent parties shall, so far as the Union is concerned, remain unchanged and continue as if no war were being waged, with the understanding however that the existing relationships and obligations between the Union and Great Britain and any other members of the British Commonwealth of Nations in so far as those relationships and obligations are the result of contractual obligations concerning the naval base at Simonstown; or of its membership of the League of Nations; or in so far as the relationships etc, may be regarded simply as flowing from the free association of the Union with other members of the Commonwealth, shall remain unaltered and shall be maintained by the Union; and that no-one shall be permitted to make use of Union territory for any purpose calculated to infringe the said relationships and obligations.[2]

The declaration was agreed to unanimously. That same day Lyons again cabled, suggesting an appeal to Mussolini, and proposing that Bruce, the High Commissioner in London, should fly to Rome with a personal message, if Chamberlain thought it would serve any useful purpose. The message found Chamberlain in bed (because of the difference in international time, it must have arrived in the small hours of the morning of 28 September).[3] The proposal was similar to one made by Lord Perth, the British Ambassador in Rome,[4]

1. Massey, op. cit., 261.
2. van den Heever, 275–6; Pirow, 227.
3. Lyons Statement of 29 September 1938; 157, *Australia, Parl. Deb., H. of R.*, 332–3.
4. *D.B.F.P.*, 3rd Series, II, no.1125.

who had already been instructed in a formal *démarche* to express the British hope that Mussolini would use his influence with Hitler to get him to accept Chamberlain's undertaking of 27 September to see that the Godesberg proposals were carried out by the Czechs.[1] After Lyons' message had been received, however, Perth was instructed to convey a personal message from Chamberlain to Mussolini asking him to support Chamberlain's new proposals for a quadripartite conference in Germany to negotiate the transfer of the Sudetenland to Germany.[2] The evidence is inconclusive, but it seems possible that Lyons' message may have had something to do with the reinforcement of Perth's original instructions.

It is clear on the evidence available that had the British Government pursued a course animated by other sentiments than those which inspired them, they would have lost the backing of South Africa, have found Australia divided and unhappy and might well have put the Canadian Government in a very difficult position; and that they had considerable advance warning of this from the Dominions High Commissioners in London, and the Dominions Governments. The advance warning of the attitude of the Dominions given at the Imperial Conference of 1937, reiterated by the Dominions High Commissioners after the occupation of Austria, is of great importance in explaining the rigidity of the British determination not to become involved in central Europe, expressed in the combination of extreme pressure on Beneš to make concessions to the demands of the Sudeten Germans, and evasiveness whenever Beneš tried to extract some assurance of Western support with which to buttress himself in making such concessions against Czech public opinion.

The knowledge of Dominions opposition to the idea of a war over Czechoslovakia is, of course, only one of the factors which went to make up the policy of appeasement which reached its culmination at Munich. There were other equally important factors in the general weakness of the British position when faced with the possibility of war, which Chamberlain and Halifax felt so strongly. The moral strength of the German nationalist case against Versailles, if judged, as they came to judge it, by that curious combination of power-political principles and Wilsonian morality which ruled international politics

---

1. *D.B.F.P.*, 3rd Series, II, no.1121, fn. 2, and 1125 fn. 2. The instructions were sent to Perth at 11.00 p.m. on the evening of 27 September.

2. *D.B.F.P.*, 3rd Series, II, nos 1140, 1159, 1161, 1165, 1166, 1167 and 1231. See also *Ciano's Diaries, 1937–38*, entry of 28 September 1938.

between the wars, and their consciousness of British military weakness were possibly more important. Most important perhaps, given these considerations, was their consciousness of the lost opportunities of 1930–36, the opportunities of reaching agreement with Hitler's predecessors, the opportunities of maintaining a Franco-Italian front against Hitler, the opportunities of tying him down with new pacts which he himself had negotiated, opportunities which French opposition, the state of British public opinion and, it should be added, Hitler's own evasiveness had denied them. All of this added up to the conviction that in 1938 they were in no state to go to war, and that to maintain Czech rule over the Sudetens until a peace conference would provide the opportunity of returning them to Germany, was no cause on which to fight one.

PART IV

Contemporary Problems

ESSAY 9

Divided Control of British Foreign Policy – Danger or Necessity?

THE appointment of Lord Home as Foreign Secretary with Mr Edward Heath as his representative, with Cabinet rank as Lord Privy Seal, in the Commons, and Mr Heath's subsequent appointment as head of the team of negotiators concerned with Britain's entry into the Common Market, gave rise to a good deal of public anxiety. Fears were widely voiced lest the arrangement prove inefficient. The bogey of divided control of foreign policy was again raised. Such anxieties are not, of course, new in British politics. When, in June 1935, Baldwin made Sir Samuel Hoare Foreign Secretary, with Anthony Eden as Minister without Portfolio for League of Nations affairs, holding Cabinet rank, yet also within the Foreign Office, Winston Churchill gave them classic expression in the House of Commons:

I am very glad indeed that the Prime Minister said that this was only a temporary experiment. I cannot feel that it will last long or ever be renewed. . . . We need the integral thought of a single man responsible for Foreign Affairs, ranging over the entire field and making every factor and every incident contribute to the general purpose on which the Cabinet has agreed. The Foreign Secretary, whoever he is, whichever he is, must be supreme in his department and everyone in that great Office ought to look to him and to him alone. . . . There is no reason why a strong Cabinet Committee should not sit with the Foreign Secretary every day in these difficult times, or why the Prime Minister should not see him or his officials at any time; but when the topic is so complicated and vast, when it is in such continued flux, it seems to me that confusion will only be made worse confounded by dual allegiances and equal dual responsibilities.[1]

There is, in fact, a whole mythology of 'dualism', 'dyarchy' as Churchill called it, in the control of foreign policy. According to this version of the constitutional developments and practices of the last eight years, every example of divided control of foreign policy has

1. Winston S. Churchill, *The Gathering Storm* (1948).

177

been unsuccessful, and the intentions behind it pernicious and un-constitutional. But it is possible to argue, without denying the force of the examples on which this mythology rests, that the ideas behind it are based on a confusion of issues and an oversimplified theory of ministerial responsibility. These ideas fasten, so it can be argued, on the role of the *individual* Minister as head of and parliamentary spokesman for his department, and neglect his role as member of a Cabinet, whose members are *collectively* responsible for government policy. There can be no complete division of interest and responsibility between members of a Cabinet who are collectively responsible for its decisions. To see the issues raised by the examples on which the mythology of 'dualism' rests as lying between unitary and divided control of foreign policy is to be mistaken.

To make this clearer one should perhaps consider the illustrations usually adduced to back the generally accepted view of the evils of 'dualism'. They are taken in most cases from the two great examples in recent years of Prime Ministerial diplomacy in conflict with Foreign Secretarial policy, the feud between Lloyd George and Curzon, and the clash between Chamberlain and Eden. In both cases these were marked by the Prime Minister's development of alternative lines of diplomatic communication with foreign governments, and alternative offices of execution, in Lloyd George's case the so-called 'Garden Suburb' and his use of his private secretaries, Edward Grigg, Philip Kerr and later Thomas Jones, and in Neville Chamberlain's case his use of Sir Horace Wilson and Sir Joseph Ball. These are not, of course, the only examples. In the second Labour Government, Ramsay MacDonald reserved the field of Anglo-American relations to himself. At the London Naval Conference of 1930 the American Secretary of State, Stimson, was forced once or twice to intervene to explain the American position on a consultative pact clearly to Arthur Henderson, the Labour Foreign Secretary, to prevent him from publicly advancing proposals (which the American delegation would have felt bound to oppose) under the mistaken impression that they were in accordance with the American line of thought.[1] In his recent *History of British Foreign Policy in the Second World War*, Sir Llewellyn Woodward has given a few similar examples of a breakdown in communication between Premier and Foreign Secretary, arising out of the Prime Minister's activities in the field of diplomacy.

1. *Henry L. Stimson Diary, Trip to Europe 1930*, III, entry of 22 March 1930.

These are not, however, examples of the evils of dual control. No one would presumably deny the Prime Minister's right to intervene in the conduct of foreign relations. The real issues at stake here are two: those of intra-Cabinet relations, and that of the proper and efficient use of the machinery of government. Good relations between members of the Cabinet are all-important to the Cabinet system as such, and for a Prime Minister to act behind his Foreign Secretary's back in the latter's field of responsibility is merely silly – and as heinous, no more or less, as his pursuit of a different policy from that of the responsible Minister in any field of ministerial responsibility. It is not so much dyarchy as anarchy. The Cabinet system of government together with the regular if not automatic circulation of all important Foreign Office papers to all Cabinet Ministers and Government departments, is designed to eliminate this kind of activity. It is worth noting, however, that during his tenure of the Foreign Office under Lloyd George, Balfour, appreciating the freedom of action open to the Prime Minister, never chose to make an issue of Lloyd George's incursions into diplomacy;[1] and that Halifax, who succeeded Eden as Foreign Secretary in February 1938, was able to rebuke Chamberlain for acting on his own without prior consultation, and secure an undertaking that it should not happen again.[2] Only where relations were strained for other reasons, in that in addition to personal conflicts, the Foreign Secretaries concerned, Curzon and Eden, chose to assert the individual responsibility of the Foreign Secretary's Office, did the practice end in direct conflict and resignation. In both cases also there was a direct conflict of policy, in Curzon's case between Lloyd George's support of the Greek invasion of Turkey and Curzon's more realistic appreciation of its inevitable and disastrous end, in Eden's case on the price to be paid for securing a

1. Curzon, true to his principles, regarded Balfour's inaction as proof of his laziness and frivolity. But Balfour was not unaware of the constitutional issues involved, and the hostility between the two men went a good deal deeper than disagreement upon such issues.

2. The occasion had to do with a talk to Lobby correspondents in which Chamberlain gave an optimistic estimate of the international scene which Halifax thought both unwarranted in fact, and likely to be unfortunate in its effects. For Halifax's letter see Keith Feiling, *The Life of Neville Chamberlain* (1946), 396–7. For Chamberlain's apology see Edward Wood, 1st Earl of Halifax, *Fulness of Days* (1957), 237–8. Halifax did, however, conclude his letter by remarking 'Nobody recognizes more readily than I do that the *ultimate* responsibility must be yours.'

cessation of Italy's anti-British policy in the Mediterranean and Middle East, and the question whether the price paid would be a once-and-for-all payment or merely the first instalment of a purchase on the 'never-never' system.

The failure of both Lloyd George and Chamberlain to use normal Foreign Office and diplomatic channels of communication with foreign governments was equally stupid and unnecessary. Their example was not followed by Ramsay MacDonald in his division of labour with Henderson. His negotiations with the United States Government in 1929–30 were handled through normal diplomatic channels, and he made effective use of Sir Robert Vansittart, who was to become Permanent Under-Secretary in the Foreign Office under him, and Sir Robert Craigie, head of the American department.

The explanations for Lloyd George's and Chamberlain's neglect of the normal machinery of government can be found in a combination of three factors, besides purely personal idiosyncrasies. First, both fell victim to the recurrent epidemic of contempt for and suspicion of 'traditional diplomacy' and its professional practitioners, attitudes which then as today confuse the necessary practices of professional diplomacy with the allegedly over-narrow social strata from which its members are recruited. Second, there were in both cases genuine and deep-rooted divisions and confusions of counsel within the country as a whole, which were reflected in the composition of the Cabinet, and whose resolution seemed even more politically perilous than a certain stretching of intra-Cabinet relations. Third, their 'usurpation' of the Foreign Secretary's role seemed to develop naturally out of the gradual evolution of the office and official personality of the Prime Minister to a status, which in the eyes of the public at least, stands considerably higher than that of even his most powerful Cabinet colleagues. This evolution has been accompanied by a corresponding devaluation in the Foreign Secretary's position in negotiations with foreign governments. The large number of foreign countries today ruled under a presidential or plebiscitary system of political leadership has hastened this process, as has the increasing appeal of 'summit' conferences.

The Cabinet system of government carries the corollary of Cabinet responsibility for and control of foreign policy as it does in any other field of governmental activity. But it allows for two differing interpretations of the role of the Secretary of State for Foreign Affairs. In the one, well summed up in Churchill's speech cited above, the

Foreign Secretary is the originator of policy proposals and the principal spokesman in the field of foreign affairs in Cabinet and Parliament. Curzon and Eden certainly held this doctrine in their hearts, though Eden had little opportunity to practise it. Austen Chamberlain under Baldwin, Hoare under Baldwin (to his own detriment) and Bevin under Attlee are perhaps its most obvious practitioners. The acceptance of such an interpretation is not without its dangers. It led Curzon and Eden so to absorb the outlook of the professional diplomatist as to think diplomatic considerations all-important and to neglect or ignore the more general considerations of democratic politics. In Eden's case this persisted into his occupancy of the office of Prime Minister, as his recently published memoirs eloquently witness.[1] It is a curious paradox that he, who is generally believed to have suffered more than most Foreign Secretaries from intervention from other members of the Cabinet into that conduct of foreign affairs which was his special responsibility, should have been one of the most flagrant offenders (if it be an offence) when he ceased to be Foreign Secretary and became Prime Minister.

There is the alternative interpretation of the Foreign Secretary's role – one much nearer the true spirit of the doctrine of Cabinet responsibility – in which the Foreign Secretary is the representative of the Cabinet acting in its name both in the day-to-day administration of foreign affairs and as the channel by which the *professional* advisers of the Government in that field can make their advice known to the Cabinet. Under this interpretation the Foreign Office and diplomatic service play the part of counsellor and executant, but responsibility for deciding policy lies with the Cabinet.

It will be seen that the first of these two interpretations of the role of the Foreign Secretary is essentially a monopolistic one. There is an excellent statement of the two viewpoints in an exchange of notes between Curzon and Churchill at a Cabinet meeting recorded by Curzon's most recent biographer.[2] Curzon wrote:

My dear Winston, I wonder what you would say if on a colonial subject I felt myself at liberty to make a speech – quite independent of the Colonial Office and critical of its chief.

and received the reply

You may say anything you like about the Colonial Office that is sincerely meant. But there is no comparison between these vital foreign matters

1. Earl of Avon, *Full Circle* (1960).
2. Leonard Mosley, *Curzon, the End of an Epoch* (1960), 216.

which affect the whole future of the world and the mere departmental topics with which the Colonial Office is concerned. For these great matters we must be allowed opinions.

Under the first interpretation of the role of the Foreign Secretary, dualism is impossible without conflict or deceit, except where the individual is momentarily content, as Curzon oddly was during the Washington Conference of 1921–22, to abdicate his claims. But under the second it is perfectly possible, and there are plenty of precedents for it. It has usually taken the form of division of function or field of activity, and despite the cases cited by the mythologists it has worked perfectly adequately. The simplest and oldest divisions arose when the Foreign Secretary was absent at a conference. Since each Secretary of State has full power to transact the business of any and every other Secretary of State, the Foreign Secretary can divide the functions of his office, concentrating the vital matters in his hands (copies of political telegrams, etc., being forwarded to wherever he is staying), and leaving the routine direction of the department to be conducted by some other Secretary of State. When Lord Salisbury attended the Berlin Conference in 1878, this practice was followed, his general duties being conducted by the Home Secretary. This in itself is not unusual. On at least three occasions, direction of the Foreign Office has been handed over to someone not a Secretary of State: in 1898 to Balfour (who was not even of Cabinet rank), during Lord Salisbury's illness; in 1917 to Lord Robert Cecil, during Balfour's absence in America (this was during the War Cabinet period when even Balfour did not, strictly speaking, have Cabinet rank); and in 1928 to Lord Cushendun during Austen Chamberlain's illness.

These are, of course, temporary divisions of function. More permanent divisions can be found in the appointment of Lord Robert Cecil as Minister of Blockade in 1916 to deal, among other matters, with all aspects of the blockade which impinged upon our foreign relations; in the appointment of the same Lord Robert Cecil, and, on his resignation in 1927, of Lord Cushendun, as Chancellor of the Duchy of Lancaster with special responsibility for disarmament negotiations and policy within the Cabinet and Foreign Office; in Lord Reading's continued tenancy of the Attorney-Generalship, an office of Cabinet rank, while acting as Ambassador in the United States, 1917–18; in the institution of Minister of State in the Middle East and in North Africa during the Second World War and the curious position of the High Commissioner for South-East Asia in postwar years; though of these last only the Minister of State in the Middle East had Cabinet rank. It should be noted that each case precisely fitted Churchill's criticism of the Eden–Hoare arrangement. The Ministers concerned in no case had their own departments but continued to work with the appropriate officials and sections in the Foreign Office. Dispatches of course were not sent in their name but in that of the Foreign Secretary. Otherwise arrangements were probably even more 'dyarchic' than those to which Churchill objected, as Hoare did not hesitate to intervene at Geneva in September 1935; though one would have presumed that representation of His Majesty's Government at the League Assembly would, above all other tasks, have fallen to the 'Minister for League Affairs'.

Such divisions raise, of course, the question of co-ordination and communication. The latter function is taken care of in part by the 'confidential print', and in part by maintaining the position of the Foreign Office and Foreign Service as the sole executants and channels of communication with foreign governments. There are, however, cases where the practices of those governments makes this impossible. The preference for the unofficial emissary or the 'volunteer diplomat', as Professor Robert H. Ferrell has called the species, is a good deal stronger outside the British Isles than it is at home. Foreign Secretaries themselves have employed, and the Foreign Office has condoned, the use of demi-official channels where official channels seemed unproductive or blocked. The most extraordinary case is probably that of Sir William Wiseman and the late Lord Murray of Elibank, who graduated from employment on intelligence matters in America to being the principal channel of communication between the Foreign Secretary and President Wilson in the years 1917–19.[1] During the Second World War the American Embassy was authorized to communicate directly with other departments of state in Britain without the mediation of the Foreign Office.

The function of co-ordination is taken care of by the development of the Cabinet committee system both at the ministerial and the departmental level. Lord Robert Cecil and Lord Cushendun, for example, took their instructions on British disarmament policy from a Cabinet committee of which they were members, headed by the Marquess of Salisbury as Lord Privy Seal. The temptation always is to substitute an overriding Minister or 'overlord', as the Ministry of

1. Sir Arthur Willert, *The Road to Safety* (1951).

Defence was substituted for the Committee of Imperial Defence; but it is a retrograde step. For the Common Market negotiations, the late Government resorted to the *ad hoc* committee system, under the chairmanship of the ubiquitous Mr Butler.

These committees, of course, reported to the Cabinet as a whole, and their membership was drawn from the Ministers, whether in or out of the Cabinet, whose departmental interests were involved in the particular sets of negotiations in question. The device of a Cabinet Committee on Foreign Policy in general has been introduced only in dubious and controversial circumstances: under Neville Chamberlain during the two years before the outbreak of the Second World War and by Sir Anthony Eden before Suez. In both cases the real working of the Committee remains obscure. Its membership, in each case, seems to have been selected on a personal basis, and not on the basis of departmental involvement in the issues to be discussed, as is the more usual practice with Cabinet committees. In both cases there have been strong suggestions that the Committee's main role, whether intended or not, was to isolate within the Cabinet those Ministers of a certain mind on current issues of foreign policy and to lend their views an authority sufficient to override any opposing views within the Cabinet. It is difficult to see quite what other role such a committee has to play. Even if these suspicions are unjustified, it is clearly an extra device standing between the full Cabinet's exercise of its collective responsibility and the individual Minister, and its relationship to the advice proffered to the Minister by his senior professional advisers in the Foreign Office and the Embassies abroad remains equally obscure.

The only real justification is that offered for the Cabinet committee system in general, namely, the need to reduce the burden on the Cabinet as a whole. Yet it is difficult to reconcile what is known or believed of its activities in each case with the doctrine of Cabinet responsibility. As Churchill remarked to Curzon, there is a difference between the vital issues of foreign policy and mere departmental matters. Matters often move too quickly for the Cabinet committee's report to the full Cabinet to be at all adequate. And actions in the field of foreign affairs can rarely be recalled or repudiated. Moreover, the overburdening of ministerial shoulders is not the only danger today nor is it easy to see how the overburdening of some Ministers, who must of necessity be the most senior, and therefore probably already more overburdened than their junior colleagues, can ease the basic problem. The alternative danger is the slowing down of the processes of decision, a danger to which the Committee of Imperial Defence, save when under the direction of a senior Minister, as under Lord Haldane in the first Labour Government, was notoriously subject.

The real problem has arisen from the widening of the scope of Britain's contacts with other countries to cover a whole range of matters under the province of other departments of State. The Committee of Imperial Defence was introduced to ensure that if resort to the *ultima ratio regum* was forced upon us, at least the other departments of State would be prepared for it. In its interwar role this aspect of its work was greatly expanded, and extra committees were added in the 1930s, to ensure that our commitments abroad and our ability to meet them did not deviate too widely from one another, a task comparable under the circumstances to that of Canute defying the waves. But foreign affairs came also to comprehend matters of international finance, currency control, trade, labour and employment, requiring the permanent co-operation, consultation and co-ordination of several departments and their heads. Negotiations on matters such as the IMF and GATT could no more be handled by the Foreign Secretary as part of the general field of foreign affairs, than could those on atomic energy. It was not until 1944 that the Foreign Office acquired its own set of economic advisers, and the machinery by which it receives advice on scientific matters is still rather obscure. For a matter like entry into the Common Market, at once profoundly technical and yet one which may cut across the whole civilian field of government activity, it is quite impossible to see how dualism can be avoided either now or in the future.

Nor need this necessarily be decried. Ultimately, the Cabinet system of responsibility, if it is to endure, must prove more important than that of the individual Minister. In the last fifty years the bulk of the real disasters of British foreign policy, such as Chanak, the near breakdown of relations with the United States in 1927–28, the Hoare–Laval plan, Munich, Palestine in 1947, Suez, have occurred when the Cabinet's attentions were not fully engaged until too late and their comprehension of the issues at stake impeded. Any device or claim which increases the likelihood of this division of attention, this impeding of comprehension, and encourages the individual Minister to regard his departmental responsibility as greater than his collective responsibility, is to be deprecated. Among such are the recurrent claims that the Foreign Secretary should always be a politician of the Palmerstonian kind, with a professional rather than a political outlook, a Curzon or an Eden. Foreign affairs are not what they were in Palmerston's day. The need is rather for a Cabinet whose members are interested and experienced both in domestic and external affairs, and a Foreign Secretary who can speak for them plainly and clearly, with knowledge and with authority. It is the Foreign Service which has the best claims for a monopoly position, not the Foreign Secretary, provided only that its processes of recruitment, training, internal organization and promotion do not seem to give such claims the lie.

Entry and Training in the
Administrative Class of the
British Foreign Service

IN an earlier essay in this collection attention was called to the changes in the nature of the social composition of the foreign-policy-making élite in Britain after 1900. It was suggested that these changes reflected a more general change in the composition of the ruling élites in general, consequent on the weakening of social divisions established by birth and the hereditary possession of wealth, and the increased possibilities open to the top level of the professional classes in the legal profession, in medicine, in education and in the armed services, to acquire sufficient capital and personal wealth to enable them not only to obtain entry but to maintain membership of the ruling élites; to buy a private education for their children of a kind hitherto only available to the aristocracy or the landed gentry, to maintain a country establishment of the appropriate size together with a house in London, to obtain entry to London clubland, and generally to maintain a way of life appropriate to the positions to which they aspired. The Foreign Office reforms of 1906 and 1919–20, it was suggested, did little more than recognize and adapt that institution to changes which were already taking place among the ruling élites in general.

Among critics of the Foreign Service[1] and its predecessors, the Foreign Office and the Diplomatic Service, it has long been the practice to condemn the narrowness of the social strata from which its membership was recruited, and to imply that only a prejudice peculiar to the Service itself prevented it throwing wide its gates to recruits from all strata of British society. Correspondingly, those who defend the Foreign Service, or who have taken part in its reforms, tend to defend those reforms for the degree to which recruitment has been 'democratized', and entry made possible to those not born of

1. Throughout this essay reference is to the administrative class (Branch A) of the Foreign Service only.

aristocratic or upper middle-class parents. On a longer view, however, such criticisms seem ill-considered, and such defences the products of guilty conscience rather than intelligence. The peculiar abilities called for by diplomacy are not necessarily concomitants of membership of any particular social stratum as such. The Foreign Service can only reflect the nature of the society which it serves. By its nature it must be drawn from the élite groups of Britain, since its job is both to represent those élites abroad, and to represent to them the nature of foreign interests, opinions and pressures in so far as those bear on the national interest. The ability to communicate freely with the élites at home is all-important; by its nature the Foreign Service is already hampered in its ability to communicate with those it represents, since its conditions of service must inevitably make it a group apart from the other élite groups in the country. Its members spend long periods of their service abroad. Friendships, even marriages often, are contracted while on foreign stations, while older friendships entered into before entry into the Service can only too easily languish for lack of sufficient contact to nurture them. All conditions combine to make the Foreign Service's system of recruitment inevitably conform to, and mirror, the system by which the ruling élites in general recruit themselves; and criticisms of the narrowness of the social strata from which the Foreign Service is recruited are both frivolous and unfair, unless they take the whole system of socio-political advancement in Britain as their background.

That being said, it is clear that to understand the new changes which are taking place in the social composition of the British Foreign Service, it is less important to understand the nature of the reforms introduced by the Foreign Service Act of 1943, than to grasp the major impact on Britain's social system of the 1944 Education Act, with its immense increase in secondary education, and its provision of what amounts virtually to free university education for all those who can secure places at British universities. The 1943 reforms were designed, in so far as they affected recruitment and training, to do away with the obligation to show proficiency in foreign languages, a proficiency only to be acquired by a period of residence in at least two foreign countries, at an expense which the conditions of the post-war world might be expected to render prohibitive. Instead, recruitment was to take place by written examination on current political and economic affairs and a prolonged screening of a kind analogous to that used for officer-cadet selection during the Second World War.

The effect of these reforms, it was said, would be to 'democratize' the system of recruitment to the Foreign Service. Its practical effects, however, may well have been to increase the intellectual calibre and character requirements demanded of would-be recruits, and thus to make the Service reflect, still more than it already did, the general intellectual–élitist nature of British political society. Acceptance by the Foreign Service became, even more than formerly, the crown *par excellence* of the private school and Oxbridge career. The other effect the new reforms had was to continue to make it possible for children of the professional classes to enter the Service. Without this the effects of the severe progressive income tax introduced in the war years and perpetuated through the 1940s, a system of taxation which bore most heavily on those whose savings came from income, might well have led to a narrowing of the social strata from which the service was recruited.[1]

The 1943 reforms in recruitment, in brief then, at best merely provided possibilities for 'democratization' of recruitment. It is the social revolution resulting from the effects of the 1944 Education Act which is beginning to be reflected in the composition of the Foreign Service today. The Act did not establish an egalitarian system of education in Britain; far from it. Rather it intensified the 'merito-cratic' element already present in the British educational system. It made more than ever for the 'career open to the talents'. This was almost immediately reflected in the jump in the number of open scholarships to the two 'prestige' universities, Oxford and Cambridge, won by children from the state-supported grammar schools. The universities equally underwent a great expansion in numbers, firstly as a result of the Government's decision to finance the university

1. In the period 1948–56, 81·9 per cent of all candidates for entry into the Foreign Service, and 90·6 per cent of the successful candidates, came from the sons of the top two classes in the Registrar-General's classified list of occupations: that is from Group I, administrators, managers, senior profes-sional and scientific occupations, 46·8 per cent and 62·4 per cent respectively; from Group II, intermediate professional managerial and technical occupa-tions, 35·1 per cent and 28·2 per cent. Only 8·1 per cent of all successful candidates, 16·5 per cent of all candidates, came from parents of Group III, highly skilled workers, foremen, supervisors, clerks, and 1 per cent in both cate-gories from parents of Group IV, skilled and semi-skilled workers. The degree of 'democratization' can probably be measured in the fact that recruitment on any scale took place from below Group I at all (Cmd. 232 (1957); *Recruitment to the Administrative Class of the Home Civil Service and the Senior Branch of the Foreign Service*).

education of any war veteran who could qualify for entry, and then to finance the university education of all those who could obtain a university place. Yet the universities, like the schools, continued to be ranged in a 'pecking order' of public esteem, Oxford and Cambridge, and to a lesser extent London, creaming off the intellectual élite from the schools (as any comparison of the proportion of students in the various universities who ended their university career with first-class honours will easily illustrate);[1] and those who observed the effects of the creaming-off process introduced under the 1944 Act in the schools by the so-called 'eleven-plus' examination, taken by all school pupils the year following their eleventh birthday, to decide what kind of secondary education they were qualified for, were much struck by the correlation between success in these examinations and a middle-class educated background.

The effect of the 1944 Education Act was to widen the base of the pyramid, but not its apex. This appeared very clearly in the postwar recruitment figures of the Foreign Service. Before 1939 entrants to the Service had come in the main from a small handful of private schools, those to which entry could only be obtained by a combination of wealth and intellectual attainment. In the first ten years after 1945, the list of private schools from which candidates were drawn increased greatly, and state-aided or state-supported grammar schools even provided 20 per cent of the entrants to the Service with their first education. The overwhelming majority of entrants, however, had passed through Oxford and Cambridge, and had received the stamp of a first-class or upper second honours degree from these universities.[2] In the period after 1955 when the impact of the 1944 Education Act had really made itself felt, grammar schools came to provide nearly 30 per cent of the entrants, and only Winchester (13 per cent) and Eton (9 per cent) provided any real proportion of the entrants from the schools from which the prewar Foreign Service entrants had been drawn. But of the 102 entrants to the Service

1. In 1954, of the students graduating from Oxford, London, Bristol, Manchester, Wales and Glasgow Universities, 42·5 per cent of all those students obtaining first class degrees in Arts subjects came from Oxford, as against 27·5 per cent, 7·25 per cent, 3 per cent, 12·5 per cent and 7·25 per cent for the other five universities.

2. These figures are taken from the annual reports of the *Civil Service Commission*, which give regularly in Appendix III, details of the schooling of successful candidates in the Foreign Office entrance examinations.

between 1956 and 1961, 50 still came from Oxford and 45 from Cambridge.[1]

The way in which the educational system on which the Service is dependent was engaged in perpetuating the pattern of the prewar years, despite the widening of entry and the increased numbers with which it was dealing, is still more apparent when an analysis is made of the subjects in which the entrants took their university final examinations. Of the 102 successful candidates in the years 1955–61, 16 per cent had studied classical languages and philosophy, and 48 per cent, no less, had taken history courses in which little or no attention is paid to the twentieth century. Modern languages accounted for 14 per cent of the entrants. Only 16 per cent had taken courses with some elements of law, economics or contemporary political studies. English, mathematics, oriental studies, geography and archaeology made up the remaining 6 per cent.[2]

This comparative lack of any formal training in economics, in social or political studies, or in scientific[3] or technological subjects has made the Foreign Service conscious in a way, unthinkable twenty years ago, of the need to continue the training of their entrants after selection. The basic training given entrants to the Foreign Service today lays immense stress on the acquisition and command of foreign languages. The Civil Service Commission handbook for 1962 states:

A knowledge of foreign languages is a basic professional qualification for members of the Foreign Service. The Commissioners, therefore, in selecting

1. Of the successful candidates in the period 1948–56, 59·7 per cent held a first degree from Oxford, only 33·6 per cent from Cambridge. Only four candidates came from London University, and five from the Scottish universities. Although 272 candidates applied from the provincial universities, none were accepted (Cmd. 232, 1957). See also the comparable figures in the *Report of the Committee on Representative Services Overseas* (the Plowden report), Cmd. 2276, *Miscellaneous No. 5* (1964), at Annex K, which show that the numbers of successful candidates from state or state-supported schools have increased far more than those from universities other than Oxford or Cambridge in the years 1952–62.

2. The figures for 1948–56 are: Classics 18·8 per cent; History 34·2 per cent; Modern Languages 18·1 per cent; Economics, Politics and Law 20·1 per cent; English, Mathematics, Science, etc., account for the remainder. See the source cited in 1 above and in the footnote to p. 189.

3. According to the Plowden report only twenty-seven members of the Foreign Service have degrees in 'Scientific and allied subjects' (Cmd. 2276 (1964), par.261).

recruits for the Senior Branch, will satisfy themselves as far as possible that candidates have the capacity to learn languages. . . . If suitably qualified candidates are available up to three extra places . . . may be filled by those, who in addition to possessing the qualities normally required for the Foreign Service, can demonstrate proficiency in particular languages specially needed by the Foreign Service. In the next five years the highest priority will be given to candidates with a knowledge of Arabic, followed by those who can demonstrate proficiency in Chinese, Japanese, Persian, Turkish, Thai or Burmese. . . .[1]

On entry to the Foreign Service (in August), the successful candidates are given a three-week general course, covering all branches of Foreign Service work, followed by a week's similar course on the Commonwealth given at the Commonwealth Relations Office. Thereafter, about half the group are sent off to learn so-called 'hard' languages. Of twenty-five entrants in 1962, four were sent to learn Arabic at the British Foreign Service School maintained at Shemlan in the Lebanon, one to learn Amharic at Manchester University, one to Tokyo University for a two-year course in Japanese, one to Hong Kong University for a similar period in Chinese, and two to learn Persian and Turkish respectively at London University's School of Oriental and African Studies. Four were sent to small private *pensions* in Europe of the type frequented by the would-be entrant into the Diplomatic Service of the interwar years, to learn French, German and Spanish. Twelve were taken directly into the departments, after a two-week course in archival practice.

This emphasis on languages does not end with the first posting. Opportunity and, where possible, financial assistance are offered where posting to a new country demands the acquisition of a second language.[2] Thus one Third Secretary, posted from Oslo where he had learnt Norwegian via London to Ankara, took four months' concentrated course work in Turkish in London before leaving for Turkey, heaving a sigh of relief when a third posting to an African state formerly part of the French Colonial Empire required nothing more arduous than a brushing-up of his rusty and long-unpractised French.

1. Civil Service Commission, *Administrative Group of Open Competitions* (1962), 10.
2. There are, of course, always cases where the postee is so heavily engaged before posting takes place that training in the new language can only be part-time. In such cases financial assistance is always possible.

The Foreign Service, however, have also been made mindful of the need to supplement their entrants' comparative lack of sophistication in contemporary political and economic studies and in basic technological and scientific knowledge. While Foreign Service personnel are in London, part-time courses in scientific subjects have in recent years been arranged on an *ad hoc* basis by the Department of Scientific and Industrial Research. Other courses on economics, on African and Latin American area studies, on the scientific aspects of export promotion, have also been arranged. All are under the continuous review of the personnel department of the Foreign Office. More senior men are also held available for secondment to the Imperial Defence College, to the NATO Staff College in Paris, to Staff Colleges in other countries in the Commonwealth or latterly and most surprisingly to the Harvard Centre of International Affairs in the United States,[1] and to St Antony's College, Oxford. A final innovation, introduced in 1962, is a residential summer school of a fortnight's duration, held at Cambridge, for senior officials of Counsellor or First Secretary rank, covering a number of aspects of current international politics in a lecture-seminar basis, in which the bulk of the lecturers come from outside the Foreign Service. The experiment was judged extremely successful, both in the lessons learnt from the outside lecturers, and in the regular and informal contact between senior personnel afforded by the residential character of the course. One may assume that so far as personnel requirements permit, the course will become a regular event in the Foreign Service's year.[2]

The recent review, however, of the Foreign Service and its allied overseas services carried out by the Plowden Committee[3] was far

1. This practice, which originated in an initiative from Harvard, began in 1958, and has continued on an annual basis since that date (see 624, *Hansard's Parl. Deb., H. of C.*, cols 100–1). In 1962, two senior Foreign Service officers were attached to the Imperial Defence College, one to the Canadian National Defence College and nineteen, including those on language courses, to the various universities. In addition forty-eight were seconded to other governmental departments, international organizations and non-governmental bodies (673, *Hansard's Parl. Deb., H. of C.*, col.7).

2. The second of these courses, held in 1963, was devoted to the subject of science in the modern world and was addressed by three of Britain's Nobel Prize Winners, Sir John Cockcroft, Lord Todd and Professor P. M. S. Blackett (*Sunday Telegraph*, 21 July 1963).

3. Cmd. 2276 (1964). See especially ch.5, and ch.3, pars 217–32.

from satisfied with this state of affairs. They found that the shortage of manpower, from which the Foreign and Commonwealth Services suffered, had prevented those who entered the Senior Service since 1945 from receiving adequate training. They criticized the annual budget for training purposes of the Foreign Service (about £25,000 annually, excluding the cost of the Foreign Service Middle East Centre for Arab Studies in the Lebanon) as being inadequate and recommended its being doubled. And having pointed out that the 1943 White Paper had envisaged a preliminary period of two and a half years' training before entrants were finally accepted, they rejected this in favour of a special course to be taken after three to four years' service. The Home Civil Service introduced in 1962 a Centre of Administrative Studies at which members of the Home Civil Service Administrative Class attend courses in a general curriculum which includes public administration, the structure of industry, economics, business administration, statistics, science and technology. More advanced courses in international finance, economic forecasting, income growth, etc., are also given. The Plowden Committee suggested the development of Special Foreign Service courses at this Centre, or the adaptation of existing courses to something closer to the needs of the new Diplomatic Service. The idea of a separate Staff College for the Diplomatic Service alone they did not consider to be feasible at the time of their inquiry or in the immediate future.

The Plowden Committee also warmly commended the mid-service courses and attachments to universities, etc., introduced after 1958. In general, they pronounced themselves in favour of increasing these attachments and summer schools, and of increased contacts with the universities and with the independent research institutes which cluster in London, such as the Royal Institute of International Affairs, the Royal Institution, the Institute of Strategic Studies, the Institute of Public Administration, etc., at the level of the staff seminar or study group. They were particularly in favour of co-operation at this level by the members of the Foreign Service's very small planning staff, the idea of both being to associate outside experts with the process of planning, either at the level of advice and discussion provided by a seminar, or at the level of the drafting of reports and recommendations in the case of the study group. This represents so great a departure from previous practice as to be worth particular mention – the more so as those recommendations had, at least so far as seminars are concerned, been implemented before the Committee's report was published.

The most important part of the Committee's recommendations, however, was their advice, since accepted, that the Foreign Service should be merged with the Commonwealth Service responsible for relations with members of the Commonwealth and the Trade Commission Service responsible since 1946 for trade relations with members of the Commonwealth into a new 'Diplomatic Service'. In matters of training and entry they adopted for this new 'Diplomatic Service' the practice of the old Foreign Service, so that it will be true to view the new Service as but the old Foreign Service 'writ large'. Second in importance was their recommendation that the Service should deliberately recruit to secure a 10 per cent margin of staff above its requirements, to allow for training, leave, postings, etc. Third were their recommendations to improve the conditions of service which led one former permanent under-secretary of state in the Foreign Office to describe them to the author as constituting a new charter for the Service. These will not, however, alter the previous picture of recruitment, and the new Diplomatic Service may be expected to follow the practices of its predecessor in recruitment to its policy-making branches.

The future pattern of Foreign Service recruitment seems now to be fairly easy to prophesy. The Service has established itself as, beyond all others, the career open to the talents. Foreign Office officials have shown themselves particularly sensitive to the charge, often repeated, that preference is given in recruitment procedures to products of Oxbridge and the private schools. On the latter they point to the increasing number of grammar school boys taken in in recent years. On the former they reply that it is only in the older universities that tutors and career advisers direct the attention of their ablest students towards a career in the Foreign Service.[1] And starting in October 1959, members of the Foreign Office have visited most of Britain's provincial universities every year to ensure that tutors and career advisers were thoroughly briefed as to the opportunities open in the Foreign Service. Their first visit, in 1959, may have been responsible for the appearance of successful candidates in the lists for 1960–61 of graduates of the Universities of London, Leeds and Wales.

1. See the letter from the Right Hon. Selwyn Lloyd, then Foreign Secretary, to Dr Thompson, Lecturer in Political Economy at the University of Edinburgh, *The Times*, 27 September 1959.

Yet it is also true that the intake in those two years was, at fifty-eight, more than the total intake for the four previous years, when up to fifteen vacancies annually were unfilled for lack of suitable candidates.[1]

The increasing numbers of the British university population, however, are already causing the older universities, willy-nilly, to see their power of creaming-off the best school leavers in the country diminish. New-plan experimental universities like those of Keele, Sussex and East Anglia are already commenting on the high calibre of students applying for entry to their faculties. Sussex, whose undergraduate courses are organized on an area-study basis, may well in three to four years' time be placing its graduates in the Foreign Service. It seems reasonable to prophesy that the older provincial universities will also begin to enjoy, if on a smaller scale, the surplus of first-class honours students which leads Oxbridge to figure so prominently as the *alma mater* of successful Foreign Service entrants. Despite the suspicions of its radical critics, it seems likely that such developments will be welcomed by the Service as a whole. Its great and unique asset in recruitment in the past has been the intellectual cachet conferred by membership, a cachet only comparable with that of recruitment to the Treasury from the top percentages of the Home Civil Service entrance examinations. Moreover, its personnel department is well aware of the increasing intellectual demands made upon its members by the increasing complexity of international problems today; and by the fact that there are today no longer any quiet posts to which failures may be transferred to end their days in honorific and dignified uselessness. Nor can the Service be expected to relish its popular image as constituting a paradise for gilded loafers, united in mutual contempt of all those outside their ranks, a 'system of outdoor relief for the British aristocracy', as one of its severest nineteenth-century critics termed it.

The widening of the bases from which its members are recruited may, however, be expected to weaken the Foreign Service in what has hitherto been one of its most important assets, the links formed by individual members of the Service with their contemporaries in other sections of Britain's élite groups as a result of contacts begun at school or university, before entry to the Service. Such links, social and informal in the strictest sense as they are, are important in two highly significant ways. Firstly, they may be expected to counter the

1. The average annual figure of vacancies is twenty-five. See Cmd. 2276 (1964), Annex I.

pressures mentioned above as being inherent in the nature of the Service, which tend to make of the Service a group apart from the other élite groups in the country. Secondly, they make it possible for members of the Service to know, to communicate with and to assess on a person-to-person basis the opinions of individual members of the other élite groups whose interests and activities impinge upon the field of Britain's foreign interests. Contact can be made on the basis of shared experience or shared acquaintanceship, where in a larger, more disparate society, such contacts can only be much more formal and governed by social considerations of status and protocol. To some considerable extent the common ground of school or university education has been supplemented in the past by the opportunities for social contact provided by the unique role of London as *the* metropolis, the centre of political, journalistic, cultural, economic and financial life alike, and by the social clubs and quasi-political, quasi-research institutes such as the Royal Institute for International Affairs, the Institute for Strategic Studies, the Royal United Services Institute, the Royal Commonwealth Society and similar bodies. These opportunities will continue, since there are no signs whatever that the dominating position of London in British life will diminish, rather the contrary. But it may well be that the Foreign Service will feel the need, in the not too distant future, actively to cultivate links with other sections of the élite groups in Britain at the level of junior entry into those élites, instead of relying on the normal processes of British social practice to establish these highly important links, on which in the latter stages of their members' careers so much may well depend in the way of informal communication and explanation between civil servant and civil servant, between civil servant and minister or minister's private secretary, between civil servant and politician, soldier or member of the press. All political society is dependent on the form of its social relationships, and the informal relationships are often of equal or greater importance than the formal. British political society has long been geared to these informal relationships, the more so as talent and merit have offered only one of the routes of entry and advancement, and that not always of major importance. The 'rise of the meritocracy' is beginning to subject the system to a number of strains and failures of function, which the Foreign Service, like the other élite groups, will have to overcome if it is to continue to function effectively. Cases such as those of Burgess and Maclean, the notorious defectors to the Soviet Union, produced by similar strains among the recruits to the élite groups in the 1930s, show how dangerous to a Service which depends by definition almost on common loyalty and a sense of common purpose, failure to recognize and adapt to such strains can be. The substitution of security procedure for trust, formal communication for informal social relationship, can lead to a paralysis of judgment, freedom of comment and recommendation which would greatly impair both the internal workings of the Service itself, and the role of the Service in the defence of the national interest. The experience of the German diplomatic service under Nazism and the more recent Calvary of the US Foreign Service under Scott MacCleod and McCarthyism are terrible warnings of the pitfalls which the Foreign Service may have to face in the next few decades.

None of this is meant to imply a criticism of the attempts being made currently to widen the cachement areas from which the Service recruits new entrants. Competition for the first-class and second-class university graduate, from industry, the professions and the Home Civil Service, is now so fierce that the Foreign Service has had to relax slightly its preference for a good honours degree as the *sine qua non* for consideration as a potential entrant. In certain circumstances they will even take a second-class honours of the lower division, a grade which was once regarded as condemning those who obtained it to the intellectual proletariat.[1] First-class ability is essential to the Foreign Service of Britain in a world where Britain's commitments seem if anything to have grown in inverse proportion to the decline in her national strength relative to the other great powers. More than ever Britain's assets are the abilities of her people. The comprehension of the external world, and the ability to ride out its tides, since governing them is no longer possible, are of the greatest national importance. The indications are that, occasional blunders such as the failure to predict Castro's victory in Cuba notwithstanding, the Foreign Service of Great Britain is today as well staffed as ever, and is recruiting an abler and more intelligent kind of Briton.

1. In 1948–56, nine candidates were accepted with a lower second-class honours degree. Six candidates provisionally accepted before the results of their university examinations were known were eliminated on their failure to secure at least second-class honours (Cmd. 232).

Security Procedures in the
British Foreign Service

IN its pattern of recruitment the Foreign Service before 1943 was governed very much by the assumption that only those already members in one way or other of the ruling élite would apply for membership of its senior grades. Entry was secured by the taking of a competitive examination. Candidates for this had to be recommended by one or two persons known to the Secretary of State, and those successful in the examination were subjected to an interview designed to ensure that the standards of the Service in intelligence, presentability, good manners, etc., were maintained.[1]

In all this, there was little or no room for security checking as it is known today. Patriotism and loyalty were assumed as automatic ingredients in those eligible for entry. 'Oddness' of the kind which led Sir Roger Casement to commit treason in 1915–16[2] or deviousness of the kind which involved J. D. Gregory in the 'francs' scandal in the 1920s[3] were rare qualities and the consequent scandals regrettable exceptions in the otherwise unblemished record of the Service. But no élite group is immune from scandal just as every family has its black sheep or its skeleton in the cupboard, and it was not thought necessary apparently for there to be any special procedures or the like to guard against its possibility. Such security checking as was done on candidates for entry was done on an unofficial word-of-mouth basis, made easy by the tutorial system of the two major universities and the ordinary network of family contacts maintained among a numerically small ruling élite. This apparent casualness in matters of personal security was matched by an equal lack of formal provision in matters of physical security. Before 1939 there was no section in the Foreign

1. See the accounts of their recruitment in Sir Maurice Peterson, *Both Sides of the Curtain* (1950); Sir David Kelly, *The Ruling Few* (1953).

2. R. C. MacColl, *Roger Casement* (1954).

3. Cmd. 3037 (1928), *Report of the Board of Enquiry appointed by the Prime Minister to investigate certain Statements affecting Civil Servants.* See also 215 *Hansard, Parl. Debs., H. of C.*, cols 47–72.

Office specifically charged with security matters. The Embassies abroad, with the exception of Paris, had no provision for security guards.[1] By 1939 this had led to a degree of penetration of British Foreign Office security in the matter of its codes and communications which is still not generally recognized. The case of 'Cicero', butler to Sir Hughe Knatchbull-Hugesson, the British Ambassador in Ankara, during the war, is well known, it is true. But far worse breaches of security occurred in Rome. In 1939 no less than three of Britain's rivals and potential opponents had broken Britain's diplomatic codes and ciphers and could listen in on all her communications. Since mid-1935, a safe-breaker in the pay of the Italian intelligence services had been regularly opening the safe in the British Embassy in Rome and abstracting copies of all diplomatic correspondence, both cabled and that which came by diplomatic bag, and passing this on not only to the Italians but also to the Minister of the Soviet Embassy, M. Helfand.[2] Much of the Italian booty had been passed on directly to the Germans in one form or the other, where it no doubt was useful confirmation of that obtained by their own means. The principal German agency for the interception of diplomatic wireless and telegraphic communication was Goering's *Forschungsamt* (Research office); and it is clear from a document extant in the files of the Under-Secretary of State in the German Foreign Ministry, that they intercepted and read correctly all the telegrams passing between London and the British Embassy in Berlin in the crisis months from September 1938 onwards.[3]

By 1939 the assumptions on which the old lack of any formal security 'vetting' (screening) procedures were based had also broken down. In 1930–31 the Communist Party of Great Britain succeeded in establishing branches in the Universities of Cambridge and London; Oxford was to fall victim in 1932. The move coincided with a hardening of opinion on the left of British politics against the system by which Britain was governed, a widely growing regard for the

1. *7th Report of Select Committee of Estimates*, Session 1953–54; *The Foreign Service, Minutes of Evidence*, 35.

2. See M. Toscano, *Pagine di Storia Diplomatica Contemporanea*, vol.II, *Origini e Vicende della Seconda Guerra Mondiale* (Milan, 1963), at ch.III, 'Problemi Particolari della Seconda Guerra Mondiale', 78. See also Lord Vansittart, *The Mist Procession*, (1958), 516.

3. Summaries are contained in a file of the Under-Secretary of State in the German Foreign Ministry, preserved in photostat in the Public Record Office, London.

Soviet Union then in the throes of the First Five-Year Plan, and growing anxiety as to the rise of Nazism in Germany, the combination of forces out of which in the mid-1930s was to come the Popular Front movement in France and the international Brigade in Spain. The strongest centre of undergraduate Communism was Trinity College, Cambridge, which produced the first Secretary of the University branch of the Communist Party of Great Britain, David Guest, the poet John Cornford who was killed in Spain, three senior officials in the party today, Emile Burns, Maurice Cornforth and James Klugmann, and two of Britain's three diplomatic defectors to the Soviet Union, Guy Burgess and Harold Philby.[1] The third, Donald Maclean, a year junior to them, was at the neighbouring college, Trinity Hall.

On evidence available today it seems a reasonable inference that these three men were recruited for Soviet Intelligence through Guy Burgess, while they were still at Cambridge.[2] Of the three only Donald Maclean entered the Foreign Service in the normal manner. As the son of a Liberal Cabinet Minister, of good family, first-class intellectual attainments, excellent manners and impressive personality, he passed easily through the mesh of the Service's traditional recruitment procedures. In ten years he was to rise to the rank of Minister, one beneath the final step of Ambassadorship, a meteoric rise which made him the 'white hope' of the Foreign Service, and is an impressive tribute to his intelligence, ability and industry. When he began actually working for the Soviets is not clear, though he must have been working for them during his period as First Secretary and Acting Counsellor in the British Embassy in Washington, that is from 1944–48, since it was from these years that the information, the known leakage of which to the Soviets led to his eventual identification, actually dated.

During the Second World War, the Foreign Office acquired its own security department, whose task was to oversee the physical and personal security of the Foreign Office at home and of British Embassies and diplomatic offices abroad, including the provision of security guards. These were supposed to be recruited and trained in Britain,[3] but in at least one case, that of the British Embassy in

1. See Neal Wood, *Communism and the British Intellectuals* (1959).
2. This was stated by the Soviet defector, Vladimir Petrov, in 1954 (Cmd. 9577 (1955), *Miscellaneous No.17. Report Concerning the Disappearance of two former Foreign Office officials*, 7).
3. *7th Report of Select Committee of Estimates*, op. cit.

Washington, the so-called security guards were in fact recruited from British citizens resident in the United States.[1] On paper the security department worked in conjunction with the personnel department where the personal security of the Foreign Service was concerned, and through four or five regional security officers acting in contact with Heads of Chancery or whoever was appointed in the individual Embassies to act as local security officer in matters of physical security. In 1948 what seems to have been a new departure was attempted with the appointment of a full-time professional security officer with a police and security background to the British Embassy in Washington, but from his own account of this, the experiment does not seem to have been a happy one,[2] and was not repeated elsewhere. It is significant in this connection that the practice was to staff the security department with career civil servants on two to three year postings rather than to use long-service professionally-trained security officers,[3] and that in 1954, when the Admiralty clerk, Vassall, who was subsequently recruited by Soviet Intelligence, was posted to the staff of the Naval Attaché at the British Embassy in Moscow, responsibility in security matters rested principally with the Head of Chancery.[4]

The experience of the security department at this period does not seem always to have been a very happy one so far as its relations with the personnel department were concerned, as the case of Guy Burgess shows. After work for the British Security Services and the BBC in liaison with the Foreign Office, Guy Burgess joined the Foreign Service as a result of his temporary employment as private secretary to the Labour Minister of State in the Foreign Office, Hector MacNeill. His entry seems to have been agreed on Mr MacNeill's recommendation and on an interview, without any detailed security check. In 1950 the security authorities informed the Foreign Office that he had been guilty of indiscreet talk while on a holiday abroad,[5] and on his posting to Washington in August 1950 the security department in the Foreign Office wrote to the Regional Security officer in the Americas, reporting this and adding that Burgess, in addition to having known Communist associates and a background of con-

1. F. J. Thompson, *Destination Washington* (1960), 162.
2. See ibid., *passim*.   3. Ibid., 200.
4. Cmd. 2009 (1963), *Report of the Tribunal appointed to inquire into the Vassall case and Related Matters*, 30.
5. Cmd. 9577 (1955), 3.

nections with the Party, was a 'man of unpleasant habits, a drunkard and would bear watching'.[1]

It is at this point that one begins to sense the breakdown of the old élite system. Maclean was by its own standards irreproachable, hard-working, brilliant, stable in most things, *sans peur et sans reproche*. Guy Burgess was a loud-mouthed unstable braggart, a drunkard and a pervert to boot. His political associations were well known, and his suitability for the ranks of the Foreign Service highly questionable at best. His record at Washington was disastrous, and after eight months he was recalled with a view to asking him to resign the Service. The élite system can only justify itself if its standards are maintained, and falling away from them or failure to meet them regarded as a dis-qualification. Overt homosexuality (Casement's ruin also) was re-garded until the 1940s as one such disqualification, public drunken-ness another. Both were present in Burgess' case and both were ignored. With Maclean, and with Philby, the third of the diplo-matic defectors to the Soviet Union, the élite system fell victim to deliberate treachery and betrayal. With Burgess it betrayed its own standards.

With the breakdown of the normal protections against treason afforded by the élite system, treason's discovery became a matter of the professional counter-espionage and security organizations. Two of these were involved in co-operation with the Foreign Service's own security department, the Security Service, usually known as M.I.5, and the counter-espionage sections of the Secret Service, known as M.I.6. Both of these date from before the First World War, and both are concerned principally with the identification of alien intelligence agents and the combating of the intelligence services employing them. The activities of the Security Service, which began as a section of Military Intelligence under the War Office, are confined to British domestic and colonial territories, and its task since its foundation in 1907 has been the observation and rendering harmless, at the appro-priate moment, of alien intelligence networks on British soil.[2] The activities of the counter-espionage branch of M.I.6 have been con-ducted abroad, and their main aim has always been to penetrate and capture individuals or sections of foreign intelligence services.[3]

1. Thompson, op. cit., 209.
2. John Bulloch, *M.I.5* (1963).
3. See Christopher Felix (*pseud.*), *The Spy and His Masters* (1963). It is to be noted that M.I.5 is also prepared to consider this within Britain, as

Neither of these organizations were concerned with the screening, or 'vetting', as it is called in British security parlance, of persons in positions of security and trust. Their job is to cover and frustrate the activities of would-be hostile intelligence agents.

In January 1949 information reached the security authorities which indicated that there had been a leakage of secret Foreign Office intelligence to the Soviet Union. There followed two years of protracted inquiries conducted on a widespread but highly secret basis, involving not only M.I.5 at home but also the counter-espionage branch of M.I.6 abroad. It is generally believed, and his ex-colleagues of wartime years have confirmed this, that it was in his capacity as M.I.6's liaison on counter-espionage matters in Washington, that Harold Philby, the third of the three defectors, became aware of the way in which the search was coming to concentrate on Maclean.[1] Philby warned Burgess, and Burgess, sent home in early May 1951, warned Maclean of the imminence of his interrogation by the security authorities, the same day that these obtained permission from the Foreign Secretary, Herbert Morrison, to undertake this interrogation.[2] That evening the two men fled the country, and with the aid of Soviet agents reached Prague and then Moscow.

The effects of the disappearance of these two men was greatly to enhance the prowess and the importance of the Foreign Office's security department. In July 1951 a Committee of Enquiry was set up inside the office to consider the existing security checks applicable to the Foreign Service.[3] This reported in favour of the thorough security vetting of all Foreign Service officers. The report was a belated acknowledgment of the need to submit the Foreign Service to the same checks which had been applied since 1948 to Civil Service employees working on matters 'vital to the security of the state'. In 1952 a standard procedure known as 'positive vetting' was introduced to cover all Foreign Service officers and all Civil Service employees

the consideration given in 1961 to the possibility of persuading the Assistant Soviet Military Attaché in London, Captain Eugen Ivanov, demonstrated. See Cmd. 2152 (1963), *Lord Denning's Report*, 83.

1. Philby resigned from the Foreign Service in 1952 and defected to the Soviets from his post as Middle Eastern Correspondent of *The Observer* and *The Economist* in January 1963. Thompson's comments, op. cit., 208–9, seem to indicate that these inquiries were going to Philby in Washington.

2. Herbert Morrison, *An Autobiography* (1961), 276; Cmd. 9577, 4; Sir Percy Sillitoe, *Cloak without Dagger* (1955), 161.

3. Cmd. 9577, 7.

in 'sensitive' positions.[1] The procedure involves checks with Security Service records, the completion of a standard questionnaire, letters to two referees chosen by the subject and a 'field investigation' into the character and circumstances of the person examined. The criteria for assessing trustworthiness were defined in a Treasury Instruction of 31 March 1954 as including membership of subversive organizations and character weaknesses liable to render a man liable to blackmail. Each case is reviewed regularly every five years and, in addition, at any time within that period 'if there is a marked change of circumstance affecting the man' under review 'likely to bear on his security rating'.[2] Review includes checks with both the individual's supervisors and with officers responsible for the security of the establishments within which he has worked.

At the same time the attention of the Foreign Service was necessarily directed to the general problem of the security of the non-Foreign Service personnel attached to British Embassies abroad, especially to those beyond the Iron Curtain. The task of convincing the Service authorities here was to prove a long and difficult one. The first move was taken in August 1952 with letters to the Intelligence Division of the three Service Ministers. At the inter-departmental committee which dealt with issues connected with Service Attachés, the Foreign Office representative argued most strongly in October 1952 for special measures to ensure that individuals selected for service in British missions behind the Iron Curtain were capable of standing up to the peculiar strains to which they would be subjected, and in April 1953 the Admiralty were provided with a long Foreign Office memorandum to act as the basis for the briefing of individuals selected for such service. In September 1953 a long memorandum embodying all current security instructions for Embassies abroad was circulated to all British diplomatic missions. It was not, however, until March 1958 that the Foreign Office secured that all Service Attachés and their staffs should be compulsorily subjected to 'positive vetting' in conformity with Foreign Service practice.[3] By this date the two worst of the Admiralty employees recruited by the Soviet Intelligence authorities, Henry Houghton at the Portland Anti-Submarine Warfare Research station and Vassall, had already passed well under Soviet control.

In the meantime the Foreign Service was busy putting its own

1. Cmd. 1681 (1962), *Security Procedures in the Public Service*, 14–15.
2. Ibid., 22; Cmd. 2009 (1963), 48. 3. Cmd. 2009 (1963), 26.

house in order. In June 1952 a wireless operator formerly attached to the British Embassy in Moscow was arrested while handing information over to the Second Secretary of the Soviet Embassy in London. Between 1952 and 1955 four members of the Service were asked to resign, including Harold Philby, and several others were shifted to non-sensitive posts. Philby himself, it should be emphasized, was really a member of the Secret Service, as was George Blake, the former Vice-Consul in Seoul, who was convicted in 1961 of having acted as a Soviet double agent since his release from Chinese captivity in 1953. Their diplomatic posts were only 'covers', and the faults in their employment cannot strictly be laid at the door of the Foreign Service.

From 1951 onwards the Foreign Service seems to have maintained a reasonably successful record in security matters, although it cannot be said that the state of affairs current in the mid-1950s in the British Embassy in Moscow during Mr Vassall's stay there, was exactly a happy one. Several warnings given as to the activities of the Soviet agent, Mikhailovsky, who recruited Vassall, were ignored by the Head of Chancery or by the Ambassador. It is also more than a little surprising that at this date there was no full-time security officer attached to an Embassy so manifestly a target for Soviet Intelligence assault, and that the Regional Security officer responsible for the Iron Curtain missions should be stationed in Vienna.[1] Nor are the figures for the annual cost of the Foreign Office Security Department and the Regional Security officers for this period all that impressive, considering the grade of Foreign Service officer who should be employed in such posts and the areas covered by the Individual Regional Officers.[2]

Nevertheless, it has to be admitted that since 1951 the only security scandals concerned with the Foreign Service, the cases of Philby and George Blake, have in reality covered not the Foreign Service but the Secret Service which in some respects uses it as a cover. The decision apparently taken in 1956 to recommend Philby to *The Observer* as a potential correspondent in the Middle East, a decision widely believed to have been prompted by the intention, later realized, of continuing to employ him as an agent for M.I.6 in

1. Cmd. 2009 (1963),, 30, 43–6.
2. The figures for the financial years 1952–53, 1953–54 and 1954–55 are £34,596, £41,309 and £46,428 respectively (546, *Hansard's Parl. Deb., H. of C.*, cols 2293–4).

the Middle East, seems on retrospect to have been appallingly ill-judged; though of course only those ultimately in the know can pronounce on the outsider's anxieties.[1]

There does, therefore, seem in general to be some justice in the conclusion of the report of the Radcliffe Committee of April 1962 on Security Procedures in the Public Service,[2] a report which points to the continuing value of the Foreign Service's consciousness of its own separate existence and status as an élite group, and confounds the gloomier prophecies of Mr John Connell as to the long-term effects of Burgess and Maclean's treachery in institutionalizing the qualities of confidence, loyalty and self-censorship, which the Foreign Service had hitherto enjoyed on an informal basis.[3]

Foreign Service Officers [wrote the Radcliffe Committee] can be in little doubt as to the reality of the various threats to security. The man who has actually had a concealed microphone detected in his dining-room wall can more readily be trained and persuaded to adopt a high standard of discipline and alertness in security matters than his counterpart in the Home Civil Service. The Foreign Service also has the advantage of being a relatively small service, whose members tend to know each other (and each other's families) personally as well as officially. This makes it possible to maintain a more effective system of personal vetting than is possible in the Home Civil Service, where little is known inside the office of a man's private life and habits.

We formed the impression that the Foreign Service is alert to the importance of Security precautions and that there is an effective security organization in the Foreign Office. Since the defection of Burgess and Maclean there has been a thorough overhaul of security procedures and this has resulted in an attitude different from that which may have prevailed in earlier years.

It is devoutly to be hoped that they are right.[4]

1. There is an alternative version of Philby's role in the Middle East, according to which he was sent deliberately by the British Secret Service's counter-espionage branch in the hope he might lead them to 'key members of the Soviet espionage network' in the area. See Edward R. F. Sheehan, 'Philby, His Rise and Fall', *Sunday Telegraph*, 18 February 1964.

2. Cmd. 1681 (1962).   3. John Connell, *The Office* (1958).

4. General misgivings aroused by the conjunction in time of the Naval Secrets case, the Vassall case, that of Philby and the Profumo affair led in January 1964 to the setting-up of a Standing Security Commission consisting of a distinguished judge, a former Secretary to the Cabinet and a former First Sea Lord to investigate any further breaches of security in the public service. See *Commonwealth Survey*, 10, no.3 (4 February 1964).

PART V

Bibliographical Section

United States Documentary Resources for the Study of British Foreign Policy, 1919–39

ANY study of this nature can only benefit from a brief introductory comment on the development of Anglo-American relations between the two wars. On the US side this was governed by the interaction between the three classic themes of US thinking on foreign policy, namely, ringmastership in the Pacific, continentalism, and leadership in Europe. On the British side one can trace a similar interaction between what, for want of better words, one might call Atlanticism, 'Imperial isolationism', and world leadership. Each of these produced their own characteristic rhythm of withdrawal from or involvement in the two main theatres of world politics between the wars, Western Europe (including the western Mediterranean) and the Far East.

To define these terms briefly: the policy of playing ringmaster in the Pacific involved the United States in the so-called 'Open Door' policy in China, in maintaining and encouraging the integrity of China, in resisting Japanese expansionism, and, as a corollary, maintaining a navy 'second to none'; 'continentalism' was the purest form of isolationism, non-intervention in the affairs of anything outside the American continent. The policy of leadership in Europe needs a little explanation when applied to the period of the interwar years. These are usually regarded as years in which isolationism was the guiding spirit in US policy.[1] Yet these were also the years of considerable US intervention on such issues as reparations, security and disarmament. The paradox can be resolved if a careful distinction is drawn between US isolationism, with its refusal to accept *commitments* in European affairs, and pure 'continentalism' which rejected even *involvement* in European affairs. The leadership in Europe which Coolidge and Kellogg, Hoover and Stimson were attempting to

1. The author has entered a dissenting note in his article 'American "Isolationism" in the 1920s; is it a useful concept?', *Bulletin of the British Association of American Studies*, n.s. no.6.

establish could perhaps be called 'moral'; it must be recognized, however, that their motives were intimately connected with the electoral cachet of such leadership and the determined activity of idealist US pressure groups.

On the British side, the term 'Atlanticism' is used to cover all those who thought in terms of a joint Anglo-US world hegemony (a thesis still capable of seducing those in authority in Britain). It should be remarked that 'Atlanticists' sometimes saw this hegemony as a new kind of British isolationism (as elements of the *Round Table* group certainly did between the wars), sometimes as a joint involvement in world affairs. The policy of world leadership usually involved clashes and misunderstanding with the United States and always involved political intervention in European affairs. The policy of 'Imperial isolationism' implied, of course, a refusal to accept commitments in Europe and, so far as possible, the avoidance of intervention into European affairs, at least into any affairs east of the Rhine. It should also be remarked that the rebuffed Atlanticist usually retreated into 'Imperial isolationism', ignorance of and antipathy towards the affairs of Europe being as marked a characteristic of this way of thinking as of the US isolationist of the purest water. Senators Borah and Hiram Johnson were in their general outlook much more akin to Lord Lothian than is at first sight apparent.

One could, perhaps, set this interaction out schematically, using the names of the Presidents and/or Secretaries of State in the United States and the Prime Ministers and/or Foreign Secretaries in Britain as the dominant figures in the direction of foreign affairs.

1917–19	Wilson. Leadership in Europe.	1917–22	Lloyd George. World leadership.
1919–20	Wilson's illness.		
1921–25	Charles Evans Hughes. Ringmaster in Pacific.	1922–23	Curzon. World leadership.
		1923	Ramsay MacDonald. World leadership.
1925–29	Kellogg. Continentalism (with a leaning towards leadership in Europe).	1924–29	Austen Chamberlain. World leadership.
1929–33	Hoover and Stimson. Leadership in Europe.	1929–34	Ramsay MacDonald. Atlanticism.

1933–39	Roosevelt. Continentalism (with a strong leaning towards the Pacific).	1934–37	Stanley Baldwin. The same, (with a strong leaning towards Imperial isolationism).
		1938–39	Neville Chamberlain. The same, only more so.

A study of this crude diagram reveals three main phases in British foreign policy: first, the period of maximum British involvement in world affairs under the two Lloyd George coalitions and the Foreign Secretaryship of Sir Austen Chamberlain, Ramsay MacDonald's first administration differing from them only in method, not in aims; secondly, the period of Ramsay MacDonald's second Labour administration and the first three and a half years of his National Government; and thirdly, the period which, through a succession of Foreign Secretaries (Simon, Hoare, Eden, Halifax), the intellectual absenteeism of Stanley Baldwin, and the conviction of Britain's weakness in face of the tasks devolving upon her which dominated Neville Chamberlain, led to the sad and sorry spectacle of the policy of 'appeasement'.

For the purposes of this paper, however, this analysis can be broken down, at least so far as the first period is concerned, into three further divisions: that of the war and the peace conference; that of the incipient clash in the Pacific, which was ended by the Washington Conference of 1921–22; and the 1924–29 period, an unhappy one in Anglo-US relations, when Kellogg's hankering after European leadership led him into direct conflict with Britain at the disarmament conference of 1927 and over the Anglo-French compromise of 1928, while his 'continentalism' left Britain to bear the brunt of Kuomintang nationalism in China in 1926. The two remaining periods in US foreign policy overlap slightly with their corresponding British periods, enough to be interesting, not enough to warrant subdivision.

A further point needs to be made concerning the relation between these two sets of themes. That between US 'leadership in Europe' and British 'world leadership' was always fraught with danger. 'Continentalism' in the United States and 'Imperial isolationism' in Britain cut down to the minimum the chance of clashes with either of the two non-isolationist themes in the other country. US 'ringmastership in the Pacific' would seem at first sight likely to clash with British 'world leadership', but in fact it did not; partly because the aims of British policy in the Far East could be accommodated to the United States' desire to play the ringmaster; partly because Britain was never in a position to devote to Far Eastern problems more than a bare minimum of her resources as a world power. 'Atlanticism' in Britain, while extremely irritating to both continentalists and isolationists in the USA, could not accept direct conflict with any US doctrine without denying its basic principles; it could, however, only co-operate truly with one – that of 'leadership in Europe'. But it should be noted that the advocates of 'Atlanticism' commanded the support of about half the Cabinet in the first and second Lloyd George coalitions, most notably in the persons of Lord Balfour, Lord Robert Cecil and later Lord Lee of Fareham. They continued to remain in touch with the centres of power, authority and information throughout the period that followed.[1]

The usefulness of the immense wealth of material in the United States available to students of British foreign policy in the interwar years is governed, at least in part, by the conjunction in positions of power or inside knowledge of advocates of US leadership in Europe and Atlanticists in Britain. And it is through the channels opened by such conjunction that the most revealing and important information has become available. But before embarking on the wealth of private papers open to research in the United States it would be as well to outline what there is available in the way of official papers.

At the time of writing, the State Department's papers up to 31 December 1932 are open without any check. Thereafter its policy as to availability is governed by the extremely haphazard filing practised by the Department in the past, by which classified and unclassified papers are mixed in the same box file without distinction. In practice this means that the small but helpful and courteous staff of the State Department's Historical Division will, if given sufficient warning, themselves look out unclassified documentary material bearing on specific queries put to them in writing. They are, however, infinitely more liberal with US citizens than with visitors, and far freer with their material when the questions asked bear on questions of US policy. One can detect in this differentiation the pressure of other countries less liberal in their conditions of access. Unlike their British counterparts, however, the State Department does not insist on reviewing the researcher's final manuscript, only on reviewing his notes.

1. Though, as is argued in Essay 2 above, their arguments did not carry very much conviction with the political leadership.

These State Department papers are at once revealing, fascinating and infuriating. Unlike their British or German counterparts, they are devoid of any commentary, marginalia, dockets or even circulation lists. There is no means of telling who saw a particular telegram, except where it was forwarded to the President, or, more rarely, to another Federal Department, for comment. Many of the divisions in US foreign policy become understandable when one sees the entire absence of anything like the British confidential print. Occasionally one finds policy memoranda prepared by members of the various Departments, but there is rarely any indication as to the documentation on which they are based. As guides to the attitudes and thinking of the policy-makers they provide little or no help. For that, one has to turn to the private letters between the professional US Foreign Service officers abroad and their departmental opposite numbers at home, some of which, though by no means all, are in the State Department files. With the State Department's files are also those of US delegations to international conferences – often, though not always, more informative.

Of other Federal Departments, this writer can speak only from personal experience of the Department of the Navy which, with a courtesy and a will to assist which was as charming as it was unexpected, permitted him to inspect not only its own files but also those of the General Board of the Navy, its senior professional advisory body, up to the end of 1936, both confidential and non-confidential material being made available to him. The latter collection included the day-to-day logs kept by the naval advisers at the various disarmament conferences, as well as the naval briefs put up for those conferences. The papers of Admiral Sims, who commanded the US Naval forces in European waters in 1917–19, and was outspokenly Anglophile in a generally Anglophobe service, are also included in their collection.

All these are concentrated in or around Washington. When the researcher turns to the papers of the Presidents and Secretaries of State he has to begin to strap on his seven-league boots. Of the five interwar Presidents, Wilson, Harding, Coolidge, Hoover and Roosevelt, only Wilson's and Coolidge's papers are in the manuscripts division of the Library of Congress. President Harding's are not available, and President Hoover's are only in process of being made available. They are in Iowa in the Hoover Library. Franklin Roosevelt's papers are in a special library in his family home at Hyde

Park, some hundred miles or more up-state in New York. Of the six Secretaries of State, Lansing's, Hughes' and Hull's papers are in the Library of Congress, the latter available only under State Department control. Colby's (Wilson's rump Secretary of State) are not available. Stimson's are in the Sterling Library at Yale and are accessible to research, though permission has to be obtained for their citation. Secretary Kellogg's are available through the Minnesota Historical Society at St Paul, Minneapolis, although this writer was unable, for reasons of time, to consult them. To these should perhaps be added the papers of Josephus Daniels, Edwin Denby and Curtis Wilbur, three Secretaries of the Navy, and of Colonel Theodore Roosevelt Jr, Assistant Secretary of the Navy 1921–25, of which all but Denby's papers are available in the Library of Congress. Denby's papers are at Detroit and were not consulted by this writer.

In addition, there are the papers of the various US Ambassadors to the Court of St James's. These are much more widely scattered. Walter Hines Page's are in the Houghton Library at Harvard. John W. Davis's papers have just been acquired by the Sterling Library at Yale and are not yet available for research. Ambassador Harvey's papers are in the Library of Duke University, North Carolina. His successor was Kellogg. Ambassador Houghton's papers are not available. Those of General Dawes are in North-Western University Library, Illinois, and are very rewarding. Neither Ambassador Bingham's nor Ambassador Kennedy's papers are yet available.

Of other diplomatic papers the most important are those of Joseph Grew, US envoy at Lausanne in 1923, Under-Secretary of State 1924–27, Ambassador in Japan 1931–41 (Houghton Library, Harvard); Frank L. Polk (Sterling Library, Yale); Leland Harrison (Library of Congress); J. Pierrepont Moffatt (Houghton Library, Harvard); and W. Cameron Forbes (Library of Congress and Houghton Library, Harvard). Mention should also be made of the papers of Admiral Hilary Pollard Jones, leading US delegate at the disarmament conferences of the 1920s (Naval Historical Foundation, Library of Congress). His Foreign Service opposite number was Hugh Gibson, whose papers are in the Hoover Library and are not available for research.

More important than these, however, are the collections of Colonel House (Sterling Library, Yale) and of Norman H. Davis (Library of Congress). House's papers are among those which have been longest available to researchers and much of the material, previously of extreme importance because all other documentary sources on the world war and the peace conference were closed, is now freely available elsewhere. But they are still a major source not only for the period of House's ascendancy with Wilson but for later periods. As a confirmed Anglophile and an ardent advocate of US leadership in Europe, House remained in close correspondence with the leading British 'Atlanticists'. His advice was sought by Hughes, Stimson and Franklin Roosevelt. He was in regular correspondence with Lord Lothian. But even more important than that, his collection includes the papers of Sir William Wiseman, the head of the British Intelligence organization in the United States up to 1919, who came to be used both by House and the British Government as a regular channel for all important communications between President Wilson and the British Cabinet, or at least its 'Atlanticist' portion. In turn he did his best to prepare Lloyd George and the remainder of the Cabinet for the impact of Wilsonian ideas and of the President himself in the autumn and winter of 1918. His importance was enhanced by the poor relations which existed between the Ambassador, Sir Cecil Spring-Rice, and both Secretary Lansing and Wilson, by the frequent absences in England of his successor Lord Reading, and by Wilson's own predilections for informal channels of information, which gave him an illusion of immediacy denied him by the bureaucratic apparatus of the State Department. The Wiseman collection contains many cables from the Foreign Office in the years 1917 and 1918. It is particularly rich in material on British policy in Russia and Siberia in 1917-18, material for which, even if the fifty-year rule is strictly operated in this country by the Public Records Office, British historians will have to wait another three to four years.

The Norman H. Davis papers are not as rich as the House collection. But this banker, financial expert and former member of the US delegation at the peace conference served both Hoover and Roosevelt as the principal US disarmament delegate and expert on Britain from 1932 to 1937. A Southerner like Colonel House, he was on the closest terms of friendship with Lord Lothian and the Astors before he began his work. Thereafter he built up relations of the closest confidence with Ramsay MacDonald, with Sir John Simon, with Anthony Eden, and with his opposite number in the Foreign Office, Sir Robert Craigie, and, at the Brussels Nine-Power Conference of 1937, with Sir Alexander Cadogan. As a result, particularly during the period when 'Atlanticism' in Britain was waning under the impact of F.D.R.'s economic and political continentalism, he was able to preserve good relations on both sides under stresses and strains greater and more potentially dangerous than those which had led, under Kellogg and Coolidge, to the bitter impasse of 1927–28. For Roosevelt himself at this time harboured the most deep-rooted suspicions of Britain. Secretary Hull did not even suspect – he believed. Without Davis' and Ambassador Bingham's painstaking interpretations of one side to the other, without their understanding and personal guarantee of the bona fides of the British Cabinet's leaders in foreign affairs at that time, it is hard to see how a major breach in Anglo-US contacts could have been avoided at a time (1934) infinitely more perilous to the Western world than 1927. After the double failure of 1937, first to secure a meeting between Chamberlain and Roosevelt and then of the Brussels Nine-power Conference on the Far East, Davis was then able to work towards the first Anglo-US staff talks in January 1938 on joint action against Japan, contacts from which were to spring the whole machinery of the ABCD conferences, of the decision to put the main US effort into Europe rather than the Pacific, and the consequent re-entry of the United States on to the European stage. Following the example set by Ramsay MacDonald, Cabinet Ministers and Foreign Office officials alike talked to him with extreme frankness about their anxieties both in Europe and the Far East, and during his absence they talked to Ambassador Bingham and to his 'number two', Ray Atherton, whose correspondence with Roosevelt, Davis and Pierrepont Moffatt is extremely rich and informative.

The material contained in these papers is particularly valuable on British policy at the peace conference, on the period of the Washington Conference, on that of the second and third Ramsay MacDonald Premierships and on the aftermath up to 1937. Its full exploitation may well lead to a revision in at least two directions of the accepted interpretation of British policy. First it shows that British hesitations with regard to full support of the League of Nations were not as baseless as contemporary enthusiasts for the League (and their followers today) believed. They were soundly based on a knowledge of the indeterminate state of American opinion on any measures against an aggressor nation – sanctions or otherwise – which might interfere with US trade. They were certainly soundly believed in, to judge by the number of times they occur in contemporary records, conversations and private correspondence.

Secondly, the papers reveal a continuing anxiety, even before 1931, as to British naval and military weakness in the Far East. After 1933 we find Baldwin saying to Norman Davis: 'If there is trouble now in the Far East, I simply do not know how we could deal with it.' In fact, in June 1934 a determined effort was made to get some kind of contractual agreement on joint action in the Far East out of Davis and Roosevelt.

In a third direction they should go a long way to enhancing and rehabilitating the reputation of Ramsay MacDonald. Bumbling in thought and rambling in expression as he so often was (an early illustration of the intolerable work-load faced by a conscientious but not abnormally healthy minister, active in the field of foreign affairs, with which the deaths of Ernest Bevin and Sir Stafford Cripps and the breakdown of Sir Anthony Eden (Earl of Avon) have now made us more familiar), he still saw clearly, dealt fairly and faced the problems of the day squarely, in a way all too rare among his contemporaries. He won the affection and trust of Henry L. Stimson, one of the few realists among US Secretaries of State in this century, and retained it until his death. He captivated F.D.R. It was, in fact, reports of his eclipse that roused the latter's suspicions so strongly in 1934. Nor was he the impractical idealist he is so often represented to be. In 1934 he fought manfully for the extra British cruisers sacrificed in 1930 to US goodwill, returning to Roosevelt's personal plea for a one third cut in naval strength a frank statement that only a one third cut in his risks could make that possible. Much can, no doubt, still be said to his detriment; and he never had to face the trials of the later 1930s. But, for all that, he emerges as a much more considerable figure in the field of foreign affairs than Simon, Hoare or the young Eden, handicapped by his colleagues; a worthy equal to Grey, Austen Chamberlain or Curzon at their best.

Lastly, these papers provide rich material for study in a field which is becoming more and more essential to an understanding of the interwar years – that of financial diplomacy: war debts, reparations, Lausanne, the World Economic Conference, the Anglo-French-US pact of 1936. The present writer had no time to do more than note the wealth of the material in this field. It is to be hoped the economic and financial historians will turn some day soon from studying the brewing industry or the practices of German central banking and tackle this infinitely rich field, where what commonly passes for knowledge is still as heavily gilded with myth and invention as the

Middle Ages once were. The most valuable material will no doubt be found in the papers of Davis, Dawes, Stimson and Franklin Roosevelt – and in those of Henry Morgenthau, extracts from which are now being published.[1]

One final note. The wealth of material available in the USA to the student of recent history derives from a combination of three factors, none of which seems to operate in Britain. First, of course, there is a much looser attitude towards official secrecy, a climate we cannot hope to achieve in this country where the trend is all in the opposite direction. The general US attitude to Government affairs, that the public has the right to know, gives priority to this principle over the maintenance even of the degree of secrecy necessary to the conduct of foreign policy, while in Britain the plea of the public interest is used to exclude Government activity from public knowledge. No adequate diplomatic Blue book has been published here since 1936, except that called into existence by the outbreak of war in 1939[2] – though we have now, of course, the excellent set of Foreign Office documents edited by Sir Llewellyn Woodward, Professor Butler and Professor Bury. Secondly, there is the public-spiritedness both of public figures and of their literary executors who seem content to leave their papers open to research under safeguards, whereas the most common British practice is to deny access to them for a period of up to fifty years or more beyond the date of their deposit. In a large number of cases the private papers of British public figures have been lost, scattered or simply burned either on the owner's death or, even more unpardonably, after he has completed his memoirs. Lastly, the librarians of the great American libraries make it their business to go after private papers whenever the owner had any connection, however shadowy, with their own institution. In this writer's own experience, the safeguards under which private papers are deposited in the United States are more than adequate to prevent muck-raking and to protect the reputation of those whose correspondence follows after.

The gain to scholarship from this public-spiritedness is immense. One has only to compare the two brilliant biographies of Franklin Roosevelt now in progress[3] and the spate of excellent studies of

1. John W. Blum, *From the Morgenthau Diaries* (Boston, 1959).
2. See Essay 13 below.
3. Arthur M. Schlesinger Jr, *The Age of Roosevelt*, I (1957), II (1960); and F. B. Freidel, *Franklin D. Roosevelt*, I (New York, 1952) – III (New York, 1956).

Wilson, to take only two examples, with the continuing absence of any biography worthy of the name to do either Stanley Baldwin or Ramsay MacDonald real justice. There are already two studies of Stimson's Secretaryship of State, one hostile and one defending him.[1] Yet another is now in progress. There is a brilliant study of the role played by peace groups in the origins of the Kellogg Pact.[2] In Britain there is as yet no serious study of our own League of Nations Union, and there is still much political polemic and little balanced study of the role of the 1933 by-election or the so-called Peace Ballot of 1935 in restraining British rearmament. The figure of Lord Robert Cecil, leader of the Conservative Right before 1914, part architect of the League of Nations, principal British delegate to the disarmament conferences up to his resignation in 1927, and a major figure in the leadership of public opinion thereafter, also lacks a biographer. Any competent student of the last forty years of British history could multiply these illustrations. British scholarship in the field of recent history compares most unfavourably with that of the United States. We understand more of the intricacies of the eighteenth-century House of Commons than we do of the system which kept a Tory majority for Neville Chamberlain after the Sandys revelations of British military unpreparedness in 1938 or the Norway débâcle in 1940. Even now the full story of the 1922 and 1931 crises has not been written from original materials,[3] although the generation of student now entering the universities was barely able to talk when the Second World War ended.

This is perhaps more of a plea that greater attention should be diverted to recent British domestic history than the theme of this essay warrants; but the two subjects are not so easily separable. The needs of British domestic politics have too often been pleaded by the defendants of Britain's foreign policy between the wars. On this the US sources, though full of reports, are often difficult to assess in the absence of information as to the original informants. Often, as in their

1. Richard N. Current, *Secretary Stimson: A study in statecraft* (New Brunswick, N.J., 1954); and Elting E. Morison, *Turmoil and Tradition: A study of the Life and Times of Henry L. Stimson* (Boston, 1960).

2. Robert H. Ferrell, *Peace in their Time: The origins of the Kellogg–Briand Pact* (New Haven, Conn., 1952).

3. Lord Beaverbrook, *The Decline and Fall of Lloyd George* (1963) and the late R. Bassett's *1931 Political Crisis* (1950), though very revealing, cannot be described as full in the strictest sense.

assessments of British motives in the disarmament field between 1922 and 1929, they are extraordinarily wide of the mark. But on British foreign policy, in Europe, in the Mediterranean and in the Far East, they form a mine of information which historians of British foreign policy between the wars can ignore today only at their peril.

Some British and Foreign Materials for the Study of the British Foreign-Policy-Making Élite since 1918

INTRODUCTORY NOTE

THE position in Great Britain as regards materials for the study of the British foreign-policy-making élite after 1918 is by no means an easy one. Public records remain officially closed to research for fifty years after the date of their creation by virtue of the Public Records Act of 1958.[1] The researcher is forced back on to three separate kinds of source material: published official documents; such private papers as are easily accessible to researchers in public archives, and have not been raided by the security authorities (as were George Lansbury's[2]) or arbitrarily closed by decision of the trustees of whatever museum to which their original owners have entrusted them;[3] and memoirs and biographies whose authors have had access to materials denied to the historian.

Of these, the published official documents fall into two categories, 'Blue books' and 'White papers' (i.e. Parliamentary Command Papers, containing contemporary diplomatic correspondence), and the postwar publication under scholarly auspices and at a snail's pace of documents bearing on British foreign policy selected from the Foreign Office archives.[4] Publication of the former category has fallen off very considerably since 1914, such publications as there have been of diplomatic correspondence covering mainly treaties,

1. See D. C. Watt, 'Foreign Affairs, the Public Interest and the Right to know', *Political Quarterly*, XXXIV, no.2 (April 1963).

2. See Raymond Postgate, *The Life of George Lansbury* (1951).

3. The Cambridge University Library and the Imperial War Museum are the worst offenders in this respect. The most grievous loss to scholarship is the closing within the fifty-year limit of the papers of Baldwin, Earl Crewe, Lord Hardinge and Sir Samuel Hoare at Cambridge.

4. Sir Rohan Butler has recently been appointed Historical Adviser to the Foreign Office to advise on ways and means of accelerating the publication of these documents (*The Times*, 1 May 1963).

exchanges of notes with other governments, proceedings of international conferences, etc. Of 'Blue books', that is major collections of diplomatic correspondence on particular topics, bound within blue covers, of which so many were published in the nineteenth century,[1] nine only were published in the twenty years 1919–39, with a further twenty-one minor collections. It is worth noting that of these latter, fourteen no less (or if Germany after the outbreak of war is counted, fifteen) deal with relations with countries then regarded as being outside the normal courtesies existing between member states of the diplomatic community:[2] of actual correspondence dealing with negotiations with states that would be recognized as belonging to the community of civilized states, there are only seven Blue books and four White papers. Since 1939 there have been less than half a dozen White papers even marginally containing reports or dispatches from or to British diplomats, and such other diplomatic material as has been published has consisted entirely of exchanges of notes with foreign governments, treaties and minutes of the meetings of international conferences. The material available for the study of the making of British foreign policy has thus dwindled drastically even over the last fifteen years.

The researcher is therefore forced back on to the memoirs and biographies of members of the élite, ministers, diplomats, senior Service officers and others. Here the field is much richer, though the quality is naturally rather variable, and the degree of usefulness of each volume is governed very much by the determination of the individual author to prefer frankness to discretion, and the pugnacity with which he managed to assert himself against the counter-pressures exerted by those whose duty it is to pass the manuscript, since both politicians and public servants are required to submit their manuscripts for official screening before publication, politicians to the Prime Minister of the day through the Secretary to the Cabinet, public servants to the permanent head of their branch of the public service.[3]

1. H. V. Temperley and Lilian Penson, *A Century of Diplomatic Blue Books, 1815–1914* (1938).
2. Russia (3); Afghanistan (2); China before the Kuomintang victories of 1927–29 (2); Egypt (3); Abyssinia (4); Germany (2). A further two are largely historical, Cmds. 5951 and 5964 on Anglo-Arab relations 1914–18, published in 1939. Only four can be strictly regarded as following in the tradition of the nineteenth-century Blue books.
3. This passage is based on information from a number of sources who have been through this procedure, the most prominent of them the late Hugh Dalton.

As a result, the value of the individual volume to the researcher may vary enormously. For those diplomatists, the majority, who remain silent during their lives and unremembered after their deaths, the ardent researcher can only refer to their own entries in such reference works as *Who's Who* or the *Foreign Office List*, their obituaries in *The Times*, and possibly a later entry in the *Dictionary of National Biography*, and hope that neither they nor their executors nor families felt obliged to celebrate the end of their professional activities with a holocaust of their private papers. Such hopes are often disappointed. British public servants are rarely conscious of their duty to their country's history and to those whose task it is to write it. One could wish it were otherwise, since the history will be written and cannot but be written the worse for such ill-advised and misplaced continuance of professional discretion beyond the limits of the grave. Britain is ill-served by such action, while they themselves remain recorded in the memoirs of others and in the diplomatic records of other countries. They alone bear the responsibility for any distortions of the record their posthumous reticence may achieve.

I. *Papers*

I. UNPUBLISHED OFFICIAL PAPERS

i. *British*

By virtue of the Public Records Act of 1958 these remain closed until fifty years after the date of their creation.

ii. *Foreign*

UNITED STATES

The archives of the Department of State are open on a restricted basis up to thirty years of the current date, and there is a further restricted period of ten years within that period. *See also Essay 12 above.*

GERMANY

All the important papers in the archives of the German Foreign Ministry and the German Reichs Chancellery, together with selected German Admiralty Papers were photostated by the tripartite Allied Commission of historians before their return to Western Germany, and copies may be inspected in the Public Records Office or the Foreign Office Library in London. Much of the Nazi material and material from the German Army Records was filmed by the American Historical Association, and may be purchased from Washington. For Britain, the first three categories available in London are the most important. Copies of all documents used as evidence in the Nuremberg trials have also been deposited with the Public Records Office.

ITALY

Selected Italian materials were microfilmed at the end of the war by their Allied captors, and copies are available for research in Washington and London.

JAPAN

The Japanese diplomatic, military and naval records were microfilmed by their American captors, and copies of these microfilms may be seen in Washington. In London there are the records of the Japanese Embassy in Rome on photostat, and copies of all the exhibits used in the Japanese War Criminal trials.

OTHER PAPERS

Conference de la Paix, 1919–20: Recueil des Actes de la Conference (Procés-Verbaux, Rapports et Documents). Parts I–VIII.
Proceedings of the Spanish Non-Intervention Committee.

2. PUBLISHED OFFICIAL PAPERS[1]

a. *Documents on British Foreign Policy, 1919–39.*

Edited by Rohan Butler, J. M. Bury and Sir Llewellyn Woodward (in progress).

b. *Blue Books*
(Major collections of diplomatic dispatches on particular subjects)

Cmd. 12 (1919). *Miscellaneous No.2.* Correspondence respecting the British Mission to South America.
Cmd. 2169 (1924). *France No.1.* Papers respecting the Negotiations for an Anglo-French Pact.

1. For a more detailed list the reader is referred to Robert Vogel, *A Breviate of British Diplomatic Blue Books, 1919–39* (McGill U.P., Montreal, 1963). Dr Vogel's list contains *all* the Treaties, exchanges of correspondence with *Foreign* Governments, etc., published by the British Government in that period. The list here printed confines itself to those official publications which, by reprinting Foreign Office dispatches between London and *British* representatives abroad, throw light on the views and methods employed by the Foreign Service, and on the *formulation* of British policy. Dr Vogel, too, does not distinguish between Blue books and White papers.

Cmd. 2458 (1925). *Protocol for the Pacific Settlement of International Disputes.* Correspondence relating to the position of the Dominions.

Cmd. 2895 (1927). *Russia No.3.* A selection of Papers dealing with the relations between His Majesty's Government and the Soviet Government, 1921–27.

Cmd. 3211 (1928). *Miscellaneous No.6.* Papers regarding the Limitation of Naval Armaments.

Cmd. 4614 (1934). *Liberia No.1.* Papers concerning affairs in Liberia, December 1930 to May 1934.

Cmd. 5143 (1936). *Miscellaneous No.3.* Correspondence showing the Course of Certain Diplomatic Discussions directed towards securing a European Settlement, June 1934 to March 1936.

Cmd. 5847 (1938). *Miscellaneous No.7.* Correspondence respecting Czechoslovakia, September 1938.

Cmd. 6106 (1939). Documents concerning German-Polish relations and the outbreak of Hostilities between Great Britain and Germany in September 1939.

c. *White papers containing diplomatic dispatches on particular subjects*

1919–39

Cmd. 8 (1919). *Russia No.1.* A collection of Reports on Bolshevism in Russia.

Cmd. 324 (1919). Papers regarding hostilities with Afghanistan, 1919.

Cmd. 586 (1920). *Miscellaneous No.2.* Correspondence relating to the Adriatic Question.

Cmd. 1214 (1921). *Miscellaneous No.9.* Correspondence respecting the New Financial Consortium in China.

Cmd. 1230 (1921). Correspondence respecting the alleged delay by British Authorities of telegrams from and to the United States.

Cmd. 1570 (1922). *Turkey No.1.* Correspondence between His Majesty's Government and the French Government respecting the Angora Agreement of 20 October 1921.

Cmd. 1572 (1922). *Egypt No.1.* Correspondence respecting Affairs in Egypt.

Cmd. 1858 (1923). *Abyssinia No.1.* Correspondence respecting Slavery in Abyssinia.

Cmd. 2435 (1925). *Miscellaneous No.7.* Papers respecting the Proposals for a Pact of Security.

Cmd. 2553 (1925). *Abyssinia No.1.* Correspondence respecting Abyssinian raids and incursions into British territory.

Cmd. 2636 (1926). *China No.1.* Papers respecting the First Firing in the Shameen Affair of 23 June 1924.

Cmd. 2874 (1927). *Russia No.2*. Documents illustrating the hostile activities of the Soviet Government and Third International against Great Britain.

Cmd. 3050 (1928). *Egypt No.2*. Papers regarding Negotiations for a Treaty of Alliance with Egypt.

Cmd. 3217 (1928). *Abyssinia No.1*. Correspondence respecting Abyssinian raids and incursions into British Territory and Anglo-Egyptian Sudan.

Cmd. 3575 (1930). *Egypt No.1*. Papers regarding the recent negotiations for an Anglo-Egyptian Settlement, 31 March to 8 May 1930.

Cmd. 4153 (1932). *Abyssinia No.1*. Papers concerning raids from Ethiopian Territory into the Anglo-Egyptian Sudan.

Cmd. 4286 (1933). *Russia No.1*. Correspondence relating to the Arrest of Employees of the Metropolitan-Vickers Company in Moscow.

Cmd. 5044 (1935). *Ethiopia No.1*. Documents relating to the Dispute between Ethiopia and Italy.

Cmd. 5957 (1939). *Miscellaneous No.3*. Correspondence between Sir Henry Macmahon and the Sherif Hussein of Mecca, July 1915 to March 1916.

Cmd. 5964 (1939). *Miscellaneous No.4*. Statements made on behalf of His Majesty's Government during the year 1918 in regard to the status of certain parts of the Ottoman Empire.

Cmd. 6115 (1939). *Germany No.1*. Final Report by the Right Honourable Sir Nevile Henderson, GCMG, on the circumstances leading to the termination of his Mission to Berlin, 20 September 1939.

Cmd. 6120 (1939). *Germany No.2*. Papers concerning the Treatment of German Nationals in Germany, 1938–39.

1939–63

Cmd. 6592 (1945). *Greece No.1*. Documents regarding the situation in Greece, January 1945.

Cmd. 6662 (1945). *France No.2*. Dispatch to HM Ambassador in Paris regarding relations between His Majesty's Government in the United Kingdom and the Vichy Government in the autumn of 1940, London, 13 July 1945.

Cmd. 7970 (1950). *Miscellaneous No.9*. Anglo-French Discussions regarding French proposals for the Western European Council, Iron and Steel Industries, March to June 1950.

Cmd. 8425 (1951). *Persia No.1*. Correspondence between His Majesty's Government in the United Kingdom and the Persian Government and related documents concerning the oil industry in Persia, February to September 1951.

Cmd. 8419 (1951). *Egypt No.2*. Anglo-Egyptian Conversations on the Defence of the Suez Canal and on the Sudan, December 1950 to November 1951.

For the study of the British foreign-policy-making elite, attention should also be called to:

Cmd. 3037 (1928). Report of the Board of Enquiry appointed by the Prime Minister to investigate certain Statements affecting Civil Servants.

Cmd. 3038 (1928). Minute by the Lords Commissioners of the Treasury and the Secretary of State for Foreign Affairs on the Report of the Board of Enquiry appointed by the Prime Minister to investigate certain statements affecting Civil Servants.

Cmd. 6420 (1943). *Miscellaneous No.2.* Proposals for the Reform of the Foreign Service.

Cmd. 9577 (1955). *Miscellaneous No.17.* Report concerning the disappearance of two former Foreign Office Officials, London, September 1955.

Cmd. 9715 (1956). Statement of the Findings of the Conference of Privy Councillors on Security.

Cmd. 232 (1957). Recruitment to the Administrative Class of the Home Civil Service and the Senior Branch of the Foreign Service: Statement of Government Policy and Report by the Civil Service Commission.

Cmd. 1681 (1962). Security Procedures in the Public Service.

Cmd. 2009 (1963). Report of the Tribunal appointed to inquire into the Vassall Case and related matters.

Cmd. 2153 (1963). Lord Denning's Report.

Cmd. 2276 (1964). *Miscellaneous No.5.* Report of the Committee on Representational Services overseas appointed by the Prime Minister under the chairmanship of Lord Plowden 1962–63.

Attention should also be drawn to:

The Select Committee on Estimates: *Seventh Report Together with the Minutes of evidence taken before Sub-Committee F and Appendices.* Session 1950–51. *The Foreign Service.*

The same: *Seventh Report Together with the proceedings of the Committee of 28 July, 20 and 25 October, 2 and 10 November and the Minutes taken before Sub-Committee E and Appendices.* Session 1953–54. *The Foreign Service.*

d. *Official Histories bearing on British defence policy, 1919–39*

HISTORY OF THE SECOND WORLD WAR: CIVIL SERIES

H. Duncan Hall, *North American Supply* (1955).

W. K. Hancock and M. M. Gowing, *British War Economy* (1949).

W. N. Medlicott, *The Economic Blockade*, vol.1 (1952).

M. M. Postan, *British War Production* (1952).

J. D. Scott and R. Hughes, *The Administration of British War Production* (1955).

HISTORY OF THE SECOND WORLD WAR: MILITARY SERIES

N. Gibbs, *Grand Strategy*, vol.I (this volume has still to appear).

J. R. M. Butler, *Grand Strategy*, vol.II (1957).

Basil Collier, *The Defence of the United Kingdom* (1957).

Major-General S. Woodburn Kirby, *The War in the Far East*, vol.I (1957).

Major-General I. S. O. Playfair, *The War in the Mediterranean*, vol.I (1954).

Sir Charles Webster and Noble Frankland, *The Strategic Bombing Offensive*, vols I and IV (1961).

COMMONWEALTH OFFICIAL HISTORIES

Paul Hasluck, *The Government and the People 1929–41* (Canberra, 1952).

Gilbert M. Tucker, *The Canadian Naval Service* (Ottawa, 1952).

F. L. Wood, *The New Zealand People at War; Political and External Affairs* (Wellington, 1958).

e. *Official papers of non-British origin containing material bearing on the content of British foreign policy, 1919–39.*[1]

DENMARK

Parliamentary Committee of Enquiry: *Betaenkning til Folketinget* I: *Bilag til Betaenkning til Folketinget*, I; *Beretning til Folketinget* II: *Bilag til Beretning til Folketinget*, II; (Copenhagen, 1945).

FRANCE

P. Mantoux (ed.), *Les Délibérations du Conseil des Quatre* (Paris, 1955).

Ministère des Affaires Etrangères:

Documents Diplomatiques. Conférence de Washington, Juillet 1921–Février 1922 (Paris, 1923).

Documents Diplomatiques. Documents relatives aux négociations concernant les garanties de sécurité contre une aggression de l'Allemagne, 10 Janvier 1919–7 Décembre 1923 (Paris, 1924).

Documents Diplomatiques. 1938–39. Pièces relatives aux événements et aux négociations qui ont précédé l'ouverture des hostilités entre l'Allemagne d'une part, la Pologne, la Grande Bretagne et la France d'autre part (Paris, 1939).

Documents Diplomatiques Français 1932–39, 2ᵉ Série (1936–39), Tome I (1ᵉ Janvier–21 Mars 1936) (Paris, 1936).

1. This list includes the principal collections only. By far the best bibliographical essay is contained in M. Toscano, *Storia dei Trattati e Politica Internazionale*, vol.I, 2nd edition (Rome, 1963).

GERMANY[1]

Documents on German Foreign Policy, 1918–45, series C and D.
Nuremberg International Military Tribunal:
Trial of the Major War Criminals (Nuremberg, 1948).
Trials of War Criminals, Cases I–XI.
Fritz Berber (ed.), *Europäische Politik im Spiegel der Prager Akten* (1942).
Deutschland–England 1933–39 (1940).
Auswärtiges Amt, *Polnische Dokumente zur Vorgeschichte des Krieges* (Berlin, 1940).
German Democratic Republic, Ministry of Foreign Affairs: *Lokarno 1925* (Berlin, 1959).

HUNGARY[2]

Historical Institute of the Academy of Sciences:

Kerekes Janos (ed.), vol.I, *A Berlin–Roma Tengely Kialakulása éz Auztria Annexiója 1936–38* (From the Berlin–Rome Axis to the Annexation of Austria) (Budapest, 1962).
Juhasz Gyula (ed.), vol.IV, *Magyerország Külpolitikája a II Vilegh/áború Kitövésének Idöszakaban, 1929–40* (Hungarian Foreign Policy at the time of the outbreak of the Second World War) (Budapest, 1962).

ITALY

Ministero degli Affari Esteri: *I Documenti Diplomatici Italiani*, Sesta Serie, 1922–35; Ottava Serie, 1935–39; Nona Serie, 1939–43.

JAPAN

International Military Tribunal for the Far East: *Trial of the Major War Criminals*, hectographed transcripts (Tokyo, 1948).

NORWAY

Royal Ministry of Foreign Affairs: *Norges forhold til Sverige under Krigen 1940–45. Aktstykken* (Norway's relations with Sweden during the war, 1940–45. Documents) (Oslo, 1947–50).

POLAND[3]

Ministry of Foreign Affairs: *The Polish White Book. Official Documents concerning Polish-German and Polish-Soviet relations 1933–39* (London, 1940).

1. See also under the Soviet Union below.
2. See ibid.   3. See also under Germany above.

General Sikorski Historical Institute: *Documents on Polish-Soviet Relations, 1939–45* (London, 1961).

PORTUGAL

Ministério dos Negócios Estrangeiros: *Dez anos de politica externa (1936–47). A naçao portuguese e a segunda guerra mundial,* Parte.1, *O rearmemento do Exército no quadro política de Aliança Luso-Britânica (1936–39)* (Lisbon, 1961–62).

SWEDEN

Foreign Ministry: *Handlingar rörande Sveriges politik under andre världskriget. Förspilet till det tyska angreppet pa Danmark och Norge den 9 April 1940* (Documents relating to Swedish policy during the Second World War. Prelude to the German aggression against Denmark and Norway on 9 April 1940) (Stockholm, 1947).

THE UNITED STATES

Department of State:

Foreign Relations of the United States (1918 onwards, yearly).
Foreign Relations of the United States: the Lansing Papers, 1914–18 (Washington, 1940).
Foreign Relations of the United States: The Paris Peace Conference (Washington, 1942–47).
Foreign Relations of the United States: Japan 1931–41 (Washington, 1943).
Foreign Relations of the United States: The Soviet Union 1933–39 (Washington, 1952).
Foreign Relations of the United States: The Conferences at Cairo and Teheran (Washington, 1961).
Foreign Relations of the United States: The Conferences at Malta and Yalta (Washington, 1955).
Foreign Relations of the United States: The Conference at Potsdam (Washington, 1960).

Joint Congressional Enquiry: *Pearl Harbour Attack. Hearings and Report* (Washington, 1946–47).

THE SOVIET UNION

People's Ministry for Foreign Affairs:
Documents and Materials relating to the Eve of the Second World War (Moscow, 1947).
The Dirksen Papers (Moscow, 1948).
La Politique Allemande 1936–43. Turquie, Hongrie, Espagne (Paris, 1946–47).

British and Foreign Materials

Correspondence between the Chairman of the Council of Ministers of the USSR and the President of the United States and the Prime Minister of Great Britain during the Great Patriotic War of 1941–45 (Moscow, 1957).

'Document: Teheran Conference of the Leaders of the Three Great Powers', *International Affairs* (Moscow), nos 7 and 8 (July and August 1961).

'The Military Negotiations between the USSR, Great Britain and France in August 1939' (in Russian), *Mezhdunarodny Zhizn*, N. II, III, (1959). (French translation in *Recherches Internationales à la Lumière du Marxisme*, N.12, March to April 1959.)

3. PRIVATE PAPERS IN GREAT BRITAIN NOW OPEN TO RESEARCH[1]

Cabinet Ministers

A. J. Balfour Papers: British Museum.

Viscount Cecil of Chelwood Papers: British Museum.

These two collections are only partially open to research, and are most informative for the periods their owners were out of office.

Austen Chamberlain Papers: University of Birmingham Library. A very valuable collection.

Hugh Dalton Diaries and Papers: British Library of Economics and Political Science, London.

H. A. L. Fisher Papers: Bodleian Library, Oxford.

Haldane Papers: Scottish National Library, Edinburgh. (Some material on the first Labour Government.)

George Lansbury Papers: British Library of Economics and Political Science, London.

Milner Papers: New College Library, Oxford. A curiously gappy collection.

Passfield Papers: British Library of Economics and Political Science, London. Of limited value.

Diplomats

None are available in public archives.

Soldiers, Sailors and Airmen

Admiral Sir Sidney Fremantle Papers: National Maritime Museum.

Field-Marshal Lord Haig Papers: National Library of Scotland.

1. This excludes Lord Beaverbrook's treasure hoard, the Bonar Law and Lloyd George Papers in process of transfer to the University of New Brunswick, Canada.

Admiral Sir Louis Hamilton Papers: National Maritime Museum.
Admiral Lord Jellicoe Papers: British Museum.
Admiral Sir Howard Kelly Memoirs and Papers: National Maritime Museum.
Captain Liddell Hart Papers: King's College, London, Military Archives.
Admiral Sir Herbert Richmond Papers: National Maritime Museum.
Admiral Thursfield Papers: National Maritime Museum.
Sir William Wiseman Papers: Sterling Library, Yale.

Others

Reginald Brett, Viscount Esher Papers: University of Liverpool Library.
Sir William H. Clarke Papers: British Library of Economics and Political Science, London.
W. H. Dawson Papers: University of Birmingham Library.
Philip Kerr, 11th Marquess of Lothian Papers: Scottish Record Office, Registry House, Edinburgh.
R. G. W. Mackay, MP, Papers: British Library of Economics and Political Science, London.
Violet Markham Papers: British Library of Economics and Political Science, London.
Sir Frederich Maze Papers: Library of the School of Oriental and African Studies.
E. D. Morel Papers: British Library of Economics and Political Science, London.
Gilbert Murray Papers: Bodleian Library, Oxford.
Wingate Papers: Durham University Library.
Spencer Wilkinson Papers: Army–Ogilby Museum, London.

II. *Memoirs and Biographies*[1]

I. THE CROWN AND ITS ADVISERS

Sir Harold Nicolson, *King George V, His Life and Reign* (1952).
John Wheeler-Bennett, *George VI, His Life and Reign* (1956).
Edward, Duke of Windsor, *A King's Story* (1951).
Reginald Brett, *Journals and Letters of Reginald,* Viscount Esher (1938).
Lord Hankey:
  Diplomacy by Conference (1946).
  The Supreme Command, 1914–18 (1961).
  The Supreme Command at the Paris Peace Conference, 1919 (1963).

1. The place of publication may be assumed to be London, except where otherwise stated. See also W. M. Matthews, *British Autobiographies,* (Los Angeles, 1955).

Sir Almeric Fitzroy, *Memoirs* (1925).
Sir Frederick Ponsonby, *Recollections of Three Reigns* (1961).

2. CABINET MEMBERS[1]

a. *The Coalition Cabinet, 1919–22*

David Lloyd George:
War Memoirs (1933–36).
The Truth about the Peace Treaties (1938).
The Truth about Reparations and War Debts (1932).
T. H. Jones, *David Lloyd George* (1951).
Frank Owen, *Tempestuous Journey* (1954).
Robert Blake, *The Unknown Prime Minister, The Life and Times of Andrew, Bonar Law* (1953).
Sir Charles Petrie, *The Life and Letters of Sir Austen Chamberlain* (1939).[2]
Lord Ronaldshay, *The Life of Lord Curzon* (1928).
Harold Nicolson, *Curzon, The Last Phase* (1934).
Leonard Mosley, *Curzon, the End of an Epoch* (1960).
Blanche Dugdale, *Arthur James Balfour* (1936).
K. Young, *Arthur James Balfour* (1963).
G. N. Barnes, *From Workshop to War Cabinet* (1924).
C. Addison:
Politics from Within, 1911–18 (1924).
Four and a half Years: a personal diary from June 1914 to January 1919 (1934).
R. J. Minney, *Viscount Addison, Leader of the House* (1950).
Earl of Birkenhead, *Frederick Erwin, Earl of Birkenhead* (1933–35).
William Camp, *The Glittering Prize, A Biographical Study of Lord Birkenhead* (1960).
Winston Churchill, *The World Crisis, the Aftermath* (1929).
Lord Long of Wraxall, *Memoirs* (1923).
Sir Charles Petrie, *Walter Long and his Times* (1936).
Vladimir Halpern, *Lord Milner and the Empire* (1952).
J. E. Wrench, *Alfred Lord Milner* (1950).
A. M. Gollin, *Proconsul in Politics* (1964).
Edwin S. Montague, *An Indian Diary* (1930).
Sir David Waley, *Edwin Montague* (Bombay 1962).
Baron Geddes, *The Forging of a Family* (1952).

1. These are listed by the first Cabinet of which the subject of the work was a member. They include members of all Cabinet ministries, not merely those listed in the Appendix.
2. A new biography of Sir Austen Chamberlain based on the Chamberlain papers is under production by Dr Douglas Johnson.

G. M. Young, *Stanley Baldwin* (1952).[1]
Wickham Steed, *The Real Stanley Baldwin* (1930).
D. S. Somervell, *Stanley Baldwin* (1953).
A. W. Baldwin, *My Father, the True Story* (1955).
Hector Bolitho, *Alfred Mond, First Lord Melchett* (1933).
Sir A. Griffith-Boscawen, *Memoirs* (1925).
Robert Jackson, *The Chief: Gordon Hewart, Lord Chief of Justice of England 1922–40* (1959).

b. *The Conservative Cabinet, November 1922*

Sir C. Mallet, *Lord Cave, a Memoir* (1931).
Randolph Churchill, *Lord Derby, 'King of Lancashire'* (1959).
L. S. Amery, *My Political Life* (1953–55).
Viscount Swinton, *I Remember* (1948).
Earl of Halifax, *Fulness of Days* (1957).
Keith Feiling, *The Life of Neville Chamberlain* (1946).
Iain Macleod, *Neville Chamberlain* (1961).

c. *The Conservative Cabinet, March 1923*

Viscount Cecil of Chelwood:
  A Great Experiment (1941).
  All the Way (1949).
M. Bechhofer, *Lord Robert Cecil und das Völkerbund* (Zurich, 1959).
Viscount Templewood, *Empire of the Air* (1957).
H. A. Taylor, *Jix – Viscount Brentford* (1933).

d. *The Labour Cabinet, January 1924*

Benjamin Sachs, *J. Ramsay MacDonald in Thought and Action* (Albuquerque, New Mexico, 1952).[2]
M. S. Venkataramani, 'Ramsay MacDonald and Britain's Domestic Politics and Foreign Relations 1919–31', *Political Studies*, VII, no.3 (October 1960).
Lauchlin MacNeill Weir, *The Tragedy of Ramsay MacDonald* (1938).
J. R. Clynes, *Memoirs, 1924–37* (1937).
General Sir F. Maurice, *Haldane, 1856–1928* (1937).
Dudley Somers, *Haldane of Sloan* (1962).
Raymond Postgate, *The Life of George Lansbury* (1951).

1. A new biography of Stanley Baldwin is under preparation by John Barnes.
2. A new biography of J. Ramsay MacDonald by David Marquand based on the MacDonald papers is under preparation.

J. H. Thomas, *My Story* (1937).
Gregory Blaxland, *J. H. Thomas, A Life for Unity* (1964).
Sidney Webb, 'The First Labour Government: A Historical Note', *Political Quarterly*, XXII, no.1 (January 1961).
Sir Patrick Hastings, *Autobiography* (1948).
Viscount Snowden, *An Autobiography* (1934).
Mrs Mary Agnes Hamilton, *Arthur Henderson* (1938).
E. A. Jenkins, *From Foundry to Foreign Office* (1933).
A. Fenner Brockway, *Socialism over 60 years, The Life of Jowett of Bradford, 1864–1944* (1946).
Josiah Wedgewood, *Memoirs of a Fighting Life* (1941).
C. V. Wedgewood, *The Last of the Radicals, Josiah Wedgewood, MP* (1951).
Lord Parmoor, *A Retrospect: Looking Back Over a Life of More than Eighty Years* (1936).
Mose Anderson, *Noel Buxton* (1952).

e. *The Conservative Cabinet, 1924–29*

Lord Eustace Percy, *Some Memories* (1958).

f. *The Labour Cabinet, 1929–31*

M. Bondfield, *A Life's Work* (1949).
Hugh Dalton, 'British Foreign Policy, 1929–31', *Political Quarterly*, II, no.4 (October to December 1931).
T. Johnston, *Memories* (1952).
Sidney Webb, 'What Happened in 1931; A Record', *Political Quarterly*, III, no.1 (January 1932).
F. Pethick-Lawrence, *Fate Has Been Kind* (1942).
V. Brittain, *Pethick-Lawrence, A Portrait* (1963).
H. Morrison, *An Autobiography* (1961).
T. Graham, *Willie Graham* (1948).

g. *The National Government, 1931–35, 1935–37*

Viscount Samuel, *Memoirs* (1945).
John Bowle, *Viscount Samuel* (1957).
Viscount Templewood, *Nine Troubled Years* (1954).
Rufus Isaacs, First Marquess of Reading, by his Son (1945).
Sir Anthony Eden, Earl of Avon, *Facing the Dictators* (1962).
Lewis Broad, *Sir Anthony Eden* (1955).
Viscount Simon, *Retrospect* (1952).
Marquess of Londonderry, *Wings of Destiny* (1943).
Viscount Norwich, *Old Men Forget* (1953).
Essayez, The Memoirs of Lawrence, Second Marquis of Zetland (1956).

h. *The National Government, 1937–39*

Viscount Maugham:
  The Truth about Munich (1944).
  At the End of the Day (1954).
Sir John Wheeler-Bennett, *John Anderson, Viscount Waverley* (1962).
Admiral of the Fleet Lord Chatfield, *It Might Happen Again* (1947).
Earl Winterton, *Orders of the Day* (1953).
R. J. Minney (ed.), *The Private Papers of Hore-Belisha* (1960).

i. *The National Government, 1939–40*

Winston S. Churchill, *The Second World War* (1948–53).
Lord Reith, *Into the Wind* (1948).

j. *The National Government, 1940–45*

Clement Attlee, *As it Happened* (1954).
Francis Williams:
  A Prime Minister Remembers (1960).
  Ernest Bevin (1952).
A. Bullock, *The Life and Times of Ernest Bevin* (1960).
Eric Estorick, *Stafford Cripps* (1949).
Colin Cooke, *The Life of Richard Stafford Cripps* (1957).
Tom Driberg, *Beaverbrook, A study in Frustration* (1956).
Colin Forbes-Adam, *The Life of Lord Lloyd* (1948).
Baron Casey, *Personal Experience, 1939–48* (1962).
Earl Woolton, *Memoirs* (1959).
Viscount Chandos, *The Memoirs of Lord Chandos* (1962).
Hugh Dalton, *Memoirs, The Fateful Years, 1931–45* (1957).

k. *The Labour Government, 1945–51*

Hugh Dalton, *Memoirs, 1945–60, High Tide and After* (1962).
W. T. Rodgers (ed.), *Hugh Gaitskell* (1964).
Emmanuel Shinwell, *Conflict without Malice* (1955).
Fred Blackburn, *George Tomlinson* (1954).
Vincent Brome, *Aneurin Bevan* (1953).
M. M. Krug, *Aneurin Bevan*, (N.Y. 1959).
Michael Foot, *Aneurin Bevan* (1962).
G. C. Eastwood, *George Isaacs* (1952).
Lord Pakenham, *Born to Believe* (1953).
Leslie Smith, *Harold Wilson: A Portrait* (1964).

British and Foreign Materials

1. *The Conservative Government, 1951–56*

Earl of Birkenhead, *The Prof in Two Worlds* (1961).
Roy Harrod, *The Prof* (1959).
Sir Anthony Eden, Earl of Avon, *Full Circle* (1960).
Lord Hill of Luton, *Both Sides of the Hill,* (1964).
John Dickie, *The Uncommon Commoner. Sir Alec Douglas-Home,* (1964).
Lord Kilmuir, *Political Adventure* (1964).
Lord Ismay, *Memoirs* (1960).

3. MEMBERS OF THE DIPLOMATIC SERVICE AND THE FOREIGN OFFICE[1]

a. *The Senior Administrative Branch*

Ainslie Douglas Ainslie, *Adventures Social and Literary* (1922).
The Diaries of Lord Bertie of Thame, 1914–18 (1924).
H. J. Bruce:
   Silken Dalliance (1946).
   Thirty Dozen Moons (1949).
Sir George Buchanan, *My Mission to Russia and other Diplomatic Memoirs* (1923).
Sir Reader Bullard, *The Camels Must Go* (1961).
Tom Driberg, *Guy Burgess: A Portrait with Background* (1956).
Sir Harold Butler, *Confident Morning* (1950).
Eric Cleugh, *Without Let or Hindrance: Reminiscences of a British Foreign Service Officer* (1950).
Sir Robert Craigie, *Behind the Japanese Mask* (n.d. 1946).
James Pope-Hennessy, *Lord Crewe, 1858–1945, the Making of a Liberal* (1955).
Colin Cooke, *The Life of Richard Stafford Cripps* (1957).
Viscount d'Abernon, *Diary of an Ambassador* (1929).
Randolph Churchill, *Lord Derby, 'King of Lancashire'* (1959).
Lawrence Durrell, *Bitter Lemons* (1957).
A. S. F. Gow, 'Sir Stephen Gaselee, KCMG, 1882–1943', *Proceedings of the British Academy*, XXIX (1944).
Baron Geddes, *The Forging of a Family* (1952).
J. D. Gregory, *On the Edge of Diplomacy* (1928).
Earl of Halifax, *Fulness of Days* (1957).
Lord Hardinge of Penshurst, *The Old Diplomacy* (1947).

1. The attentive reader will note some duplication between this and the preceding section where Cabinet Ministers subsequently served as Ambassadors. The list is arranged alphabetically in accordance with the name of the author of an autobiography or the subject of a biography.

Sir Nevile Henderson:
  Failure of a Mission (1940).
  Water under the Bridges (1945).
Dr Rudi Strauch, *Sir Nevile Henderson* (Bonn, 1959).
Sir Samuel Hoare, *Ambassador on Special Mission* (1946).
Sir Robert Hodgson, *Spain Resurgent* (1953).
Sir Thomas Hohler, *Diplomatic Petrel* (1942).
Lord Howard of Penrith, *Theatre of Life, 1863–1936* (Boston, 1935–36).
Rufus Isaacs, First Marquess of Reading, by his Son (1945).
Sir David Kelly, *The Ruling Few* (1953).
Sir Alec Kirkbride, *A Crackle of Thorns* (1956).
Sir Ivone Kirkpatrick, *The Inner Circle* (1959).
Sir Hughe Knatchbull-Hugessen, *Diplomat in Peace and War* (1949).
Stephen Lawford, *Youth Uncharted* (1935).
Valentine Lawford, *Bound for Diplomacy* (1963).
Sir Reginald Leeper, *When Greek meets Greek* (1950).
Sir Francis Lindley, *A Diplomat off Duty* (1947).
Sir H. C. Luke, *Cities and Men* (1956).
J. R. M. Butler, *Lord Lothian (Philip Kerr), 1882–1940* (1960).
Sir Fitzroy Maclean, *Eastern Approaches* (1949).
Charles Bigham Mersey, *A Picture of Life (1941)*.
Harold Nicolson, *Peacemaking 1919* (1933).
Viscount Norwich, *Old Men Forget* (1953).
Sir Lancelot Oliphant, *Ambassador in Bonds* (1946).
Sir Owen O'Malley, *The Phantom Caravan* (1954).
Sir William J. Onderyk, *Ways and Byways in Diplomacy* (1959).
Lord Eustace Percy, *Some Memories* (1958).
Sir Maurice Peterson, *Both Sides of the Curtain* (1950).
Sir Alec Randall, *Vatican Assignment* (1956).
Sir George Rendell, *The Sword and the Olive* (1957).
Lord Rennell of Rodd, *Social and Diplomatic Memories; Third Series, 1902–19* (1925).
Sir Andrew Ryan, *The Last of the Dragomans* (1951).
Bernard M. Allen, *Sir Ernest Satow: A Memoir* (1933).
Sir Walford Selby, *Diplomatic Twilight* (1953).
Sir Clarence Skrine, *World War II in Iran* (1962).
Lord Strang, *At Home and Abroad* (1956).
Sir Geoffrey Thompson, *Front-Line Diplomat* (1959).
Sir John Tilley, *London to Tokyo* (1942).
Lord Vansittart:
  Lessons of My Life (1943).[1]
  The Mist Procession (1958).

1. A political biography of Lord Vansittart based on the Vansittart papers is under preparation by Ian Colvin.

British and Foreign Materials

Sir Victor Wellesley, *Diplomacy in Fetters* (1945).
Sir Arnold Wilson:
  Loyalties (1930).
  Mesopotamia (1931).
  South-West Persia (1941).
Sir Michael Wright, *Disarm and Verify* (1964).

b. *Consular Officers*

Sir Gerald Campbell, *Of True Experience* (1949).
Ernest Hamblock, *British Consul: Memories of Thirty Years' Service in Europe and Brazil* (1938).
Sir Walter Risley Hearn, *Some Recollections: Memories of thirty-five years in the Consular Service* (1928).
Sir William Meyrick Hewlett, *Forty Years in China* (1943).
Arnhold Wienholt Hodson:
  Seven Years in Abyssinia (1927).
  Where Lions Reign (1929).
Arthur Keyser, *Trifles and Travels* (1943).
G. H. Selous, *Appointment to Fez* (1956).

c. *The King's Messengers (Diplomatic Couriers)*

George P. Antrobus, *King's Messenger, 1918–40; Memories of a Silver Greyhound* (1941).
Piers William North, *Reminiscences of a Younger Son* (1957).
Michael O'Brien Tuohig, *Diplomatic Courier* (1960).
Sir Walter Windham, *Waves, Wheels, Wings* (1943).

d. *Novels by Foreign Service members and attachés illustrative of conditions in the Foreign Office, etc.*

Lawrence Durrell, *Mountolive* (1959).
Andrew Graham, *A Foreign Affair* (1958).
Mary Hocking, *The Winter City* (1961).
Mary McMinnies, *The Visitors* (1958).
Harold Nicolson, *Public Faces* (1932).
Hugh Thomas, *The World's Game* (1957).

e. *Military and Naval Attachés*

Admiral Guy Gaunt, *Yield of the Years* (1940).
General Richard Hilton, *Military Attaché in Moscow* (1949).

Percy H. H. Massey, *Eastern Mediterranean Lands* (1923).
Henry Dundas Napier, *Experiences of a Military Attaché* (1924).
Major-General Stuart Piggott, *Broken Thread* (1950).
Colonel F. A. Wellesley, *Recollections of a Soldier-Diplomat* (1940).

4. SOLDIERS, SAILORS AND AIRMEN[1]

a. *Soldiers*

Robert Blake, *The Private Papers of Douglas Haig, 1914–19* (1952).
John Terraine, *Douglas Haig* (1963).
General Sir Wellesley D. G. Brownrigg, *Unexpected* (1942).
Sir Christopher Caldwell, *Field-Marshal Sir Henry Wilson: his Life and diaries* (1927).
Basil Collier, *Brasshat* (1961).
Colonel C. H. Ellis, *The Transcaspian Episode* (1963).
Sir Hubert Gough, *Soldiering On* (1954).
Lord Ismay, *Memoirs* (1960).
Major-General Sir John Kennedy, *The Business of War* (1957).
General Sir Leslie Hollis, *One Marine's Tale* (1956).
Field-Marshal Lord Ironside, *Archangel, 1918–19* (1953).
The Ironside Diaries, 1937–40 (1962).
Sir Edward Spears, *Assignment to Catastrophe* (1954).
Sir Arthur Bryant, *The Turn of the Tide* (1957).
Colonel Roger Hammett Beadon, *Some Memories of the Peace Conference* (1933).
Major-General Carton de Wiart, *Happy Odyssey* (1955).
Field-Marshal Viscount Montgomery of Alamein, *Memoirs* (1958).
Sir Arthur Willert, *The Road to Safety* (1953).
Col. the Hon. Sir Arthur Murray, *At Close Quarters* (1946).
General Sir Charles Harington, *Tim Harington Looks Back* (1940).
General Sir Frederick Morgan, *Peace and War* (1961).
Major-General Stuart Piggott, *Broken Thread* (1950).
Colonel R. Meinertzhagen: *Army Diary, 1899–1926* (1960).
                                    Diary of a Black Sheep, (1964).
Bernard Fergusson, *Wavell, Portrait of a Soldier* (1961).
Viscount Wavell, *Allenby, Soldier and Statesman* (1946).
John Connell, *Wavell, Scholar and Soldier,* (1964).

1. In this and the following sections 5–8 I have included only works known to me to include material relevant to the theme of this book. I have made no attempt to list *all* the memoirs and biographies which might otherwise come under this heading.

b. *Sailors*

Captain Augustus Agar, *Footprints in the Sea* (1959).

Admiral W. S. Chalmers, *The Life and Letters of Reginald, Earl Beatty* (1951).

Admiral of the Fleet Lord Chatfield, *It Might Happen Again* (1947).

Admiral of the Fleet the Earl of Cork and Orrery, *My Naval Life, 1888–1941* (1942).

Lionel Dawson, *Sound of the Guns; Rear-Admiral Sir Walter Cowan, RN* (1949).

Admiral of the Fleet Viscount Cunningham of Hyndhope, *A Sailor's Odyssey* (1951).

Vice-Admiral Sir Barry Domville, *By and Large* (1947).

Admiral Sir Frederick Dreyer, *The Sea Heritage* (1955).

A. J. Marder, *Fear God and Dread Nought*, vol.III (1959).

Admiral Sir Sidney R. Fremantle, *My Naval Career, 1850–1928* (1949).

Admiral Sir William James, *The Sky was always Blue* (1951).

Admiral Sir Reginald Bacon, *The Life of John Rushworth, Earl Jellicoe* (1936).

Admiral Sir Roger Keyes, *The Naval Memoirs* (1935).

Cecil Aspinall-Oglander, *Roger Keyes* (1951).

Rear-Admiral W. S. Chalmers, *Full Cycle, The Life of Sir Bertram Ramsey* (1960).

Victoria, Baroness Wester Wemyss, *The Life and Letters of Lord Wester Wemyss* (1935).

Rear-Admiral Noel Wright, *Sea of Memory* (1947).

c. *Airmen*

Andrew Boyle, *Trenchard, Man of Vision* (1962).

Sir P. Joubert, *Fun and Games*, (1964).

Sir John Slessor, *The Central Blue* (1956).

Sir Frederick Sykes, *From All Angles* (1943).

Air Vice-Marshal Arthur S. Gould Lee, *Special duties* (1946).

John Laffin, *Swifter than Eagles. A Biography of Air Chief Marshal Sir John Salmond*, (1964).

P. R. Reid, *Winged Diplomat: The Life Story of Air Commodore Freddie West, VC, CBE, MC* (1962).

5. MEMBERS OF THE COLONIAL AND CIVIL SERVICES

Lord Belhaven, *The Uneven Road* (1955).

Norman and Helen Bentwich, *Mandate Memories, 1918–1948*, (1964).

Sir William Beveridge, *Power and Influence* (1953).

Philip Graves, *The Life of Sir Percy Cox* (1940).
Sir H. Hamilton, 'Sir Warren Fisher and the Public Service', *Public Administration*, XXIX (Spring 1951).
Sir Hugh Foot, *A Start in Freedom* (1964).
P. H. Grigg. *Prejudice and Judgement* (1948).
Harold Ingrams, *Arabia and the Isles* (1942).
Sir Charles Johnson, *The View from Steamer Point*, (1964).
Sir Alexander McFadyean, *Recollected in Tranquillity* (1964).
Lady Mildred Murray, *The Making of a Civil Servant; Sir Oswald Murray, GCB, Secretary to the Admiralty, 1917–36* (1940).
Sir E. Denison Ross, *Both Ends of the Candle* (1943).
Lord Salter:
  Personality in Politics (1947).
  Memoirs of a Public Servant (1961).
Ronald Storrs, *Orientations* (1937).
Sir Stuart Symes, *Tour of Duty* (1946).
Sir Stephen Tallents, *Men and Boy* (1947).
Sir Cecil M. Weir, *Civilian Assignment* (1953).

6. DOMINIONS AND COMMONWEALTH STATESMEN

The Memoirs of the Aga Khan (1954).
Ernest Watkins, *R. B. Bennett* (1964).
Sir Robert Laird Borden; His Memoirs (Toronto, 1938).
Sir Michael Blundell, *So Rough a Wind* (1964).
Lord Casey, *Personal Experience, 1939–45* (1962).
W. S. Wallace, *The Memoirs of Sir George Foster* (Toronto, 1957).
C. M. van den Heever, *General J. B. M. Hertzog* (Johannesburg, 1946).
Oswald Pirow, *James Barry Munnick Hertzog* (1958).
W. S. Hughes, *The Splendid Adventure* (1929).
William Farmer Whyte, *William Morris Hughes, His Life and Times* (Sydney, 1957).
R. Macgregor Dawson, *William Lyon Mackenzie King* (Ottawa, 1931).
T. W. Pickersgill, *The Mackenzie King Record* (Toronto, 1961).
Vincent Massey, *What's Past is Prologue* (1964).
W. R. Graham, *Arthur Meighen* (Toronto, 1960).
K. P. S. Menon, *The Flying Troika* (1963).
W. R. Riddell, *World Security Through Conference* (Toronto, 1947).
Sarah Gertrude Millin, *Smuts* (1936).
W. K. Hancock, *Smuts, The Sanguine Years* (1962).
Sir Roy Welensky, *Welensky's 4,000 Days* (1964).

7. JOURNALISTS, FOREIGN CORRESPONDENTS AND THE
PRESS

Sir Linton Andrews, *Linton Andrews; The Autobiography of a Journalist*
(1964).
Norman Angell:
 The Steep Places (1947).
 After All (1951).
Anon., *The History of The Times*, vol.IV (1952).
Lord Beaverbrook:
 Men and Power, 1917–18 (1956).
 The Decline and Fall of Lloyd George, 1921–22, (1963).
Tom Driberg, *Beaverbrook, a Study in Frustration* (1956).
Vernon Bartlett, *This is my Life* (1937).
Sir Robert Bruce Lockhart:
 Comes the Reckoning (1947).
 Friends, Foes and Foreigners (1957).
 Giants Cast Long Shadows (1960).
Sir Valentine Chirol, *Fifty Years in a Changing World* (1927).
Claud Cockburn:
 In Time of Trouble (1956).
 Crossing the Line (1958).
Mrs W. L. Courtney, *The Making of an Editor, W. L. Courtney, 1880–
1928* (1930).
Sir Evelyn Wrench, *Geoffrey Dawson and Our Times* (1955).
Sefton Delmer:
 Autobiography: vol.I, *Trail Sinister* (1962).
        vol.II, *Black Boomerang* (1963).
H. A. Taylor, *Robert Donald* (1934).
P. H. Brand (ed.), *The Letters of John Dove* (1938).
Paul Einzig, *In the Centre of Things* (1959).
Willi Frischauer, *European Commuter* (1964).
Katherine Garvin, *J. L. Garvin* (1948).
G. E. R. Gedye, *Fallen Bastions* (1939).
Mary Agnes Hamilton:
 Remembering My Good Friends (1944).
 Uphill All the Way (1953).
R. Wilson Harris, *Life So Far* (1954).
F. W. Hirst by his Friends (1958).
Sir Roderick Jones, *A Life in Reuters* (1957).
A. L. Kennedy, *Britain Faces Germany* (1937).
J. R. M. Butler, *Lord Lothian (Philip Kerr), 1882–1940* (1960).
C. J. Hambro, *Newspaper Lords in British Politics* (1958).

Desmond Chapman-Huston, *The Lost Historian. A Memoir of Sir Sidney Low* (1935).
Reginald Pound and Geoffrey Harmsworth, *Northcliffe* (1959).
G. Ward Price, *Extra-Special Correspondent* (1957).
Colonel Repington, *After the War* (1923).
Lord Riddell, *An Intimate Diary of the Peace Conference and After* (1923).
Lord Rothermere, *Warnings and Predictions* (1939).
J. L. Hammond, *C. P. Scott of the Manchester Guardian* (1934).
Divers Authors, *C. P. Scott and the Making of the Manchester Guardian* (1946).
G. R. Slocombe, *A Mirror to Geneva* (1937).
J. A. Spender, *Life, Journalism and Politics*, (1927).
Wilson Harris, *J. A. Spender* (1946).
Freya Stark, *Dust on the Lion's Paw: Autobiography, 1939–45* (1961).
H. Wickham Steed, *Through Thirty Years, 1892–1922* (1924).
Mike Williams-Thompson, *On the Record: an interim Memoir* (1960).
Sir Evelyn Wrench:
   Struggle, 1914–19 (1935).
   I Loved Germany (1940).
   Immortal Years (1945).

8. OTHER PERSONALITIES

King Abdallah, *My Memoirs* (1949).
Arthur Marwick, *Clifford Allen, Open Conspirator* (1964).
Maurice Collis, *Nancy Astor* (1960).
Michael Astor, *Tribal Feeling* (1963).
Sir Charles Belgrave, *Personal Column* (1960).
E. Burgoyne, *Gertrude Bell from her Personal Papers, 1914–26* (1961).
Sir William Beveridge, *I Fight to Live* (1947).
Lord Boothby, *My Yesterday, Your Tomorrow* (1962).
John Buchan, *Memory Hold the Door* (1940).
J. Lonsdale Bryans, *Blind Victory* (1951).
Victoria de Bunsen, *Charles Roden Buxton, A memoir* (1940).
John Rowland and Basil, Second Baron Cadman, *Ambassador for Oil, the Life of John, First Baron Cadman* (1960).
Earl of Birkenhead, *The Prof in Two Worlds* (1961).
Roy Harrod, *The Prof* (1959).
Lord Citrine, *Men and Work*, (1964).
J. M. Greaves, *Corder Catchpool* (1953).
W. R. Hughes, *Indomitable Friend* (1956).
Baron Croft, *My Life of Strife* (1948).
Red Cross and Berlin Embassy, 1915–26, Extracts from the diaries of Viscountess d'Abernon (1946).

British and Foreign Materials

H. R. P. Dickson, *Kuwait and its Neighbours* (1956).
Sir John Glubb, *A Soldier with the Arabs* (1951).
G. P. Gooch, *Under Six Reigns* (1958).
F. J. Tritton, *Carl Heath, Apostle of Peace* (1951).
H. N. Brailsford, *The Life and Work of J. A. Hobson* (1948).
W. S. Hewins, *Apologia of an Imperialist* (1939).
Thomas Jones, CH, *A Diary with Letters, 1931–50* (1954).
R. F. Harrod, *The Life of John Maynard Keynes* (1951).
Lord Keynes:
   Two Memoirs (1949).
   The Economic Consequences of the Peace (1920).
Lt.-Colonel F. H. Kisch, *Palestine Diary* (1958).
Colin Forbes-Adam, *Life of Lord Lloyd* (1948).
Lord Mottistone, *Fear and Be Slain* (1931).
Katherine Marjorie Murray, Duchess of Atholl, *Working Partnership. The Life of John George, Eighth Duke of Atholl* (1958).
Lord Murray of Elibank, *At Close Quarters* (1946).
K. D. D. Henderson, *The Making of the Modern Sudan; the Life and Letters of Sir Douglas Newbolt of the Sudan Political Service* (1953).
Sir Henry Clay, *Lord Norman* (1957).
Conor Cruse O'Brien, *To Katanga and Back* (1962).
Sir Francis Oppenheimer, *Stranger Within: Autobiographical Pages* (1961).
Frank Pakenham, *Peace by Ordeal* (1935).
Sir Charles Petrie, *The Power Behind the Prime Ministers* (1958).
Henry St John M. Philby:
   A Pilgrim in Arabia (1943).
   Arabian Days (1948).
Lord Reith, *Into the Wind* (1948).
Sidney Reuben Robertson, *Making Friends for Britain: an incursion into diplomacy* (Buenos Aires, 1948).
Sir Thomas Russell Pasha, *Egyptian Service, 1902–46* (1949).
S. Salvidge, *Salvidge of Liverpool* (1934).
R. Henriques, *Marcus Samuel, First Viscount Bearsted and Founder of the Shell Transport and Trading Company, 1853–1927* (1960).
Sir Percy Sillitoe, *Cloak without Dagger* (1955).
Lord Strabolgi, *Sailors, Statesmen and Others* (1933).
Gerald Sparrow, *Not Wisely but too Well* (1961).
H. Montgomery Hyde, *The Quiet Canadian, Sir William Stephenson* (1962).
Ronald W. Clark, *Tizard,* (1964).
Sir Miles Thomas, *Out on a Wing,* (1964).
Gerald Pawle, *The War and Colonel Warden: Based on the Recollections of Commander C. R. Thompson, CMG, OBE, RN(ret.) Personal Assistant to the Prime Minister, 1940–45* (1960).
F. J. Thompson, *Destination Washington* (1960).

Ernest Thurtle, *Time's Winged Chariot: Memoirs and Comments* (*1945*).
Herbert A. Grant Watson, *An Account of a Mission to the Baltic States in 1919* (1958).
Margaret Cole (ed.), *Beatrice Webb's Diaries, 1922–40* (1952).
Sir Arthur Willert, *The Road to Safety: A Study in Anglo-American Relations* (1952).
Sir Ronald Wingate, *Not in the Limelight* (1959).

9. FOREIGN DIPLOMATISTS, OR MILITARY REPRESENTA-TIVES AND OTHERS STATIONED IN LONDON, 1919–45.

a. *Austria*

George Franckenstein, *Diplomat of Destiny* (New York, 1940).
Lothar Wimmer:
    Expériences et Tribulations d'un diplomate autrichien entre deux guerres, 1929–38 (Neuchâtel, 1946).
    Zwischen Ballhausplatz und Downing Street (Vienna, 1958).

b. *France*

Comte de St Aulaire, *Confession d'un vieux diplomate* (Paris, 1953).
Prince Xavier de Bourbon, *Les Accords secrets franco-anglais de décembre 1940* (Paris, 1949).
Géneral Charles de Gaulle, *Mémoires de Guerre* (Paris, 1954–59).
Louis Rougier:
    Mission sécrete à Londres. Les accords Pétain-Churchill (Geneva, 1946).
    Les Accords secrets franco-britanniques. Histoire et Imposture (Paris, 1954).
Jacques Soustelle, *Envers et Contre Tous* (Paris, 1947–50).

c. *Germany*

Albrecht Bernstorff zum Gedächtnis (privately printed, n.p., 1952).
Kurt von Stutterheim, *Die Majestät des Gewissens. In Memoriam Albrecht Bernstoffs* (Hamburg, 1962).
Herbert von Dirksen, *Moskau, Tokyo, London* (Stuttgart, 1949); Eng. trans., *Moscow, Toyko, London* (1951).
S. S. Fitz Randolph, *Der Frühstucks-Attaché aus London* (Stuttgart, 1954).
Margarete Gärtner, *Botschafterin des guten Willens* (Bonn, 1955).
Fritz Hesse, *Das Spiel um Deutschland* (Munich, 1953); Eng. trans., *Hitler and the English* (1954).
Erich Kordt, *Nicht aus den Akten* (Stuttgart, 1950).
Wolfgang zu Putlitz, *Unterwegs nach Deutschland* (Berlin, 1956); Eng. trans., *The Putlitz dossier* (1957).

British and Foreign Materials

Joachim von Ribbentrop, *Zwischen London und Moskau* (Leoni am Starnberger See, 1953); Eng. trans., *The Ribbentrop Memoirs* (1954).
General Baron Geyr von Schweppenburg, *The Critical years* (1952).
H. G. Sasse, *100 Jahre Botschaft in London*, (Bonn, 1963).

d. *Italy*

Giusseppe Bastianini, *Uomini, Cose, Fatti, Memorie d'un Ambasciatore* (Milan, 1959).

e. *Japan*

Marmoru Shigemitsu, *Japan and Her Destiny* (1958).
Shigeru Yoshida, *The Yoshida Memoirs, The Story of Japan in Crisis* (Boston, 1962).

f. *Poland*

Count Edward Raczyński, *In Allied London* (1962).
W. *Sojusniczym Londynie; Dziennik Ambassadora Edwarda Raczyńskiego, 1939–1945* (1960).

g. *Sweden*

Erik Palmenstierna, *Atskelliga Egenheter* (Stockholm, 1942).

h. *The Soviet Union*

C. Nabokoff, *Ordeal of a Diplomat* (1921).
George Bilainkin, *Ivan Maisky: Ten Years Ambassador* (1944).
Ivan Maisky:
Journey into the Past (1962).
Who helped Hitler? (1964).

i. *The United States*

Thomas C. Irwin, 'Norman H. Davis and The Quest for Arms Control, 1931–1938', (Ph.D. thesis, Ohio State University 1963).
Harold B. Whiteman Jr, 'Norman H. Davis and the Search for International Peace and Security, 1917–44' (Ph.D. thesis, Yale 1958).
Charles G. Dawes, *Journal as an Ambassador to Great Britain* (New York, 1939).
Bascom N. Timmins, *Portrait of an American, Charles G. Dawes* (New York, 1953).
Frank W. F. Johnson, *George Harvey, a passionate Patriot* (New York, 1929).

Robert E. Sherwood, *The White House Papers of Henry Hopkins* (1948–49).

C. Seymour, *The Intimate Papers of Colonel House* (Boston, 1926–29).

Richard J. Whalen, *The Founding Father, John Kennedy*, (New York, 1964).

David Hunter Miller, *My Diary at the Paris Peace Conference* (New York, 1924).

Robert Murphy, *Diplomat among Warriors* (1964).

B. J. Hendrich, *The Life and Letters of Walter Hines Page* (New York, 1922–26).

Elting E. Morison, *Admiral Sims and the Modern American Navy* (Boston, 1942).

John Gilbert Winant, *A Letter from Grosvenor Square* (1947).

III. *Monographs bearing on the British foreign-policy-making élite, etc.*

Anon:

'Men of the Foreign Office: the experts who help to frame and implement British policy overseas', *The Sphere*, June 1950.

'The Foreign Service', *Manchester Guardian*, 26 October, 28 October and 3 November 1955.

F. T. A. Ashton-Gwatkin, *The British Foreign Service*, (Syracuse, N.J., 1950).

Max Beloff, *New Dimensions in British Foreign Policy, A Study in British Administrative Experience, 1947–59* (1961).

Nora Beloff, *The General Says No* (1963).

Donald G. Bishop, *The Administration of British Foreign Relations* (Syracuse, N.J., 1962).

J. Blondel, *Voters, Parties and Leaders. The Social Fabric of British Politics* (1963).

Charles M. Brown, *A Short History of the British Embassy in Washington, D.C., U.S.A.* (Washington, D.C., 1930).

Philip W. Buck, *Amateurs and Professionals in British Politics, 1918–59* (Chicago, 1959).

Philip W. Buck and M. B. Travers, *Control of Foreign Relations in modern Nations*, (1957).

J. Rives Childs, 'The Evolution of British diplomatic Representation in the Middle East', *Royal Central Asian Society Journal*, XXVI (October 1939).

John Connell (pseud.), *The Office, a Study of British Foreign Policy and its makers, 1919–51* (1958).

Gordon A. Craig and Felix Gilbert (eds.), *The Diplomats, 1919–39* (Princeton, N.J., 1953).

Frans Gosses, *The Management of British Foreign Policy before the First World War* (1948).

H. R. G. Greaves, *The Parliamentary Control of Foreign Affairs* (New Fabian Bureau, 1933).

W. L. Guttsman, *The British Political Elite* (1963).

Sir William Hayter, *The Diplomacy of the Great Powers*, (1960).

Angelo Hüsler, *Contribution à l'Étude de l'Élaboration de la Politique Etrangére Britannique, 1945–1956*, (Geneva, 1961).

R. Heussler, *Yesterday's Rulers. The Making of the British Colonial Service* (Syracuse, N.J., 1963).

R. F. V. Heuston, *Lives of the Lord Chancellors, 1885–1940* (1964).

Sir Thomas Hohler, 'British Representation in the East', *Royal Central Asian Society Journal*, XXVIII, (1941).

Sir David Kelly, 'British Diplomacy' *in* Stephen D. Kertesz and M. A. Fitzsimons, (Eds.), *Diplomacy in a Changing World*, (Notre Dame, 1959).

Christopher Mayhew, 'The British Diplomat' *in* Karl Braunias and Gerald Stourzh, (Eds.), *Contemporary Diplomacy; Beiträge aus dem Internationalen Diplomaten-Seminar Klessheim*, (Graz, 1959).

Col. Lord Murray of Elibank, *Reflections on Some Aspects of British Foreign Policy between the Two World Wars* (Edinburgh, 1946).

R. T. Nightingale, *Personnel of the British Foreign Office and Diplomatic Service, 1851–1929* (Fabian Tract No.232, 1930).

Cecil Parrott, 'The Foreign Office Library', *Library World*, LXI, no.720 (June 1960).

Clive Parry, 'The Foreign Office Archives', *International Relations*, II, no.4 (October 1961).

Peter G. Richards, *Honourable Members. A Study of the British Back Bencher* (1964).

Richard Sallett:
'Wie das Foreign Office arbeitet', *Aussenpolitik*, IV, Nr.3, March 1953.
Das diplomatische Dienst: seine Geschichte und Organisationen in Frankreich, Gross-Britannien und den Vereinigten Staaten (Stuttgart, 1953).

Lord Strang:
The Foreign Office (1955).
The Diplomatic Career (1962).

Sir John Tilley and Stephen Gazelee, *The Foreign Office* (1933).

Hermann Volle, 'Die britische Diplomatie im Wandel der Nachkriegszeit. Der auswärtige Dienst und die Aenderung der britischen Gesellschafts Struktur', *Europa-Archiv*, vol.v, no.16 (20 August 1950).

Sir Charles Webster, *The Art and Practice of Diplomacy* (1961).

Sir Arthur Willert, 'The Foreign Office from Within', *Strand Magazine*, February 1936.

Beckles Willson:
  Friendly Relations: A Narrative of Britain's Ministers and Ambassadors to America, 1791–1930 (Boston, 1934).
  The Paris Embassy (1928).
F. G. M. Willson, 'Routes of Entry of New Members of the British Cabinet, 1868–1958', *Political Studies*, VII, October 1959.
Neill Wood, *Communism and the British Intellectuals* (1959).
Sir Llewellyn Woodward:
  'The Foreign Service'; in J. E. Maclean (ed.), *The Public Schools and University Education* (1936).
  British Foreign Policy during the Second World War (1962).
Kenneth Younger:
  'Public Opinion and British Foreign Policy', *International Affairs*, XL, no.1, January 1964.
  'Public Opinion and Foreign Policy', *British Journal of Sociology*, VI, no.2, June 1955.

IV. *Monographs, etc., dealing with Security Affairs in Britain*

John Bulloch, *M.I.5* (1963).
John Bulloch and Henry Miller, *Spy Ring: the Naval Secrets Case* (1962).
Christopher Felix, *The Spy and his Masters* (1963).
M. Toscano, 'Problemi Particolari della Storia della Seconda Guerra Mondiale', in *Pagine di Storia Diplomatica Contemporanea* (Milan, 1963), vol.II.
Dame Rebecca West, *The Vassall Story* (1963).
H. H. Wilson and Harvey Glickmann, *The Problem of Internal Security in Great Britain, 1948–53* (N.Y., 1954).

Some Members of the British Foreign-Policy-Making Élite, 1916-56[1]

1. Leading Cabinet Members[2] and Ministers not in the Cabinet

1. THE COALITION GOVERNMENT, 1916–18, 1919–22

D. Lloyd George, Premier 1916–22.
A. Bonar Law, Exchequer 1916–19, Privy Seal 1919–21.
A. Balfour, Foreign Office 1916–19, Lord President 1919–22.
Viscount Milner, Minister without Portfolio 1916–18, War Office 1918–19.
A. Chamberlain, India Office 1916–18, Minister without Portfolio 1918–19, Exchequer 1919–21, Privy Seal 1921–22.
Sir E. Geddes, Admiralty 1917–19.
W. Long, Colonial Office 1916–19, Admiralty 1919–21.
Lord Lee of Fareham, Admiralty 1921–22.
W. Churchill, Munitions 1917–19, War Office 1919–21, Colonial Office 1921–22.
E. Montague, India Office, 1918–22.
Sir F. Smith, Lord Birkenhead, Attorney-General 1916–19, Lord Chancellor 1919–22.
S. Baldwin, Board of Trade, 1921–22.
Marquess Curzon, Lord President 1916–19, Foreign Office 1919–22.

2. THE CONSERVATIVE GOVERNMENT, 1922–24

A. Bonar Law, Premier 1922–23.
S. Baldwin, Exchequer 1922–23, Premier 1923–24.
Marquess of Salisbury, Lord President 1922–24.

---

1. The compilation of this list has been greatly aided by the recent appearance of D. Butler and Jennifer Freeman, *British Political Facts, 1900–60* (1963). In the lists here printed, the names italicized are those for whom memoirs or biographical studies are listed in the bibliographical essay (13) immediately preceding.

2. This list only comprehends those whom the author believes to have actually played a significant part in the formulation of British foreign policy. For a full list of Cabinet and other ministers see Butler and Freeman, op. cit.

Viscount Cave, Lord Chancellor 1922–24.
Lord Robert Cecil, Privy Seal 1923–24.
Marquess Curzon, Foreign Office 1922–24.
L. Amery, Admiralty 1922–24.
Earl of Derby, War Office 1922–24.

3. THE LABOUR GOVERNMENT, 1924

J. R. MacDonald, Premier and Foreign Office.
Viscount Haldane, Lord Chancellor.
P. Snowden, Exchequer.
Viscount Chelmsford, Admiralty.
A. Henderson, Home Office.
J. Clynes, Privy Seal.
J. H. Thomas, Colonial Office.

4. THE CONSERVATIVE GOVERNMENT, 1924–29

S. Baldwin, Premier 1924–29.
Marquess Curzon, Lord President 1924–25.
Marquess of Salisbury, Privy Seal 1924–29.
Sir A. Chamberlain, Foreign Office 1924–29.
W. Churchill, Exchequer 1924–29.[1]
W. Bridgeman, Admiralty 1924–29.
Sir S. Hoare, Air Ministry 1924–29.
L. Amery, Colonial Office 1924–29, Dominions Office 1925–29.
Earl of Birkenhead, India Office, 1924–28.
Viscount Cecil (Lord Robert Cecil), Duchy of Lancaster, 1924–27.
Lord Cushendun, Duchy of Lancaster 1927–29.
Sir P. Lloyd-Graeme (Sir P. Cunliffe-Lister), Board of Trade 1924–29.

5. THE LABOUR GOVERNMENT, 1929–31

J. R. MacDonald, Premier 1929–31.
A. Henderson, Foreign Office 1929–31.
P. Snowden, Exchequer 1929–31.
A. Alexander, Admiralty 1929–31.
J. H. Thomas, Privy Seal 1929–30, Dominion Office 1930–31.
Lord Passfield (Sidney Webb), Dominions Office 1929–30, Colonial Office
   1929–31.
W. Graham, Board of Trade 1929–31.

1. There is as yet no adequate account either by memoir or biography of
this section of Sir Winston Churchill's political career.

Appendix

6. THE NATIONAL GOVERNMENT, 1931–35

J. R. MacDonald, Premier 1931–35.
S. Baldwin, Lord President 1931–35.
P. Snowden, Exchequer 1931, Privy Seal 1931–32.
N. Chamberlain, Exchequer 1931–35.
Marquess of Reading, Foreign Office 1931.
Sir J. Simon, Foreign Office 1931–35.
Sir B. Eyres-Monsell, Admiralty 1931–35.
Sir P. Cunliffe-Lister, Board of Trade 1931, Colonial Office 1931–35.
W. Runciman, Board of Trade 1931–35.
Marquess of Londonderry, Air Ministry 1931–35.
J. Thomas, Dominions Office 1931–35.
Sir S. Hoare, India Office 1931–35.
Viscount Hailsham, War Office 1931–35.
A. Eden, Privy Seal 1933–35 (not in Cabinet).

7. THE NATIONAL GOVERNMENT, 1935–40

S. Baldwin, Premier 1935–37.
N. Chamberlain, Exchequer 1935–37, Premier 1937–40.
Viscount Halifax, War Office 1935, Privy Seal 1935–37. Lord President 1937–38, Foreign Office 1938–40.
Lord Runciman, Board of Trade 1935–37, Lord President 1938–39.
Sir S. Hoare, Foreign Office 1935, Admiralty 1936–37, Home Office 1937–39, Privy Seal 1939–40, Air Ministry 1940.
A. Eden, Minister without Portfolio 1935, Foreign Office 1936–37, Dominions Office 1939–40.
Sir J. Anderson, Privy Seal 1938–39, Home Office, 1939–40.
Sir K. Wood, Health 1935–38, Air Ministry 1938–40, Privy Seal 1940.
A. Duff Cooper, War 1935–37, Admiralty 1937–38.
Earl Stanhope, Admiralty 1938–39, Lord President 1939–40.
W. Churchill, Admiralty 1939–40.
Sir P. Cunliffe-Lister (Lord Swinton), Air Ministry 1935–38.
Sir J. Inskip, Minister for the Co-ordination of Defence 1936–39, Dominions Office 1939.
Lord Chatfield, Minister for the Co-ordination of Defence 1939–40.
Earl Winterton, Duchy of Lancaster 1938–39.
O. Stanley, Board of Trade 1937–40, War 1940.
Sir J. Reith, Information 1940.
Lord E. Percy, Minister without Portfolio 1935–36.
L. Hore-Belisha, Transport 1936–37, War 1937–40.

8. THE COALITION GOVERNMENT, 1940–45

a. *Cabinet*

W. Churchill, Premier and Minister of Defence 1940–45.

N. Chamberlain, Lord President 1940.

Sir J. Anderson, Lord President 1940, Exchequer, 1943.

C. Attlee, Privy Seal 1940–42, Dominions 1942–43, Lord President 1943–45.

Sir S. Cripps, Privy Seal 1942–45.

Viscount Halifax, Foreign Office, 1940.

A. Eden, War 1940, Foreign Office 1940–45.[1]

O. Lyttelton, Board of Trade 1940, Minister of State resident in the Middle East 1942, Production 1943–45.

R. Casey, Minister of State resident in the Middle East 1942–43.

H. Dalton, Economic Warfare 1940–42.

L. Amery, India and Burma Office 1940–45.

b. *Ministers not of Cabinet rank*

A. Duff Cooper, Information 1940–41.

B. Bracken, Information 1942–45.

H. Dalton, Board of Trade 1942–45.

H. Macmillan, Minister resident at Allied Headquarters, North West Africa, 1942–43.

J. Llewellyn, Minister for Supply resident in Washington 1942–43.

B. Smith, Minister for Supply resident in Washington 1943–45.

Lord Swinton, Minister resident in West Africa 1942–44.

H. Balfour, Minister resident in West Africa 1944–45.

Lord Moyne, Minister of State resident in the Middle East 1944.

Sir E. Grigg, Minister of State resident in the Middle East 1944–45.

9. THE CONSERVATIVE 'CARETAKER GOVERNMENT', 1945

W. Churchill, Premier and Minister of Defence.

Sir J. Anderson, Exchequer.

A. Eden, Foreign Office.

Viscount Cranborne, Dominions Office.

L. Amery, India and Burma Office.

B. Bracken, Admiralty.

1. The volume of Lord Avon's memoirs covering this period of his career had not appeared as this went to press.

10. THE LABOUR GOVERNMENT, 1945–51

C. Attlee, Premier 1945–51, Defence 1945–46.

H. Morrison, Lord President 1945–51, Foreign Office 1951.

H. Dalton, Exchequer 1945–47, Duchy of Lancaster 1948–50.

Sir S. Cripps, Board of Trade 1945–47, Economic Affairs 1947–50, Exchequer 1947–50.

E. Bevin, Foreign Office 1945–51, Privy Seal 1951.[1]

A. Alexander, Admiralty 1945–46, Defence 1946–50, Duchy of Lancaster 1950–51.

Lord Addison, Dominions and Commonwealth Relations Office 1945–47, Privy Seal 1947–51.

P. Noel-Baker, Commonwealth Relations Office 1947–50.

P. Gordon Walker, Commonwealth Relations Office 1950–51.

E. Shinwell, Fuel and Power 1945–47, War 1947–50 (not in Cabinet), Defence 1950–51.

A. Bevan, Health 1945–51.[2]

H. Wilson, Board of Trade 1947–51.

Lord Pethick-Lawrence, India and Burma 1945–47.

Earl of Listowel, India Office 1947–48.

Lord Pakenham, Duchy of Lancaster 1947–48, Civil Aviation 1948–50.

John Hynd, Duchy of Lancaster 1945–47 (not in Cabinet).

11. THE CONSERVATIVE GOVERNMENT, 1951–55

Sir W. Churchill, Premier 1951–55, Defence 1951–52.[3]

R. Butler, Exchequer 1951–55.

Sir A. Eden, Foreign Office 1951–55.

Earl Alexander, Defence 1952–54.

H. Macmillan, Housing 1951–54, Defence 1954–55.

Lord Ismay, Commonwealth Relations Office 1951–52.

Marquess of Salisbury, Lord Privy Seal 1951–52, Commonwealth Relations Office 1957, Lord President 1952–55.

O. Lyttelton, Colonial Office 1951–54.

P. Thorneycroft, Board of Trade 1951–55.

Viscount Swinton, Commonwealth Relations Office 1952–55.

A. Lennox-Boyd, Colonial Office 1954–55.

Lord Cherwell, Paymaster-General 1951–53.

1. The volume of Alan Bullock's official biography covering this period of Bevin's career had not appeared as this went to press.

2. The volume of Michael Foot's official biography covering this period of Bevan's career had not appeared as this went to press.

3. There is no adequate record of this period in Sir Winston Churchill's career.

Sir A. Salter, Economic Affairs 1951–52 (not in Cabinet).
Sir D. Maxwell-Fyfe (Lord Kilmuir), Home Office 1951–54, Lord Chancellor 1954–55.

11. *The Foreign Service and Foreign Office*

1. HM PRINCIPAL AMBASSADORS

Paris

Earl of Derby (1918), *Lord Hardinge* (1920), *Marquess of Crewe* (1922), Sir W. Tyrrell (1927), Sir G. Russell Cook (1934), Sir Eric Phipps (1937), Sir R. Campbell (1939), *Duff Cooper* (1944), Sir O. Henry (1948), Sir Gladwyn Jebb (1954).

Washington

Marquess of Reading (1918), *Sir A. Geddes* (1920), *Sir Esmé Howard* (1924), Sir Ronald Lindsay (1930), *Marquess of Lothian* (1939), *Viscount Halifax* (1941), Lord Inverchapel (1946), Sir O. Franks (1948), Sir Roger Makins (1952).

Berlin[1]

Lord d'Abernon (1920), Sir R. Lindsay (1926), Sir H. Rumbold (1928), Sir E. Phipps (1933), *Sir N. Henderson* (1937–39), General Sir B. Robertson (1946), *Sir I. Kirkpatrick* (1950), Sir F. Hoyer Millar (1953), Sir C. Steel (1957).

Rome

Sir G. Buchanan (1919), Sir R. W. Graham (1921), Sir E. Drummond, Lord Perth (1933), Sir P. Loraine (1939–40), Sir Noel Charles (1954), Sir V. Mallett (1947), Sir A. Clarke (1953).

Tokyo

Sir C. N. E. Eliot (1920), *Sir J. Tilley* (1926), Sir F. Lindlay, (1931), Sir R. Clive (1934), *Sir R. Craigie* (1937–41), Sir M. Dening (1951).

Moscow

Sir G. Buchanan (1910–18), *R. Bruce-Lockhart* (1919), Sir R. McCleod Hodgson (1924), Sir Esmond Ovey (1929), Viscount Chilston (1933),

---

1. From 1952 onwards the British Embassy was accredited to the Federal Republic of Germany and stationed at Bonn.

Appendix

Sir W. Seeds (1939), *Sir S. Cripps* (1940), Sir A. Clark Kerr, Lord Inverchapel (1942), *Sir M. Peterson*, (1946), *Sir D. Kelly* (1949), Sir A. Gasgoigne (1951), Sir W. Hayter (1953).

Ankara

Sir H. Rumbold (1920), Sir R. Lindsay (1925), Sir G. Clerk (1924), Sir P. Loraine (1933), *Sir H. Knatchbull-Hugessen* (1939), *Sir M. Peterson*, (1944), *Sir D. Kelly* (1946), Sir N. Charles (1949), Sir K. Helm (1951), Sir J. Bowker (1954).

2. PERMANENT UNDER-SECRETARIES AND DEPUTY UNDER-SECRETARIES IN THE FOREIGN OFFICE

a. *Permanent Under-Secretaries*

Lord Hardinge (1916), Sir E. Crowe (1920), Sir W. Tyrrell (1925), *Sir R. Vansittart* (1930), Sir A. Cadogan (1938), Sir O. Sergent (1946), *Sir W. Strang* (1949), *Sir I. Kirkpatrick* (1953).

b. *Deputy Under-Secretaries*

Sir V. Wellesley (1925), Sir H. Montgomery (1930), Sir L. Oliphant (1936), Sir A. Cadogan (1936), Sir O. Sergent (1939), Sir W. Monckton (1940), *Sir R. H. Bruce-Lockhart* (1941), Sir D. J. Montagu-Douglas-Scott (1946), O. C. Hervey (1946), Sir E. L. Hall-Patch, (1946), *Sir I. Kirkpatrick* (1948), Sir R. Makins (1948), Sir G. Jebb (1949), Sir H. Caccia (1949), Sir A. Clarke (1950), Sir P. Dixon (1950), Sir F. Hoyer Millar (1950), Sir F. Roberts (1951), Sir R. Barclay (1953), Sir J. Ward (1950), Sir D. Arden (1956), Sir P. Dean (1956), Sir P. Gore-Booth (1956), Sir d'A. Reilly (1956).

c. *Assistant Under-Secretaries*

Sir W. Tyrrell (1918), Sir R. Lindsay (1921), Sir H. Montgomery (1922), *J. D. Gregory* (1925), *R. G. Vansittart*, (1928), L. Oliphant (1929), G. A. Mounsey (1929), Sir O. Sergent (1933), C. H. Smith (1933), Sir F. G. A. Butler (1933), *Sir R. L. Craigie* (1935), D. J. Montagu-Douglas-Scott (1938), *W. Strang*, (1939), Sir H. J. Seymour (1940), W. M. Codrington (1940), Sir R. H. A. Leeper (1940), N. B. Ronald (1942), Sir M. Palairet (1943), O. C. Hervey (1943), V. F. W. Cavendish-Bentinck (1944), E. L. Hall-Patch, (1944), *N. M. Butler* (1944), J. I. C. Crombie (1944), Sir R. I. Campbell (1950), R. G. Lower (1945), C. F. A. Warner (1946), H. M. G. Jebb (1946), M. E. Dering (1946), J. M. Troutbeck (1946), H. A. Caccia (1946), R. M. Makins (1947), F. S. A. Ashton-Gwatkin (1947), F. R. Hoyer Millar (1947), M. R. Wright (1947), C. H. Bateman

(1948), W. G. Hayter (1948), R. B. Stevens (1948), W. I. Mallett (1949), F. K. Roberts (1949), Sir A. Noble (1949), H. A. Clarke (1949), d'A. Reilly (1949), J. G. Ward (1950), O. C. Morland (1950), R. H. Scott, (1950), R. J. Bowker (1950), Sir F. E. Evans (1951), P. Mason (1951), J. W. Nicholls (1951), G. W. Harrison (1951), R. K. Barclay (1951), J. E. Coubon (1952), P. H. Dean (1953), W. D. Allen (1953), R. Allen (1953), R. L. Speaight (1953), C. A. E. Shuckburgh (1954), P. F. Grey (1954), I. T. M. Pink (1954), D. A. H. Wright (1955), H. Beeley (1956), A. D. M. Ross (1956), Viscount Hood (1956).

d. *Joint Permanent Under-Secretaries, German Section*

Sir W. Strang (1947), *Sir I. Kirkpatrick* (1949), Sir D. Gainer (1950).

III. *Leading Civil Servants, etc.*

I. SECRETARIES TO THE CABINET

Sir M. Hankey (1916), Sir E. Bridges (1938), Sir N. Brook (1947).

2. SECRETARIES TO THE COMMITTEE OF IMPERIAL DEFENCE

Sir M. Hankey (1912), *Lord Ismay* (1938).

3. PERMANENT UNDER-SECRETARIES TO THE TREASURY

Sir W. Fisher (1919), Sir H. Wilson (1939), Sir R. Hopkins (1942), Sir E. Bridges (1945), Sir N. Brook and Sir R. Makins (1956).

4. BOARD OF TRADE

Sir S. Chapman and Sir W. Marwood (1919), Sir S. Chapman and Sir H. Payne (1919), Sir S. Chapman (1920), Sir H. Hamilton (1927), Sir W. Brown (1937), Sir A. Overton (1941), Sir J. Woods (1945), Sir F. Lee (1951).

5. SECRETARIES TO THE ADMIRALTY

Sir D. Murray (1917), Sir R. Carter (1936), Sir H. Markham (1940), Sir J. Long (1947).

6. SECRETARIES TO THE WAR OFFICE

Sir R. Brade (1914), Sir H. Creedy (1920), *Sir J. Grigg* (1939), Sir F. Bovenschen and Sir E. Speed (1942), Sir E. Speed (1945), Sir E. Turner (1949), Sir E. Playfair (1956).

Appendix

7. SECRETARIES TO THE AIR MINISTRY

Sir A. Robinson (1917), Sir W. Nicholson (1920), Sir C. Bullock (1937), Sir D. Banks (1936), Sir A. Street (1939), Sir W. Brown (1945), Sir J. Barnes (1947), Sir M. Dean (1955).

8. DOMINIONS AND COMMONWEALTH RELATIONS

Sir C. Davies (1925), Sir E. Hardinge (1930), Sir C. Parkinson (1940), Sir E. Machtig (1940), Sir A. Carter (1947), Sir P. Liesching (1949), Sir E. Laithwaite (1955).

9. DEFENCE

Sir H. Wilson Smith (1947), Sir H. Parker (1948), Sir R. Powers (1956).

10. PRIVY COUNCIL

Sir A. Fitzroy (1899), *Sir M. Hankey* (1923), Sir R. Howarth (1938), Sir E. Leadbitter (1942), F. Fernau (1951), W. Agnew (1953).

11. GOVERNORS OF THE BANK OF ENGLAND

Sir B. Cokayne, Lord Cullen of Ashborne (1918), *Montagu Norman, Lord Norman* (1920), Lord Catto (1944), Lord Cobbold (1949).

12. THEIR MAJESTIES' PRIVATE SECRETARIES

Lord Stamfordham (1910–31), Sir C. Wigram, Lord Wigram (1931–36), Sir A. Hardinge (1936–43), Sir A. Lascelles (1943–52), Sir M. Adeane (1953).

IV. *Chiefs of the Armed Services*

1. CHIEFS OF NAVAL STAFF

Sir R. Wemyss (1917), *Earl Beatty* (1919), Sir C. Madden (1927), Sir F. Field (1930), *Sir E. Chatfield, Lord Chatfield* (1933), Sir R. Backhouse (1938), Sir D. Pound (1939), *Sir A. Cunningham, Lord Cunningham* (1943), Sir J. Cunningham (1946), Lord Fraser of North Cape (1948), Sir R. McGrigor (1951), Earl Mountbatten (1955).

2. CHIEFS OF THE IMPERIAL GENERAL STAFF

Sir H. Wilson (1918), Earl of Cavan (1922), Sir G. Milne (1926), Sir A. Montgomery Massingbird (1933), Sir C. Deverell (1936), Viscount Gort

(1937), *Sir E. Ironside* (1939), Sir J. Dill (1940), *Sir A. Brooke, Lord Alanbrooke* (1941), *Viscount Montgomery* (1946), *Sir W. Slim* (1948), Sir J. Harding (1952), Sir G. Templar (1955).

3. CHIEFS OF AIR STAFF

Sir H. Trenchard (1918), *Sir J. Salmond* (1930), Sir G. Salmond (1933), Sir E. Ellington, (1933), Sir C. Newall (1937), Sir C. Portal (1940), Sir A. Tedder, Lord Tedder, (1946), *Sir J. Slessor* (1950), Sir W. Dickson (1953), Sir D. Boyle (1956).

v. *Ministers of State, Parliamentary Under-Secretaries*

1. MINISTERS OF STATE

R. K. Low (1943), W. Mcbone (1945), P. J. Noel-Baker (1945), H. MacNeill (1949), K. G. Younger (1950), S. Lloyd (1951), Marquess of Reading (1953), A. Nutting (1954), A. Noble (1956).

2. PARLIAMENTARY UNDER-SECRETARIES OF STATE

Rt Hon. Sir L. Worthington-Evans (1918), C. B. Hemsworth (1919), Col. Sir H. Greenwood Bt (1919), F. G. Kellaway (1920), *Sir P. Lloyd-Graeme* (1921), *Sir W. J. Hicks* (1922), R. McNeill (1922), Lieut.-Col. A. Buckley (1923), Arthur Ponsonby (1924), W. Lunn (1924), A. Samuel (1924), Rt Hon. R. MacNeill (1924), G. T. Locker-Lampson (1925), D. H. Hacking (1927), *H. Dalton* (1929), G. M. Gillett (1929), *R. A. Eden* (1931), Sir H. Young (1931), Lieut.-Col. David J. Colville (1931), Earl Stanhope (1934), Capt. Euan Wallace (1935), Earl of Plymouth (1936), R. H. Hudson (1937), R. A. Butler (1938), H. Johnstone (1940), R. K. Low (1941), Rt Hon. G. H. Hall (1943), G. Spencer Summer (1945), Lord Dunglass (1945), Lord Lovat (1945), H. MacNeill (1945), C. P. Mayhew (1946), Lord Henderson (1948), E. A. T. Davies (1950), Marquess of Reading (1951), A. Nutting (1951), A. D. Dodds Parker (1953), R. H. Turton (1954), Lord J. Hope (1954), Hon. W. D. Ormsby-Gore (1956).

Index

Abyssinia, 105, 108, 109, 154, 158, 166
Acheson, Dean, 67, 72
Adams, Sir Ronald, 113
Adams, Vivyan, MP, 125
Admiralty, *see* Navy Department
Africa, 160
Aga Khan, 164, 168
Agriculture and Fisheries, Department of, 7
Air Department, 3, 27, 41, 90, 102, 112, 118
Alanbrooke, Field-Marshal Lord, 42, 50
Alexander, A. V. (Lord), 57, 65, 68
Alexander, H. G., 125
'All Aid to Britain Short of War' movement, 46
All-People's Association, 121
All Souls College, 2, 161
Allen of Hurtwood, Lord, 124, 125, 126, 127, 128, 133
Allen, Professor H. C., 19–20, 25
Allies, The, 34, 111, 144
Alsace-Lorraine, 127
Alsop, Joseph, 46, 76
Alsop, Stewart, 76
Amau, Mr, 89, 90
Amery, Leo, 29, 32, 60, 148, 151, 161
Anderson, John, *see* Waverley, Viscount
Anderson, Mose, 124
Anglo-American Financial Agreement of 1946, 54, 57, 60, 61, 63, 65, 66, 67, 68, 69, 76
Anglo-German Naval Agreement, 123, 127, 128
Anglo-Japanese Alliance, 22, 38, 46
Anglo-Venezuelan Frontier Dispute, 21
Armour, 46
Army, British, 50, 111–12, 113
Army Council, 113

Army Department, 3, 22, 27, 28, 34, 41, 90, 107, 113, 118, 203
Ashton-Gwatkin, F. S. A., 5, 101
Asia, 25, 99
Asquith, Lord, 26, 32, 41
Astor, Hon. Michael, 26, 119
Astor, Nancy, Viscountess, 26, 119
Astor family, 26, 119
Athenaeum Club, 2
Atherton (US diplomat), 46
Atholl, Duchess of, 133
Attlee, Earl, 57, 64, 68, 74, 75, 132, 181
Austin, Alfred, 28
Australia, 61, 143, 144, 146, 149, 154, 155, 156, 160, 161, 164, 167–9, 170, 172, 173
Austria, 34, 44, 72, 73, 84, 92–3, 104, 105, 114, 117, 122, 127, 134, 167, 173
Avon, Earl of, 41, 44–5, 49, 50–1, 101, 102, 115, 128, 131, 135, 160, 161, 163, 164, 165, 166, 177, 178, 179, 181, 183, 184, 186

Bacon, Admiral Sir Reginald, 151
Baldwin, A. W., 43
Baldwin, Stanley, 1st Earl, 3, 4, 26, 29, 32, 39, 41, 43, 88, 96, 98, 108, 111, 153, 161, 165, 177, 181
Balfour, Arthur James, 28, 33–4, 39, 60, 179, 182
Ball, Sir Joseph, 178
Bank of England, The, 6, 48, 68
Bank of International Settlements, 6
Banker, The, 68
Bartlett, Vernon, 125
Bärtschli, Hans E., 142
Baruch, Barney, 66, 67, 79
Battle of Britain, 115
Beatty, Admiral of the Fleet Earl, 31, 39, 103, 107
Beaverbrook, Lord, 3, 12, 134

Index

Belgium, 78, 149
Benckendorff, Count, 25
Beneš, Dr, 168, 173
Berber, Dr Fritz, 124, 125, 126
Berle, Adolf, 46, 47
Berlin Conference 1878, 182
Bertie of Thame, Lord, 33
Bevan, Aneurin, 19, 57, 59, 60, 64, 65, 76
Bevin, Ernest, 57, 58, 65, 72, 74, 75, 132, 181
Biggs-Davison, John, MP, 42
Bilainkin, George, 133
Bingham, Robert, 88, 89, 90, 92, 155
Birkenhead, F. E. Smith, 1st Earl of, 33, 37
Birmingham Post, 11
Birmingham University, 4
Blackett, Professor P. M. S., 193
Blake, George, 206
Blomberg, General von, 127
Blum, J. M., 166
Boer War, The, 22, 29
Bolshevism, 145
Bonham Carter, Lady Violet, 133
Borden, Sir Robert, 140, 143, 144, 146, 150
Bourne, Dr, 28
Brady, Robert A., 56
Brand, Robert, 1st Lord, 29
Brebner, J. Bartlet, 38, 146
Bremner, Marjorie, 20, 24
Bretton Woods Agreement, 65
Bridgeman, W., 41
Bridges, Lord, 104
Bristol University, 190
British Broadcasting Corporation (BBC), 2
British Communist Party, 62
British Defence White Paper, 1935, 47
British Empire, 28, 29, 36, 47, 105, 107, 140, 141, 143, 144–5, 147, 148, 151, 152, 157, 160, 162, 164, 168, 169, 171
British Expeditionary Force, 107, 109
British Foreign Service School, 192
British Left, The, *see* Labour Party

British Legion, 128, 132
British Library of Economics and Political Science, *see* London School of Economics
British Right, The, *see* Conservative Party
Brogan, Professor Denis, 19
Brown, Vice-Admiral Sir Harold, 113
Bruce, Stanley, 1st Viscount Bruce of Melbourne, 169, 170, 171, 172
Bryan, William Jennings, 27, 31, 47
Bryant, Sir Arthur, 42, 50
Bryce, Lord, 22, 26, 30, 39, 47
Buchan, John, 1st Lord Tweedsmuir, 29
Bullard, Sir Reader, 41
Bullitt, William C., 46
Bulloch, John, 203
Bullock, Alan, 132
Bunsen, Maurice de, 31
Bunsen, Victoria de, 124
Burgess, Guy, 197, 201, 202–3, 204, 207
Burns, Emile, 201
Butler, Sir Harold, 49, 98
Butler, Sir James, 26, 127, 128
Butler, J. R. M., 119
Butler, R. A., MP, 184
Buxton, Charles Roden, MP, 124, 125
Byrnes, James, 56, 74

Cabinet, The, 3, 5, 6, 12, 13, 26, 27, 36, 40, 44, 45, 63–4, 65, 68, 70, 74, 76, 77, 83, 84, 85, 86, 87, 88, 89, 90, 92, 93, 94, 95, 97, 100, 102, 103, 107, 108, 111, 113, 114, 118, 119, 133, 135, 139, 140, 142, 144, 145, 146, 153, 159, 161, 165, 170–1, 172, 177–86
Cadman, John, 1st Baron, 39
Cadman, Basil, 2nd Baron, 39
Cambridge University, 189, 190, 191, 195, 196, 200
Campaign for Democratic Socialism, 10
Campaign for Nuclear Disarmament, 2

Campbell, A. E., 23
Campbell, Charles S., 21, 27
Canada, 29, 38, 60, 140, 141, 143,
    145, 146, 147, 149, 151, 152, 153,
    154, 155, 156, 157, 160, 161, 164,
    167, 170, 173
Canadian National Defence College,
    193
Canadian Parliament, 140
Canterbury, Archbishop of, 128
Carlton Club, 2
Carnock, Arthur Nicolson, 1st Lord,
    42
Carr, E. H., 48
Carson, Sir Edward, 33
Carter, Gwendolen, 139
Casement, Sir Roger, 199, 203
Castro, Dr, 198
Catchpool, Corder, 124, 128, 129
Catchpool, St John, 125
'Cato', 119
Cazalet, Victor, 119, 129
Cecil, Lord Robert (Viscount Cecil
    of Chelwood), 31, 133, 182, 183
Celler, Representative, 61, 66
Celovsky, Boris, 159
Central Africa, 74
Ceylon, 113
Chalmers, W. S., 103
Chamberlain, Sir Austen, 4, 5, 41,
    43, 110, 133, 142, 148, 149, 151,
    181, 182
Chamberlain, Hilda, 106
Chamberlain, Joseph, 22, 29, 140,
    162
Chamberlain, Neville, 12, 29, 41, 42,
    44, 45, 85, 90–1, 93, 98, 102, 106,
    107, 108, 110, 111, 112, 115, 118,
    119, 130, 131, 133, 135, 156, 157,
    161, 162, 163, 165, 166–8, 170,
    171, 172, 173, 178, 179, 180, 184
Chanak crisis, 147, 148, 185
Chancellor of the Exchequer, 3
Chatfield, Admiral of the Fleet Lord,
    85, 103–4, 106, 107
Chatham House, *see* Royal Institute
    of International Affairs
Cherwell, Lord, 6

Chiang Kai-shek, 89
Chicago, 25
Chiefs of Staff, 74, 84, 85, 86, 103,
    106, 107, 110, 111, 114, 115, 155
China, 8, 47, 57, 72, 90, 92, 105, 112,
    156, 164, 206
China Station, 8–9
Chirol, Valentine, 23
Christian Scientists, 124
Church of England, Convocation,
    128
Churchill, Winston S., 28, 33, 37, 42
    44, 47, 49, 52, 63, 64, 66, 67, 103,
    110, 131, 133, 134, 145, 160, 162,
    177, 180–1, 183, 184
Ciano, Count Galeazzo, 173
'Cicero', 200
Chief of the Imperial General Staff
    (CIGS), 113
Civil Defence, 106
Civil Service, 3, 5, 15, 55, 85, 100,
    104, 118, 142, 204
Civil Service Commission, 190, 191–2
Clay, Sir Henry, 48
Clayton, Will, 56, 60, 63, 67, 73
Cleveland, Stephen Grover (US
    President), 21
Cliveden, set, the, 26, 119, 161
Coalition Government, 32–4, 35, 37
Coalition Government, Second, 41,
    88, 145, 147
Cockburn, Claud, 119, 132
Cockcroft, Sir John, 193
Cocks, Seymour, MP, 133
Cold War, the, 57, 79
Cole, G. D. H., 60, 61
Collier, Basil, 84, 86, 106, 107
Collis, Maurice, 26, 119
Colombia, 30
Colonial Conference, 140, 141, 143,
    147
Colonial Office, 7
Colonies, 152
Comintern, 132
Committee of Enquiry on the future
    of the capital ship, 110
Committee of Imperial Defence
    (CID), 5, 7, 85–6, 103, 106, 109,

139, 140, 141, 142, 143, 153, 184, 185

Committee of Imperial Defence, Chiefs of Staff Sub-Committee, 7, 139, 153, 154

Common Market, *see* European Common Market

Commonwealth, the, 46, 60, 61, 62, 83, 96, 139–74, 192, 193

Commonwealth Civil Service, 14, 194, 195

Commonwealth Conference, 2

Commonwealth Relations Office, 7, 160, 192

Communist Party of Great Britain, 62, 119, 200–2

Communists, 62, 70, 132, 200–1, 202

Connell, John, 207

Conservative Party, 10, 20, 21, 22, 24, 26, 27, 28, 29, 30, 32, 41, 42, 49, 69, 115, 131, 133, 151

Contemporary Review, 11

Conwell-Evans, Philip, 124, 127, 128, 129

Cooke, Colin, 77, 78, 132

Cooke, Ramsay, 147

Coolidge, Calvin (US President), 39

Cooper, A. Duff, 41, 108, 135, 171

Co-operative Party, 57

Cornford, John, 201

Cornforth, Maurice, 201

Council for Foreign Relations in USA, 39, 46

Cowdray, Weetman Pearson, 1st Viscount, 33

Craigie, Sir Robert, 41, 88, 109, 180

Crewe, 1st Marquess of, 25

Cripps, Sir Stafford, 57, 65, 68, 74, 75, 77, 78, 132

Cromer, Evelyn Baring, 1st Earl of, 28

Crossman, R. H. S., 61, 62, 66

Crown, the, 10, 13, 14

Cuba, 29, 198

Cunliffe-Lister, Sir Philip (1st Earl of Swinton), 41, 108, 110

Cunningham of Hyndhope, Admiral of the Fleet Viscount, 8, 50

Cuno, Wilhelm von, 122

Curtis, Lionel, 29, 48

Curzon, George, 1st Marquess, 25, 28, 34, 36, 37, 145, 146, 148, 178, 179, 181, 182, 184, 186

Cushendun, Ronald McNeill, 1st Lord, 182, 183

Czechoslovakia, 12, 44, 76, 105, 114, 134, 155, 157, 159–74

Dafoe, J. W., 98, 147

Daily Herald, 94, 134

Daily Telegraph, 11, 55, 134

Daily Worker, 132

Dalton, Hugh (later Lord), 54, 56, 57, 60, 61, 63–4, 65, 67, 68, 69, 73–5, 77, 132

Darwin, Charles, 23

Davis, Norman H., 9, 46, 87–8, 89, 91–2, 93, 94, 95, 96, 97, 98, 167–8

Dawes loan, 6

Dawson, Geoffrey, 12, 29, 32, 97, 119, 133, 134, 161, 163, 167, 170, 171

Dawson, R. MacGregor, 147

Defence, Minister of, 3, 74, 103, 112

Defence, Ministry of, 3, 183–4

Defence Requirements Sub-Committee (DRC), 86, 87, 89, 90, 106, 107, 108, 109, 110, 111, 113, 118

Defence White Papers, 108, 110, 114

Democratic Party in US, 56

Denby, Edwin (US Secretary of the Navy), 37

'Denning Report', 204

De Valera, Eamon (Eire President), 68

Dicey, Edward, 28

Dilke, Sir Charles, 28

Dill, General, 113

Diplomatic Service, 3, 4, 5, 22, 28, 34, 41, 159, 181, 187, 192, 194, 195

Disraeli, Benjamin, 162

Dixon, Sir Pierson, 6

Dollfuss, Engelbert (Austrian Chancellor), 92, 122, 126

Dominions, the, 38, 84, 97, 105, 139–74

Index

Dominions Office, 148, 160
Douglas, Lewis (US Ambassador in London), 77
Douglas-Home, Sir Alec, 177
Dreyer, Admiral Sir Frederick, 150
Dugdale, Blanche, 33
Dulanty, J. W. (Irish High Commissioner in London), 170, 171
Dulles, Allen, 46
Dulles, John Foster, 46, 50
Dunkirk, 115
Durand, Sir Mortimer, 22, 28

East Anglia University, 196
Economic Commission to Europe (ECE), 6
Economist, The, 2, 55, 70, 125, 204
Eden, Sir Anthony, *see* Avon, Earl of
Education Act, 1944, 188, 189, 190
Edward VIII, King of England, 14, 131; as Prince of Wales, 128; as Duke of Windsor, 129
Egypt, 2, 10, 28, 51, 61, 113
Eire, *see* Ireland
Eisenhower, General Dwight, 50
Eliot, Elizabeth, 25
Ellington, Sir Adrian, 107
Elliot, W. Y., 139, 153
Empire Parliamentary Association 121
English Speaking Union, 34, 121
Epstein, Leon D., 20, 24, 51, 62, 64, 66, 76
Esher, Reginald Brett, 2nd Viscount, 14, 33, 34, 35, 36
Eton College, 190
Europe, 23, 27, 28, 30, 39, 43, 45, 56, 62, 63, 71, 72–3, 78, 83, 88, 89, 90–1, 93, 97, 99, 119, 127, 141, 142, 145, 149, 154, 157, 158, 159–74, 178, 192
European Common Market, 2, 3, 6, 13, 51, 60, 177, 184, 185
European Economic Community (EEC), *see* European Common Market
European Free Trade Association (EFTA), 6

European Recovery Programme, *see* Marshall Plan
Evans, Emrys, 133
Eyres-Monsell, Sir Bolton, 41, 88–9, 108

Fabian Society, 2, 58
Fagan, George M., 40
'Fair Deal', the, 76
Far East, 43, 63, 64, 83, 84, 86, 89, 90–1, 93, 94, 96, 106, 107, 109, 146, 151, 154, 155, 159, 160, 162
Fashoda incident, 22
Federation of British Industries, 92
Feiling, Keith, 42, 91, 107, 111, 157, 163, 179
Feis, Herbert, 42, 46, 63
Felix, Christopher, 203–4
Fergusson, Sir Donald, 103
Ferrell, Professor Robert H., 161, 183
Field, Noel, 94
Financial Times, 11, 155
First World War, 8, 112, 120, 139, 144, 203
Fisher, Admiral of the Fleet Lord, 23, 28, 86
Fisher, H. A. L., 22
Fisher, Sir Warren, 5, 85, 93, 100–16, 131
Fitzsimons, M. A., 19, 61, 76
Fleet Air Arm, 86
'Focus', 133, 135
Foot, Dingle, MP, 133
Forbes-Adams, Colin, 29
Foreign Affairs, Secretary of State for, *see* Foreign Secretary
Foreign Office, 3, 4, 5, 7, 11, 12, 22, 27, 31, 33, 36, 37, 39, 41, 42, 45, 48, 75, 92, 95, 97, 100, 101, 106, 110, 118, 123, 128, 131, 142, 147, 155, 159, 166, 179, 180, 181, 182, 183, 184, 185, 187, 195, 202, 204
Foreign Office Lists, 24
Foreign Secretary, 3, 4, 25, 28, 33, 34, 44, 72, 74, 102, 112, 145, 147, 177, 179, 180, 182–6

Foreign Service, 3, 4, 5, 14, 28, 31, 34, 41, 101, 119, 160, 183, 186, 187–207
Foreign Service Act, 1943, 188
Forrestal, James, 70, 71, 77
Forster, W. Arnold, 125
Fortnightly, the, 11
Forward, 55
Foster, Sir George, 143 146
Fox, Annette Baker, 53, 63
Fox, William T. R., 53, 63
France, 14, 23, 28, 38, 40, 43, 75, 83, 105, 107, 114, 120, 121, 132, 134, 145, 149, 155, 164, 165, 166, 167, 168, 171, 174
Freeman, E. A., 28
French Popular Front, 132, 201
French Right, 21
Fry, M. G., 146
Fulbright, Senator, 67

Gaitskell, Hugh, 10, 60
Galbraith, John K., 38, 146
Gallacher, Willie, MP, 62
Gardner, Richard W., 48, 56, 57, 61, 65, 67, 68, 70, 71
Gärtner, Dr Margarete, 120–3, 126, 128, 129, 130, 131
Garvin, Joseph, 26, 29, 97, 119
Garwood, Ellen Clayton, 56, 73
Geddes, Sir Auckland, 37
Geddes brothers (Auckland, 1st Lord, and Sir Eric), 33
Gelber, L. M., 21
General Agreement on Tariffs and Trade (GATT), 6, 185
Geneva Disarmament Conference, 1927–29, 8, 9
Geneva Naval Conference, 40
Geneva Protocol, 148, 149
George V, King of England, 13, 14
George V Jubilee, 148
George VI, King of England, 14
German Labour Corps, 130
Germany, 12, 14, 23, 28, 30, 31, 33, 34, 35, 37, 43, 44, 73, 74, 83, 84–5, 86, 90–1, 92–3, 94, 98, 99, 100–16,

117–35, 140, 143, 154, 155, 156, 161–74, 200
Gibraltar, 113
Gibson, Harvey Dow, 46
Gilbert, Martin, 100, 119, 159
Gladstone, William Ewart, 22
Glasgow Herald, 11
Glasgow University, 190
Gleeson, S. Everett, 44
Goebbels, Dr, 166
Goerdeler, Karl, 134
Goering, Hermann, 200
Gollin, A. M., 26
Gooch, G. P., 125, 140
Gordon, Donald C., 140
Gordonstoun, 122
Gort, Field-Marshal Viscount, 113
Gott, R. W., 100, 119, 159
Gowing, M. M., 86, 108, 109, 111, 112, 114
Granzow, Dr Brigitte, 118
Greece, 8, 71, 73–5, 179
Greenwood, Arthur, MP, 130
Gregory, J. D., 199
Grew, Joseph, 46, 92
Grey of Fallodon, Edward, 1st Viscount, 22, 23, 25, 31, 32, 33, 34, 35, 36, 139, 141, 144, 157
Grigg, Edward, 1st Lord Altrincham, 29, 32, 178
Guardian, The, 2, 11, 55, 123, 134
Guedalla, Philip, 133
Guest, David, 201

Hahn, Dr Kurt, 122
Haig, Field-Marshal Earl, 33, 36
Haight, J. McVickers, 44
Hailsham, Douglas Hogg, 1st Viscount, 108
Haldane, Richard, 1st Viscount, 26, 185
Halifax, Edward Wood, 1st Earl of, 42, 108, 135, 161, 163, 165, 168, 169, 171, 173, 179
Hall, H. Duncan, 139, 153, 156
Halle, Dr Ernst von, 120–1
Hamilton, Alexander, 30
Hamilton, Sir Horace, 104

Hancock, W. K., 86, 108, 109, 111, 112, 114
Hankey, Maurice, 1st Lord, 5–6, 33, 85, 86, 95, 101, 109, 110, 115, 140, 141, 142, 154
Hardinge of Penshurst, Charles, 1st Lord, 22, 28, 33
Harriman, Averil, 70, 71
Harris, R. Wilson, 125, 133
Harrison, Tom, 66
Harrod, R. F., 48, 49, 78
Harvard Centre of International Affairs, 193
Harvard University, 69
Harvey, Frank, 13
Hasluck, Paul, 155, 156
Haushofer, Albrecht, 127
Haxell, Simon, 119
Hay-Pauncefote Agreement on the Panama Canal, 22
Headlam-Morley, Agnes, 48
Heath, Carl, 125
Heath, Edward, MP, 3, 177
Heever, C. M., van den, 156, 165, 172
Heindel, R. H., 19, 21
Helfand, M., 200
Henderson, Arthur, 178, 180
Henderson, Sir Nevile, 131
Henry, 55
Herter, Christian, 46
Hertzog, General J. B. M., 156, 165, 169, 172
Hindenburg, President Field-Marshal von, 122
Hitler, Adolph, 45, 84–5, 92, 99, 104, 114, 115, 117, 118, 119, 122, 123, 126, 127, 128, 129, 130, 133, 134, 155, 156, 157, 164, 165, 167, 168, 170, 171, 172, 173, 174
Hoare, Sir Samuel (1st Viscount Templewood), 13, 41, 42, 102, 108, 109, 110, 131, 135, 156, 177, 181, 183
Hoare–Laval Plan, 109, 131, 185
Hodson, H. V., 98
Hoesch, Leopold von, 14, 128
Hoffmann, Paul, 77, 78

Hohenlohe, Countess Stephanie von, 123
Holstein, Friedrich von, 23
Home, 14th Earl of, *see* Douglas-Home, Sir Alec
Home Civil Service, 5, 14, 101, 189, 194, 196, 198, 207
Home Civil Service, Centre of Administrative Studies, 194
Home Secretary, 182
Hong Kong, 47, 113
Hong Kong University, 192
Hoover, Herbert (US President), 26, 31, 40, 42, 46
Hore-Belisha, Leslie, 112, 113, 135
Horne, Sir Robert, 33
Hose, Commodore, RCN, 153
Houghton, Henry, 205
House, Colonel, 34, 36, 93, 144
House of Lords, 5, 100, 104
House of Representatives, 56
Howard, Sir Esmé (later 1st Lord Howard of Penrith), 31, 148
Hughes, Charles Evans, 13, 37, 38, 39
Hughes, R., 108, 113, 156
Hughes, W. R., 124
Hughes, William, 38, 143, 144, 146, 168
Hull, Cordell, 46, 56, 90, 92, 93, 94, 95, 96, 98, 155
Hurley, General Patrick, 47
Hurst, Sir Cecil, 36, 43
Hutchinson, Lt.-Col. Graham Seton, 123

Ickes, Harold, 55
Imperial Conference, 38, 140, 141, 143, 146, 147, 148, 151, 152, 154, 155–6, 164, 165, 167, 173
Imperial Defence College, 153, 193
Imperial General Staff, 141
Imperial War Cabinet, 142, 143, 144, 149–50
Imperial War Conference, 142, 143, 149
India, 28, 47, 61, 65, 84, 160, 164
India Act, 131
India Office, 7, 160

Index

Indo-China, 51
Inskip, Sir Thomas, 110, 111–12, 113, 114, 135, 165
Institute for Strategic Studies, 2, 194, 197
Institute of Public Administration, 194
International Labour Organization, 49
International League of Women, 121
International Military Tribunal, 122
International Monetary Fund (IMF), 6, 69, 77, 78, 185
International Trade Organization, 60, 68
Iran, 51, 113
Iraq, 39
Ireland, 14, 37, 68, 157
Ironside, Field-Marshal Lord, 113
Ismay, General Lord, 110
Italo-Abyssinian crisis, 13, 42, 108, 154, 158, 166
Italy, 43, 73, 76, 83, 85, 105, 109, 115, 154, 155, 156, 165, 166, 174, 180, 200
Ivanov, Captain Eugen, 204

Jacobs, Alaric, 60, 66
James, Sir William, 109
Japan, 8, 38, 41, 43, 47, 64, 83–99, 105, 107, 109, 111, 112, 115, 117, 145, 146, 154, 155, 156, 161, 164
Jellicoe, Admiral of the Fleet Earl, 31, 150, 151
Jews, 26, 135
Johnson, Douglas, 5
Johnson, Franklyn Arthur, 141
Johnstone, Tom, MP, 130
Jones, Joseph M., 72
Jones, Sir Roderick, 123
Jones, T. H., 26
Jones, Thomas, 178
Jordan, 51

Kanzi Kato, Admiral, 84
Keele University, 196
Kellogg Pact, 42
Kelly, Sir David, 41, 199

Kelly, Admiral Sir Howard, 8, 9
Kemp, Commander P. K., 87, 107, 111, 114
Kennan, George, 73
Kennedy, Tom, MP, 130
Kenworthy, Commander J. M., RN, MP, see Strabolgi, Lord
Kenya, 113
Kerr, Philip, see Lothian, Marquess of
Keyes, Admiral Sir Roger, 8, 89
Keynes, John Maynard, 1st Lord, 6, 48, 49, 54, 64, 65, 67, 120, 164
King, W. R. Mackenzie, 147, 148, 170
Kipling, Rudyard, 28
Kirby, Maj.-Gen. S. Woodburn, 84, 85, 106, 156
Klugmann, James, 201
Knatchbull-Hugessen, Sir Hughe, 200
Korea, 57
Korean War, 63, 80
Krupps works, 121

Labour Government, First, 185
Labour Government 1929–31, 128, 178
Labour Government, 1945–51, 50, 53–80
Labour Party, 19, 20, 21, 35, 36, 51, 53, 54, 59, 69, 75–6, 79–80, 124, 129, 132, 133, 164
Labour Party Conference, 59, 132
Lammers, Dr, 124
Land, Admiral E. S., 39
Langer, W. L., 44
Lansbury, George, 129, 132
Laski, Harold, 61
Laval, Pierre, 109, 131
Law, Bonar, 3, 12, 41
Law, Robert, MP, 125
Lawford, Valentine, 131
Lawrence, Sir Alexander, 129
Layton, Sir Walter, 125, 133
League of Nations, 7, 41, 42, 43, 45, 72, 84, 85, 89, 122, 144, 148, 149, 154, 158, 164, 166, 177, 183

League of Nations Union, 2, 125, 126
Leahy, Admiral, USN, 9
Lebanon, 51
Lee of Fareham, Arthur, 1st Viscount, 38, 39
Lee, Jennie, MP, 60
Leeds University, 195
Legge-Bourke, G., 101
Leith-Ross, Sir Frederick, 6
Lend-Lease, 47, 63, 64
Lewis, Wilmot, 94
Liberal Party, 19, 20, 22, 26, 27, 30, 31, 35, 36, 41, 131, 133
Lindsay, Sir Ronald, 39, 98
'Link', the, 130
Lippmann, Walter, 46
Listener, The, 2
Lithuania, 129
Little, Admiral Sir Charles, 8, 9, 88
Lloyd George, 12, 32, 33, 35, 37, 41, 97, 129, 142, 145, 146, 178, 179, 180
Lloyd George, 1st Lord, 29
Lloyd, Selwyn, 195
Locarno Agreement, 5, 149, 164
Locker-Lampson, Commander, MP, 133
Lodge, Senator, Henry Cabot, 22–3, 38, 39
London Council for Labour, 58
London Naval Conference, 40, 83, 88, 89, 91, 93, 97, 98, 109, 178
London Naval Treaty, 84, 87–8, 111, 152
London School of Economics, 54
London University, 190, 191, 192, 195, 200
Londonderry, Charles, 7th Marquess of, 108, 119
Long, Walter, 142
Lothian, Philip Kerr, 11th Marquess of, 26, 29, 32, 39, 93, 95, 96, 97, 98, 99, 117, 119, 124, 127, 129, 133, 161, 178
Lovett, Robert A. (US Under-Secretary of State), 71
Lymington, Gerard, Viscount (later 9th Earl of Portsmouth), 123

Lyons, Joseph A. (Prime Minister of Australia), 169, 171, 172, 173

MacBrien, Brigadier J. H., 150
McCallum, R. B., 36, 120
McCarthy, Senator, 57, 80, 198
MacCleod, Scott, 198
MacColl, R. C., 199
MacDonald, Malcolm, 169, 170, 171, 172
MacDonald, Ramsay, 10, 14, 32, 40, 87–8, 92, 93, 94, 95, 96, 97, 108, 126, 127, 133, 148, 151, 178, 180
McKenna, Reginald, 26
Maclean, Donald, 197, 201, 203, 204, 207
Macleod, Iain, 45, 91, 106, 107, 163
MacNeill, Hector, 202
Maiski, Ivan, 119, 133
Malaya, 113
Malcolm, Gen. Sir Neill, 175
Mallalieu, W. C., 73, 74
Mallalieu, W. E., 79
Malta, 113
Manchester University, 190, 192
Manchuria, 83, 92, 105
Mansergh, P. N. S., 139, 162, 163
Marder, A. J., 23, 140
Marshall, General George, 70, 71, 73, 75, 76, 78
Marshall Plan, 48, 63, 68–9, 70, 71, 72, 76, 77, 79
Martin, L. W., 19, 35
Martin, Kingsley, 133
Marwick, Arthur, 124, 125, 126, 127
Marxism, 58, 61
Masaryk, Jan, 76
Massey, Vincent, 143, 161, 167, 169, 170, 171, 172
May, Ernest R., 31, 33
Mayhew, Christopher, 77
Meade, Professor James, 6
Meaney, Neville Kingsley, 144–5
Mediterranean area, 160, 162, 180
Meighen, Arthur, 146, 152
Memel, German minority in, 129
Menzies, Robert Gordon, 169
Mexico, 22, 30

M.I.5, 203, 204
M.I.6, 203, 204, 206
Middle East, 38, 51, 74, 162, 180, 182, 183, 207
Mikhailovsky (Soviet agent), 206
Miller, J. D. B., 139
Milner, Alfred, 1st Viscount, 28, 29, 33, 37, 60, 142
Minney, R. J., 112, 113, 114
Moffatt, J. Pierrepont, 47, 91, 92, 93, 94
Monroe Doctrine, 23, 160
Montagu, Edwin, 33
Mooney, Neville Kingsley, 46
Moore, Colonel, 119, 129
Morel, E. D., 121
Morgenthau, Henry, 34, 55, 56, 166
Morrison of Lambeth, Herbert, Lord, 57, 58, 75, 204
Moscow Conference of Foreign Ministers, 1947, 73
Moseley, Sir Oswald, 123
Mosley, Leonard, 181
Mottistone, John Seely, 1st Lord, 101
Mowat, R. B., 48
Muenzenberg, Willi, 132
Munich crisis, 44, 114, 159–74, 185
Murray, A, C., 3rd Viscount Elibank, 35, 101, 183
Murray, Professor Gilbert, 133
Mussolini, Benito, 45, 156, 164, 172, 173
Mutual Guarantee, Draft Treaty of, 149

Namier, Sir Lewis, 48, 119, 123, 159
National Assistance Rates, 11, 41, 42, 43, 44, 46
National Association of Manufacturers (US), 76
National Government, 14, 85, 131
National Health Service, 67
National Liberal Club, 2
National Maritime Museum, Greenwich, 9
National Peace Council, 126
Naval secrets case, 202, 206, 207

Naval Staff College, 153
Navy, Secretary of State for the, 3
Navy Dept, 3, 22, 27, 28, 31, 34, 41, 43, 83, 86, 87, 90, 91, 93, 103, 111, 112, 113, 118, 141, 142–3, 149, 150–3, 159, 205
Navy Estimates, 108
Nazis, 14, 47, 85, 92–3, 117–19, 122, 124, 128, 132, 198, 201
Near East, 51, 145
Nelson, Harold, 144
Nenni, Pietro, 76
Neurath, Baron von, 122, 156, 164, 165, 167
New Deal, the, 48, 55, 56
New Fabian Bureau, 129
Newfoundland, 22, 141
New Statesman, 2, 55, 61, 70, 133
New York Times, 71
New Zealand, 61, 84, 141, 142–3, 146, 149, 154, 155, 158, 160, 164, 170
News Chronicle, 125, 134
'Next Five Years Group', 126
Niblack, Vice-Admiral, USN, 13
Nicolson, Sir Harold, 13, 42
1922 Committee, 2
Nineteenth Century and After, the, 11
Noel-Baker, Philip, MP, 125, 133
Noel-Buxton, Noel, 1st Lord, 124, 125, 128
Norman, Montagu, 6, 48
North, Admiral Sir Dudley, 8
North Africa, 50, 182
North Atlantic Treaty Organization (NATO), 50, 153
NATO Staff College, 193
Northcliffe, Alfred Harmsworth, 1st Viscount, 30, 33, 34
Norwich, Viscount, *see* Cooper, A. Duff
Novo, J. de, 38
Nuremberg Laws, 132

Observer, The, 2, 26, 55, 94, 97, 98 119, 161, 204, 206
Oceania, 160
O'Connor, Raymond G., 40, 83

Index

Official Secrets Act, 20
Oliver, F. S., 29, 30
Ollivier, M., 143, 147, 151
Organization for European Economic Co-operation (OEEC), *see* European Common Market
Osgood, Robert E., 24
Overseas Trade, Department of, 5, 102
Oxford Union, 126
Oxford University, 189, 190, 191, 195, 196, 200

Pacific Conference, 146
Page, Walter Hines, 32
Pakenham, Francis, Lord (later 7th Earl of Longford), 58
Palestine, 74, 113, 185
Palmerston, Henry, 3rd Viscount, 186
Panama Canal, 22
Paris Conference, 36, 96, 144
Paris Conference of Foreign Ministers, 74, 75
Parliament, 10, 26, 55, 65, 66, 69, 96, 108, 109, 129, 131, 181
Parliamentary Labour Party, 57
Parliamentary Opposition, 3
Pauncefote, Sir Julian, 38
Pax Britannica, 30, 160
Pax Romana, 30
Pelling, Henry, 19, 20, 21
Percy of Newcastle, Lord Eustace Percy, 1st Lord, 22, 26, 46, 47
Perley, Sir George, 143
Perth, Eric, 16th Earl of, 5, 100, 101, 172, 173
Peterson, Sir Maurice, 36, 41, 199
Petrie, Sir Charles, 43
Petrov, Vladimir, 201
Philby, Harold, 201, 203, 204, 206–7
Philippines, the, 29
Phillips, William, 37, 89, 98
Pilgrim Trust, 34, 39
Pirow, Oswald, 169, 172
Plowden Report, 191, 193, 194–5
Poland, 76
Poland, Treaty with, 127

Political Quarterly, 55, 60, 62, 66
Political Science Quarterly, 73
Polk, Frank L., 37
Pope, Senator, 97
Pope-Hennessy, James, 25
Post Office, the, 7
Postan, M. M., 87, 109, 112
Postgate, R., 132
Potsdam Conference, 56, 63
Powicke, F. J., 48
Pratt, Admiral, USN, 38
Prime Minister, 3, 14, 41, 45, 179, 180
Profumo affair, 207
Prothero, Sir George Walter, 48
Prussia, 20
Public Commission for Refugees, 49
Public Records Act, 1958, 15
Public Records Office, 28

Quakers, 124
Quebec Conference, 63

Radcliffe Committee Report, 207
Rajchman mission to China, 1933, 72
Rapidan, Ramsay MacDonald's visit to, 1929, 40
Rappaport, Armin, 19
Reading, Rufus Isaacs, 1st Marquess of, 33, 34, 36, 37, 39, 122, 182
Reichs Chancellor, 121
Reichstag, 132
Republican Party in US, 40, 57
Reuters, 123
Rhineland, 14, 105, 121, 145, 158, 164
Rhodes, Cecil, 29
Rhodes Trust, 127
Rhondda, David Thomas, 1st Viscount, 33
Ribbentrop, Joachim von, 125, 127, 129
Riddell, George, 1st Lord, 12, 33
Ritter, G., 134
Robbins, Professor (Lord), 6, 65
Roman Empire, 30
Roman history, 29

Roosevelt, Franklin D., 42, 43, 44–7, 52, 55, 63, 88, 89, 91, 92, 93, 95, 96, 97, 98, 166
Roosevelt, Theodore (US President), 9, 22, 23, 28, 31, 39
Roosevelt, Col. Theodore, Jr, 38, 39
Root, Elihu, 38, 39, 40
Rosebery, Archibald, 5th Earl of, 26
Rothermere, Harold Harmsworth, 1st Viscount, 30, 33, 123, 134
Round Table, the, 11, 29, 60, 95, 119, 142
Rousseau, J. J., 35
Rowland, John, 39
Rowse, A. L., 161
Royal Air Force, 50, 90, 107, 111, 113, 114
Royal Commonwealth Society, 2, 197
Royal Institute of International Affairs, 2, 29, 39, 48, 95, 96–7, 99, 124, 125, 127, 194, 197
Royal Institution, 194
Royal Navy, 8, 109, 111, 140, 149–50, 152
Royal United Services Institute, 2, 197
Rumbold, Sir Horace, 118
Runciman, Walter, 1st Viscount, 168
Russell, E. C., 152
Russia, 23, 30, 33, 66, 90, 157, 166. *See also* Soviet Union

St Antony's College, Oxford, 193
Salem, Kurt Hahn's school at, 122
Salisbury, James, 4th Marquess of, 183
Salisbury, Robert, 3rd Marquess of, 22, 27, 162, 182
Salter, Sir Arthur, MP, 133
Sandys, Duncan, MP, 133
Sazonov, Sergey D., 25
Schleicher, General von, 122
Schlesinger, Arthur M., Jr, 46
Scientific and Industrial Research, Department of, 193
Scotsman, The, 11
Scott, J. D., 108, 113, 156

Second World War, 6, 47, 48, 49, 63, 64, 114–15, 170, 178, 182, 183, 184, 188, 200, 201
Security Service, 203
Seeley, Sir John, 28
Selby, Sir Walford, 5, 101
Seligman, Sir Charles, 92
Semmel, Dr Bernard, 41
Shanghai, International Settlement of, 8, 84
Sheehan, Edward R. F., 207
Shepherd, Miss P. M., 40
Shinwell, Emanuel, 57, 65
Shwadran, B., 38, 39
Sillitoe, Sir Percy, 204
Simon, Sir John, 88, 89–90, 93, 96, 97, 98, 108, 127, 128, 135, 167, 168–9
Sinclair, Sir Archibald, 133
Singapore, 8, 84, 87, 111, 113, 151, 155
Sino-Japanese War, 9, 156
Slessor, Sir John, 112
Smith, Ben, MP, 130
Smith, Norman, MP, 60
Smuts, Field-Marshal J. C., 48, 95, 96–7, 98–9, 143, 144, 148, 151, 161, 164, 169
Snyder, John Wesley (US Secretary of the Treasury), 69, 71, 78
Socialism, 53–80
Socialist Commentary, 55, 61
Somerville, Vice-Admiral F. J., 8
South Africa, 29, 141, 143, 145, 146, 149, 151, 154, 155, 156, 157, 161, 162, 164, 168, 169, 170, 172, 173
South-East Asia, 183
Soviet Union, 61, 62, 76, 118, 167, 198, 201, 202, 203, 204, 206
Spaak, Paul-Henri, 60
Spanish-American War, 21, 23, 28
Spanish Civil War, 105, 201
Spanish Popular Front, 132
Spectator, 2, 55, 121, 125, 133
Spencer, Charles, 124, 129
Spier, Eugen, 133, 134, 135
Spring-Rice, Sir Cecil, 22, 30, 31, 32, 33

Index

Stalin, Joseph, 73
Stalinism, 62
Standley, Admiral, USN, 9
Stead, W. T., 23, 28
Stephenson, Sir William, 217
Sterling Area, 61, 62, 65
Stimson, Henry Lewis, 14, 40, 178
Stockholm Socialist Congress, 35
Stokes, R. R., MP, 60
Storry, R. W., 84
Strabolgi, 10th Lord, 36
Strang, William, 1st Lord, 41, 42
Stresemann, Gustav von, 122
Sudan, 51, 113
Suetsugu, Admiral, 84
Suez crisis, 2, 10, 50, 51, 184, 185
Sumner, B. H., 48
Sunday Telegraph, 193
Sunday Times, 2, 55
Supply, Ministry of, 109
Sussex, University of, 196
Sutherland, Colonel (Canadian Minister of National Defence), 153
Swinton, Earl of, *see* Sir Philip Cunliffe-Lister
Sykes, Sir Percy, 22

Taft, William Howard (US President), 40
Taylor, A. J. P., 21, 26
Taylor, Senator, 67
Temperley, Harold, 140
Templewood, Viscount, *see* Sir Samuel Hoare
Te Water, Charles (South African High Commissioner), 161, 169, 170, 171
Thomas, J. P. L., 115
Thompson, Dr A. E., 195
Thompson, F. J., 202, 203, 204
Three-Power Naval Conference, Geneva, 152
Tilley, Sir John, 48
Tillmann, Seth W., 144
Times, The, 2, 6, 10, 12, 23, 26, 29, 32, 51, 55, 95, 96–7, 119, 128, 134, 160, 161, 170, 195

Tobias, Fritz, 132
Todd, Alexander, Lord, 193
Tokyo University, 192
Toscano, M., 200
Toynbee, Arnold Joseph, 48
Trade, Board of, 5, 6
Transport, Ministry of, 7
Transport and General Workers Union, 58
Treasury, the, 5, 6, 48, 68, 74, 101, 102, 103, 104, 110, 111, 112, 113, 154, 196, 205
Treasury Inter-Services Committee, 110
Trenchard, Marshal of the RAF Viscount, 114
Trevelyan, G. M., 32
Tribune, 55, 62, 64, 76
Trinity College, Cambridge, 201
Trinity Hall, Cambridge, 201
Tritten, F. J., 125
Truman, Harry (US President), 55, 57, 63, 64, 68, 72, 75, 76
Truman Doctrine, 72, 75
Tucker, Gilbert M., 140
Tucker, W. R., 132
Tunstall, Brian, 140
Turkey, 34, 71, 73–5, 105, 162, 179
Tyrrell, William, 1st Lord, 5, 101

Union for Democratic Control, 10, 35, 40, 121
United Nations, 7
United Nations Relief and Rehabilitation Administration (UNRRA), 73
United States, 8, 19–52, 53–80, 83–99, 105, 144, 145, 146, 152, 154, 155, 160, 161, 165, 169, 180, 182, 185, 198
United States Congress, 21, 31, 37, 38, 39, 55, 57, 59, 60, 61, 62, 66, 67, 68, 69, 76, 77, 79
United States Naval Archives, 37
United States Navy, 9, 38, 92, 93, 95
United States Senate, 36, 37, 61, 67, 88, 93, 112
Upper Silesia, 145

Vallance, Aylmer, 60
Vandenberg, Senator, 57
Vansittart, Robert, 1st Lord, 4, 5, 14, 31, 32, 39, 42, 85, 86, 88, 90, 93, 102, 106, 107, 109, 115, 118, 131, 180, 200
Vassall, John, 202, 206, 207
Venezuela, 28
Versailles Peace Conference, 12, 36, 48
Versailles Treaty, 36–7, 43, 46, 49, 83, 119, 120, 121, 122, 128, 130, 134, 144–5, 164–5, 173
Vickers-Armstrong, 121
Vinson, Fred, 56, 67, 69

Wales, University of, 190, 195
Waley, Sir David, 6
Wall Street, 64
Wallace, Henry (US Vice-President), 55
War Debts and Reparations, 83
War Office, *see* Army Department
Ward, Sir Joseph, 158
Washington Conference, 12, 38, 146, 151, 182
Washington Naval Treaty, 87–8, 151
Washington Treaties, 38
Waterhouse, Captain Charles, MP, 10
Watkins, Ernest, 79
Watt, D. C., 19, 103, 117, 123, 124, 156
Waverley, John Anderson, 1st Viscount, 131
Webster, Sir Charles, 48
Wedgewood, C. V., 129
Wedgewood, Col. Josiah, MP, 129
Week, The, 132
Weir, William, 1st Viscount, 113
Welles, Sumner, 44
Wellesley, Sir Victor, 48
Wester Wemyss, Admiral of the Fleet Lord, 31, 36

Wester Wemyss, Victoria, Lady, 31
Wheeler-Bennett, Sir John, 14, 125, 131, 159
White's Club, 2
Who's Who, 25
Whyte, W. Farmer, 38, 146
Wigram, Clive, 1st Lord, 14, 131
Wilde, Oscar, 26
Willcock, H. D., 66
Willert, Sir Arthur, 32, 35, 183
Williams, John H., 78
Willson, Beckles, 22
Wilson, Sir Horace, 6, 100, 115, 171, 178
Wilson, Hugh, Jr, 42, 46
Wilson, Woodrow (US President), 19, 22, 26, 30–8, 40, 46, 47, 52, 56, 144, 173, 183
Winchester College, 190
Windrich, Elaine, 19
Windsor, Duchess of, 129
Windsor, Duke of, *see* Edward VIII
Winkler, Henry R., 19, 35
Wirtschaftspolitische Gesellschaft, 121–2, 134
Wiseman, Sir William, 35, 183
Wood, F. L., 84, 156, 158
Wood, Neal, 201
Woodward, Sir Llewellyn, 47, 63, 133, 178
Wootton, Graham, 128
World Bank, 6, 77
World Disarmament Conference, 83, 85, 122, 148–9
World Economic Conference, 122
Wrench, Sir Evelyn, 29, 34, 119, 121, 167, 170

Yarnell, Admiral, USN, 9
Yorkshire Post, 11
Young, Eugene J., 39
Young, G. M., 108
Young loan, the, 6

Zilliacus, Konni, MP, 76